MW00989664

Understanding DSGE

Celso José Costa Junior

Escola de Economia de São Paulo, FGV
Departamento de Economia, UEPG

Vernon Series in Economic Methodology

www.vernonpress.com

Vernon Press is an imprint of Vernon Art & Science Inc.

In the Americas:	*In the rest of the world:*
Vernon Press	Vernon Press
1000 N West Street,	C/Sancti Espiritu 17,
Suite 1200, Wilmington,	Malaga, 29006
Delaware 19801	Spain
United States	

Library of Congress Control Number: 2015952652

Vernon Series in Economic Methodology

ISBN 978-1-62273-133-6

Contents

PART II   Extensions

Para Dair, Priscilla e Manuela:
obrigado pela paciência, amor e apoio.

Preface

When one resolves to write a book, and hopes that it will be well accepted, one issue arises that should definitely be addressed: "What makes this book different from those that have gone before?" This preface seeks to answer this question.

Dynamic Stochastic General Equilibrium (DSGE) models have become a point of reference in modern macroeconomics. What currently makes this methodology so important is its ability to answer any question regarding the behavior of a particular economic phenomenon.

If, on the one hand, the theoretical development of DSGE models is not overly complex to understand, on the other, their practical application is rather more difficult. The literature on this subject presents important, yet obscure points, which are difficult to comprehend. Generally, articles begin with a presentation of the agents' object functions and of the equations that solve the maximization problem, while their resolution is not shown. In many cases, it is difficult to identify both the exact theoretical model and its application. Thus, the most important part of this type of exercise is overcoming these barriers of obscurity.

Although this methodology has become so popular in the current economic literature, there is no manual that reveals, step-by-step, how this "black box" works. This deficiency poses an important challenge, as many young researchers give up this line of research on account of the initial difficulty.

Some books, although not manuals as such, aid in understanding this methodology. Wickens's "Macroeconomic Theory: A Dynamic General Equilibrium Approach" (2011) presents a view of modern macroeconomics that seeks to integrate macroeconomics and microeconomics. It is firmly rooted in general equilibrium models and demonstrates an understanding of the changes that macroeconomic methods are facing. The following four books follow practically the same logic. They begin with a basic model and, as one progresses through the book, several types of friction are incorporated. The books are: "Computational Macroeconomics for the Open Economy" by Lim and McNelis (2008); "The ABCs of RBCs" by McCandless (2008); "Monetary Policy, Inflation, and the Business Cycle" by Galí (2008); and "Introduction to Dynamic Macroeconomic General

Equilibrium Models" by Torres (2014). There are a further two books that deal with the methodology's "behind the scenes" aspects: "Structural Macroeconometrics" by DeJong and Dave (2007), and "Methods for Applied Macroeconomic Research" by Canova (2007).

In short, this work takes the best bits from each of the aforementioned books: Lim and McNelis (2008) – organization; McCandless (2008) – presentation of log-linearization and solutions; and Torres (2014) – educational methodology, in a quest for tools that are useful for overcoming initial obstacles to the study of DSGE modeling and persuading young researchers to work with this methodology. In principle, this is not a macroeconomics book per se, but one that presents the tools used in the development of these models. The idea is that it acts as a complement to the books mentioned in the previous paragraph while at the same time presenting the models in greater detail, offering a step-by-step course. The target audiences are advanced undergraduate students, graduate students and experienced economists prepared to learn this methodology. The book begins with a basic Real Business Cycle model and, gradually, the frictions of a standard DSGE model are incorporated: imperfect competition, price and wage frictions, habit formation, non-Ricardian agents, investment adjustment costs, capacity underutilization costs, and lastly, government.

Chapter 1
Introduction

Why tell a story using models instead of telling a story using words? According to Professor Fábio Kanczuk of São Paulo University:

> "To the older generation of any era, Macroeconomics means telling stories, believing they derive from an accounting equality, without realizing that they are but exactly that: identities. Confusing what is endogenous with what is exogenous, equilibrium with disequilibrium.... To the younger generation, it is important to think in terms of equilibrium and to identify the exogenous shocks, in order to then be able to tell the story. Otherwise, it appears so dishonest that even some consultants would be ashamed. In this case, even with its harsh limitations, DSGE helps us to think. There are people who are intelligent enough to do without models and can perform the identification in their heads. When I try to do that, I notice that I often get confused. I also notice that other people get confused, but don't realize it". (Blog AC3L, 2013)

In short, a model consists of mathematical expressions that have unique, precise definitions. This does not occur when only words are used. Thus, once a mathematical expression is defined, it is represented by a rigid set of rules that concern the relationships that can be made, with no room for subtext or metaphors. This is why a well-defined structure is needed, even when telling stories.

During the years that followed Kydland and Prescott's (1982) seminal article, RBC theory provided the main reference structure for the analysis of economic fluctuations, becoming the center of macroeconomic theory. The impact of the RBC revolution lies in its methodology, which established the use of DSGE models as a central tool for macroeconomic analysis. Behavioral equations describing aggregate variables were replaced by first-order conditions of intertemporal problems faced by households and firms. Ad hoc assumptions in the formation of expectations were replaced by rational expectations.

However, this methodology was initially criticized for limiting itself to the analysis of only one type of shock (productivity shocks) and only one type of economic structure (perfect competition), besides not recognizing any role for monetary policy. Therefore, from the perspective of central banks, it was hard to see how these models could contribute to the monetary policy debate. Twenty years later, this controversy has been completely dispelled. The main reason for this is that the technological innovation overlying RBC models introduced frictions that allowed Keynesian principles and new shocks to be incorporated. The success of these new models allowed major economic institutions to develop their own DSGE models, as did the Brazilian Central Bank (SAMBA), the European Central Bank (NAWM), the Bank of Canada (ToTEM), the Bank of England (BEQM), the Bank of Japan (JEM), the Bank of Chile (MAS), and the International Monetary Fund (GEM), among others.

The acceptance of this methodology is due to its coherent analysis structure. This coherence is a result of the acceptable behavior that agents maximize when making decisions, and of rational expectations. Its dynamic mechanism is another attraction, as these models are able, clearly and transparently, to represent the intertemporal movement of economic variables. Lastly, these models are not subject to the Lucas critique (Lucas, 1976). For this reason, central banks are striving to make DSGE more and more useful in the analysis of economic policy. To this end, they are taking into account an increasingly sophisticated financial sector (with financial vulnerability and collateral restrictions) and are progressively perfecting the understanding of forecasting.

According to Chari *et al.* (2009), in order for a model to contribute to economic policy analysis, it needs to have two essential characteristics. The first is that the estimated parameters should be structural parameters of the economy, so that they are not affected by policy changes, and the second is that the exogenous shocks used in the model should have a coherent and relevant interpretation. They also state that there are two main approaches for models that meet these two requirements. The first seeks to keep the model as simple as possible with respect to the number of parameters, variables and dynamics. The other is aligned with Christiano *et al.* (2005) and Smets and Wouters (2003), who seek a so called "adjustment principle". In this sense, this second approach argues for the inclusion of several estimation mechanisms with the aim of improving adherence to observed data, such as different types of rigidity and shocks. Thus, the models that are concerned with bringing theory and reality closer together follow this second tradition. They propose frictions and shocks to a degree that is sufficient and necessary for better adjustment to the observed data.

> **Definition 1.0.1** (Adjustment principle). *According to Kocherlakota (2007), by this principle, the better a model's projected data adheres to observed data, the more preferable it is for policy analysis.*

The idea of Representative Agents and Lifespan

It is a fact that every consumer is different in relation to his/her preferences for goods and services. The same holds true for firms with regard to the technology used in the production process. In other words, agents in an economy are heterogeneous. However, considering these characteristics, a potential theoretical problem of flexibility emerges, rendering the theoretical modelling of each economic agent's individual choices impossible. Furthermore, it would be impossible to know each individual agent's exact choices. The fact is that any economic model is a simplified description of a complex phenomenon.

The solution found was to group economic agents into larger categories, for example, in the case of a study regarding consumers, forming groups with similar consumption characteristics (high, average and low-income consumers) would be recommended. This procedure within DSGE modelling is called introducing a representative agent. In this approach, it is assumed that a large quantity of identical economic agents exists. This is clearly a significant simplification of reality. However, by adopting such a procedure, macroeconomic modelling is a lot simpler, at least enough to fulfill the purpose of macroeconomic studies, such as how household consumption reacts to rising interest rates.

Thus, the aim of DSGE modelling is to build relatively small theoretical models (using representative agents) that include households, firms, government, the financial sector and the foreign sector. Aggregating these types of agent enables one to see how they interact, allowing for a detailed analysis of a certain macroeconomic policy effects.

Now that the issue of how economic agents are defined in DSGE models has been described, it is necessary to consider each agent's lifespan, which, for the purpose of these models, means the temporal reference that agents use to make their decisions. It is assumed that they have infinite time horizons. Obviously, firms and governments do not exist forever. However, when a government decides upon its budget, it does not expect that it will cease to exist. Firms act likewise; when deciding their budgets, they do not consider that they will go bankrupt in the future. This assumption in relation to consumers is simpler. Although it is assumed that each consumer has a finite lifespan, when considering the family structure in which members periodically are born and die, the "family" representative agent becomes infinite.

Teaching DSGE models in undergraduate and graduate courses

Macroeconomics is complex, and complex systems, as is common knowledge, are difficult to analyze. However, is the macroeconomics being taught in undergraduate courses consistent with reality? Are models such as the IS-LM and Mundell-Fleming models, among others, really able to represent how the macroeconomy works? Is the macroeconomics taught in undergraduate courses different from that taught in postgraduate courses?

At the beginning of the 1970s, macroeconomic theory received a jolt. The neoclassical synthesis model, which was almost universally accepted as the basic paradigm up to the end of the sixties, is today not considered scientifically respectable. The popularity of this model began to wane because of to its inability to explain certain economic events, especially failing to appropriately deal with factors such as inflation and supply shocks. The waning enthusiasm for these models is also a result of the theoretical and empirical progress of an alternative approach to the behavior of households and firms, grounded in the concepts of optimization of agents' behavior and market adjustments.

Although models based on the neoclassical synthesis have fallen out of favor with economists over the last 25 years, they continue to be the main tools used in undergraduate course textbooks. Although it is true that some manuals now include material about macroeconomics with microfoundations (Romer, 2012; Blanchard and Fischer, 1989 and Benassy, 2011 for graduate courses; and Barro, 1997; Williamson, 2008 and Barron *et al.*, 2006 for undergraduate courses, among others) it is still insufficient, even in postgraduate courses. In summary, modern macroeconomics is not being taught in an orderly manner owing to a lack of textbooks that direct the study of this methodology systematically.

Generally speaking, mathematics cannot be accredited with being the reason for modern macroeconomics barely being taught in undergraduate economics courses, as the basic tools in these models (derivatives, maximization, etc.,) are taught in the majority of courses, even undergraduate courses. Textbooks such as "Fundamental Methods of Mathematical Economics" by Chiang and Wainwright (2005) or "Mathematics for Economists" by Simon and Blume (1994), very popular in math classes and in economics courses, fulfill the necessary and sufficient conditions for a good understanding of macroeconomic modelling.

Dynare

Dynare is a software platform for handling a wide range of economic models, in particular DSGE models and overlapping generations (OLG) models. The models solved by Dynare include those relying on the rational expectations hypothesis, wherein agents form their expectations about the future in a way consistent with the model. But Dynare is also able to hand models where expectations are formed differently: at one extreme, models where agents perfectly anticipate the future; at the other, models where agents have limited rationality or imperfect knowledge of the state of the economy and, hence, form their expectations through a process of learning.

This platform offers an easy way to describe these models, capable of performing simulations given the calibration of the model parameters or forecasting these parameters given a dataset. In practice, the user will write a text file containing the list of variables, dynamic equations, computing tasks and the desired graphical or numerical outputs.

Dynare is a free software, which means that it can be downloaded free of charge, that its source code is freely available, and that it can be used for both non-profit and profitable purposes. It is available for the Windows, Mac and Linux platforms and is fully documented by way of a user guide and reference manual. Part of Dynare is programmed in C++, while the rest is written using the Matlab programming language. The latter implies that commercially-available Matlab software is required in order to run Dynare. However, as an alternative to Matlab, Dynare is also able to run on top of Octave (basically a free clone of Matlab). The development of Dynare is mainly done at Cepremap by a core team of researchers who devote part of their time to software development.

In short, Dynare is a preprocessor and collection of routines that operate on Matlab, which has advantages for reading and writing DSGE models, almost as if one were writing an academic article. Not only does this make the presentation of models easier, it also easily allows for code sharing. Figure 1.1 is an overview of how Dynare works. Basically, the models and its related attributes, such as the shock structure, are written equation by equation in a text editor. The result is a file.mod [1]. This file is loaded by Matlab, which initiates Dynare's preprocessor, translating the file.mod so it can be used by Matlab's routines to solve or estimate the model. Finally, the results are shown by Matlab.

The structure of the book

As mentioned in the preface and in this introduction, the aim of this book is that it should be a training course on DSGE, seeking an applied format. The chosen presentation methodology includes brief theoretical presentations of each chapter's assumptions, and the presentation and development of the underlying model. Then, agents' optimization problems are presented along with policy equations, after which the steady state is determined and the log-linearized equations found. To complete the model, the shocks of the proposed problem are discussed.

---

[1] An important guide on how to write files.mod is Griffoli (2011).

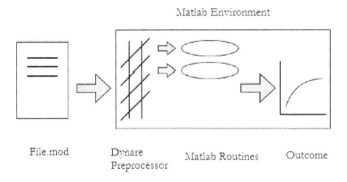

Matlab Environment

File.mod   Dynare   Matlab Routines   Outcome
                 Preprocessor

Figure 1.1: The file.mod is read by Dynare's preprocessor, which calls the Matlab routines required to perform the desired operations and display the results. Source: Modified from Griffoli (2011).

The idea is to try to eliminate the superfluous, an arduous task since everything seems essential. There are often many ways to present or solve a problem, for example: this book uses the Lagrange method for solving optimization problems; however, some economists prefer to use dynamic programming. What is important is that the results are the same. Aspects of this kind will be left aside, with further reading being recommended for readers seeking alternative techniques.

To facilitate didactic understanding, this book employs certain features that reinforce the basic theory. These features are:

- Definition: the part of the text that introduces a new expression, specifying its meaning. Each time a theoretical element is important to understanding a chapter's methodology, it will be shown as a definition.

- Theoretical result: the result of a problem that should be specified by the reader. For a better understanding of the dynamic development of DSGE models, it is necessary to have a knowledge of the main equations that form the model. To this end, this feature seeks to reinforce the importance of some expressions.

- Assumption: the attribution of a certain characteristic to the proposed model.

- Preposition: a justified (and demonstrated) mathematical statement.

- File.mod: the chapter model written in Dynare's simulation format. To make the study of each model easier, at the end of each chapter, they are presented in the .mod format.

- Presentation of problem solutions: in this book, we chose to present the solution of problems step by step. This is due to the lack of detail in textbooks that deal with this methodology.

Besides these features, the reader will find some important differences between this book and other textbooks with regard to topic approach and organization. This work is organized in seven chapters, including this introduction. From chapters 2 to 7, the model's structure is developed progressively, including new frictions and other economic agents.

The first part of this book presents three basic models: the RBC model, the NK model with price frictions, and the NK model price and wage frictions. The idea is to begin with a simpler model and then, as the chapters progress, new frictions are introduced. In this part, the main focus is on the development of the tools and basic ideas presented here.

The main aim of part II is to introduce frictions in households, firms and the government sector so that the model approximates reality or, in other words, so that the model meets the adjustment principle. To this end, frictions in intertemporal consumption choices, in access to the "financial market", in investments and in installed capacity will be included. With regard to the first type of friction, the concept of habit formation will be used. As for restrictions on the financial market, so-called non-Ricardian families will be incorporated. The other two types of friction are related to investment adjustment costs and the underutilization of maximum installed capacity.

This book was originally intended to be read from beginning to end. However, researchers who already possess some knowledge of DSGE models may go directly to the chapters of interest, keeping in mind that every assumption or idea taken from a previous chapter will have its source duly indicated.

Part I

Basic principles

Chapter 2

Real Business Cycle (RBC) model

This chapter presents a simple Real Business Cycle (RBC) model, assuming perfect competition and fully flexible prices in all markets.

Real business cycle theory states that supply shocks (technological shocks) are what generate economic fluctuations, and uses a neoclassical growth model as a reference for the economy's long-term behavior. The model's basic structure is relatively simple. It describes the behavior of two types of agent: households and firms. In practice, there is a very large number of households that are treated as if they were identical. Thus, one may use the term "representative household" or simply "household". As for firms, the same logic applies: there is a large number of firms, however, they possess the same technology and can thus be typified as a representative firm. It is appropriate to mention that this type of model is not limited to these two economic agents (households and firms). A "complete" model would consist of five agents: households, firms, fiscal and monetary authorities, the foreign sector and financial institutions.

Brief theoretical review: Real Business Cycles

In order to present the basic ideas involved in this type of model, this section demonstrates how households solve two problems of choice: intratemporal consumption-leisure and intertemporal consumption-savings. It also deals with how firms choose the inputs used in the production process. Basically, in all cases, the marginal rate of substitution is compared to relative price. For the first problem, a model with two goods (consumption and leisure), and how optimal choice occurs within this trade-off, will be analyzed. The second problem will be presented using a simple two-period intertemporal model. Lastly, a firm's profit maximization problem is demonstrated. The ideas presented in this section are simple, but suffice to demonstrate how these choices are made within this model and in the rest of the book.

Model with two "goods": consumption and leisure

In this initial study of consumer theory, it will be assumed that there are two large categories of consumer good, "good 1" and "good 2". Because of to the interest in studying how consumers choose what they consume, one must define how these agents earn their income. The most obvious way is to think that consumers obtain income from their labor. Thus, an individual may choose to work a certain number of hours, receiving wage W per hour. Presumably, work is a consumer "bad", that is, agents do not like to work because the more they do, the less time they have for leisure. Thus, with the aim of adapting the model to standard consumer theory, instead of considering a "bad" (work), one must consider a "good" (leisure), defined as the number of hours left after subtracting the time spent working from the total number of available hours in a certain period[1].

Indifference curves (consumption-leisure)

The two factors that provide an individual with utility are consumption (C) and leisure, $u(C, leisure)$. Here, both consumption and leisure will be treated as goods, even though leisure is somewhat intangible[2]. Initially, it is useful to think of the general properties of a utility function $u(C, leisure)$ as the standard properties of consumer theory. Thus, the utility function is assumed to have the following properties:

---

[1] Leisure + Work = total available time.

[2] Leisure can be analyzed as a good, being a function of the opportunity cost, availability and preferences. The question then arises, "what is the opportunity cost of leisure?" The cost of spending hours watching television is basically the amount of money that one would receive if one were working instead. Therefore, the opportunity cost of one hour of leisure should be the same as the wage for one hour's work. Availability is directly related to the amount of household income and preference is related to a household's sensitivity to demand for leisure given changes in income or wages (Ehrenberg and Smith, 2000).

1. Strictly increasing, $\frac{\partial u}{\partial C} > 0$ and $\frac{\partial u}{\partial leisure} > 0$; and

2. Diminishing marginal returns, $\frac{\partial^2 u}{\partial C^2} < 0$ and $\frac{\partial^2 u}{\partial leisure^2} < 0$.

> **Definition 2.1.1** (Indifference curve). *An indifference curve shows a grouping of consumer bundles for which an individual is indifferent. In other words, all bundles provide the same utility.*

With these assumptions, it is possible to plot an indifference curve map for consumption and leisure, as illustrated in Figure 2.1. Each indifference curve possesses the standard properties of consumer theory. Specifically, each curve has a negative slope, is convex to the origin and may not cross another indifference curve.

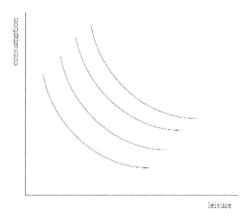

Figure 2.1: Indifference curve map for consumption and leisure.

Although these two goods (consumption and leisure) are not on the goods market (one cannot really buy leisure), there is still a well-defined idea of a "marginal rate of substitution" (MRS) between them. The MRS measures how many units of a good one is willing to give up in exchange for another good. On a graph, the MRS is the slope of the indifference curve.

Definition 2.1.2 (Marginal Rate of Substitution). *The negative slope of an indifference curve of a bundle formed by two goods, X and Y, is referred to as the Marginal Rate of Substitution (MRS) at that point. That is,*

$$MRS_{X,Y} = -\left.\frac{\partial Y}{\partial X}\right|_{U=U_1} = -\left.\frac{MU_X}{MU_Y}\right|_{U=U_i}$$

where MU_X and MU_Y represent the marginal utilities in relation to goods X and Y, respectively, and the $|_{U=U_i}$ notation indicates that the slope is calculated along the indifference curve U_i.

In short, in the consumption-leisure model, the marginal rate of substitution of leisure with consumption, represented by $MRS_{\text{Leisure},C}$, is the rate at which a consumer is willing to give up leisure for consumer goods.

Budget constraints

An indifference map is not sufficient to study a consumer's optimal choice. To this end, the individual's budget constraint is required. Here, the amount of income an individual has to spend on consumption depends on how much he/she chooses to work. For the purposes of this study on budget constraint, suppose an individual has 60 hours available per week for work and leisure[3].

Assuming that an individual can work the amount of hours he/she likes (L), receiving an hourly wage W, total weekly income is:

$$Y = LW$$

---

[3]Of the 168 hours (24 x 7) in a week, the weekends and hours intended for the individual's subsistence (bathing, meals, etc.) are being subtracted. So the number of daily and weekly hours available for work-leisure are 12 hours and 60 hours (12 x 5) respectively.

As previously mentioned, the number of work hours (L) plus the number of leisure hours per week, must be equal to 60 hours, $L = 60 - leisure$. Thus, income can be written as a function of leisure:

$$Y = (60 - leisure)W$$

Another simplifying assumption is that individuals spend all their income on consumption, not saving anything. Each consumer good, c, can be bought on the market for the price P. Thus, an individual's consumption in each period is:

$$Pc = Y$$

Combining the two previous expressions, we arrive at the following budget constraint:

$$Pc = (60 - leisure)W$$

In this expression, an individual takes the prices of consumer goods (P) and hourly wages (W) as a given, choosing the level of consumption and amount of leisure. Rearranging the previous budget constraint,

$$\underbrace{\overbrace{\underbrace{Pc}_{\text{consumer goods}} + \underbrace{W\,leisure}_{\text{leisure}}}^{\text{destination of income}} = \underbrace{60W}_{\text{total disposable income}}}$$

it can be seen that the period's total disposable income ($60W$) is used to acquire consumer goods (Pc) and leisure ($W\,leisure$). As mentioned above, leisure is not directly bought or sold on the market. However, wages are the opportunity cost of leisure; each hour spent on leisure is an hour that could have been spent working. Thus, from an economic point of view, in which opportunity costs are explicitly considered, wages are the price of leisure.

A budget constraint describes the set of choices available to a consumer, but reveals nothing about the choice to be made within this set. To plot the budget constraint on a graph, as in Figure 2.1, the equation must be rearranged in the following way:

$$c = \left(\frac{60W}{P}\right) - \left(\frac{W}{P}\right) leisure$$

The budget constraint is a line with a vertical intercept of $\left(\frac{60W}{P}\right)$ and slope $-\left(\frac{W}{P}\right)$. When $c = 0$ the horizontal intercept is *leisure* = 60, showing that if an individual does not want to consume any goods, he/she will use all of his/her time for leisure.

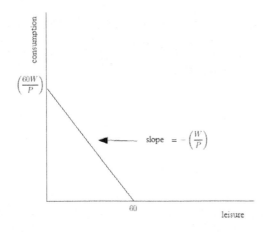

Figure 2.2: Budget constraint line for the consumption-leisure model..

Individuals' decisions regarding consumption and work

To obtain optimal choice, the interaction of individuals' preferences (indifference curve maps) with their budget constraints must be considered. Formally, an individual's problem is:

$$\max_{c,L} u(c, L)$$

subject to,

$$Pc = WL$$

Many optimization problems can be solved using the Lagrangian method:

$$\mathcal{L} = u(c, L) - \lambda(Pc - WL)$$

With the following first-order conditions:

$$\frac{\partial \mathscr{L}}{\partial c} = \frac{\partial u}{\partial c} - \lambda P = 0$$

$$\frac{\partial \mathscr{L}}{\partial L} = \frac{\partial u}{\partial L} + \lambda W = 0$$

Combining the two previous expressions:

Theoretical result 2.1.1 (Supply of Labor).

$$\underbrace{\frac{\partial u/\partial L}{\partial u/\partial c}}_{MRS\ L\text{-}c} = \underbrace{-\frac{W}{P}}_{Relative\ price\ L\text{-}c}$$

On a graph, at point E (figure 2.3), leisure-consumption's marginal rate of substitution is equal to leisure-consumption's relative price[4]. On the other hand, at point D, leisure-consumption's relative price ($\frac{W}{P}$) exceeds leisure-consumption's marginal rate of substitution. If this occurs, an individual will be better off working more (enjoying less leisure) and using the additional income to expand consumption. Thus, with the increased acquisition of consumer goods, leisure-consumption's MRS increases. When this initial difference ceases to exist (point E), there is no more incentive for an individual to increase his/her level of work. In other words, the leisure-consumption bundle represented by point D belongs to indifference curve U_1, following the budget constraint line towards point E. It should be noted that, of all the points on the budget constraint line, it is this point that is tangential to the highest indifference curve (U_2). Therefore, given his/her budget constraint, the individual will be in a better situation at point E than at point D.

---

[4]The reader must remember that, for graphical analysis, it is better to use the consumption-leisure instead of the consumption-work locus, as the first pair represents two "goods", whereas the second pair represents a "good" and a "bad".

Definition 2.1.3 (The problem of the household). *To maximize utility, given a fixed amount of income, an individual will buy the amount of goods that depletes his/her total income equating to the physical rate of tradeoff between any two goods (MRS) and the rate at which a good can be exchanged for another on the market (relative price).*

Definition 2.1.4 (Optimal result of the problem of the household). *The optimal consumption bundle is the point that represents the pair of goods that is on the highest indifference curve and is within the individual's budget constraint.*

In summary, each individual chooses a combination of consumption and leisure that maximizes his/her utility. Thus, an individual chooses the pair $(C^*, leisure^*)$ (figure 2.3) for which the budget constraint is the tangent of an indifference curve.

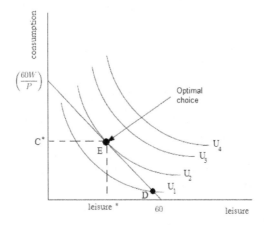

Figure 2.3: Optimal choice of consumption and leisure.

Labor supply function

When an individual optimally chooses to spend H hours of his/her
time on leisure then, at the same time, he/she is choosing to spend
$L = 60 - H$ hours of his/her time working. Therefore, the individual
is supplying L hours of work to this market. Evidently, the choice of
the amount of labor in figure 2.3 depends on the level of wages (W).
Thus, the budget constraint is $c = 60w - wH$, where $w = \frac{W}{P}$ is the
real wage.

Initially, it will be assumed that real wages are at a very low level
(w_1). At this starting point, the optimal choice will be point A (figure
2.4). This choice is associated with the amount of labor L_1. Now
suppose that real wages increase, $w_2 > w_1$. The new optimal choice
is point B. At this point, the individual enjoys less leisure compared
to point A ($L_2 > L_1$).

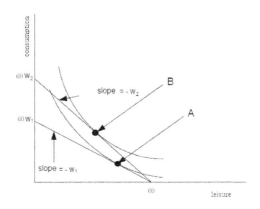

Figure 2.4: With a rise in real wages from w_1 to w_2, the individual chooses
more consumption and less leisure.

Now suppose that the real wage increases to w_3. The optimal
choice at this new real wage level is at point C (figure 2.5). Comparing point C to point B, the individual does not adjust his/her
amount of labor hours when real wages rise from w_2 to w_3. Thus, at
this wage level, the individual works L_3 hours, with $L_3 = L_2 > L_1$.

Consider yet another rise in real wages ($w_4 > w_3$).). At this
point, real wages are high enough that the individual does not increase his/her amount of work to keep the same level of consumption. At this level of wages, it is reasonable to expect that the indi-

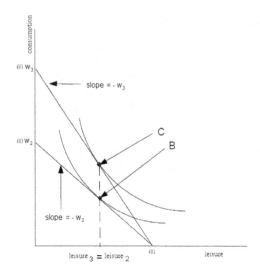

Figure 2.5: With a rise in real wages from w_2 to w_3, the individual chooses more consumption and the same amount of leisure.

vidual chooses to spend less time working and more time on leisure ($L_4 < L_3$). In figure 2.6, an increase in wages causes the optimal choice to move from point C to point D. At this point, the individual works fewer hours than at point C.

Substitution and income effects

The effects of changes in real wages on optimal leisure choice can be separated into two components: a substitution effect and an income effect. Both effects have a general significance within economics and can indeed be applied to any optimal choice problem.

In the context of this consumption-leisure model, the substitution effect of higher real wages leads the individual to choose less leisure (work more). In other words, because of to the higher level of wages, the opportunity cost of leisure has risen. Thus, the individual would tend to demand less leisure. Conversely, the income effect of higher real wages causes the individual to choose more leisure (less work). That is, because of to the higher income that a higher level of real wages affords, the individual would choose

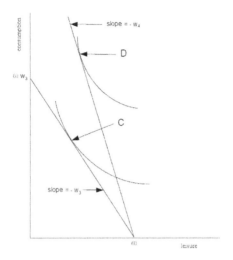

Figure 2.6: With a rise in real wages from w_3 to w_4, the individual chooses more consumption and more leisure.

a higher level of consumption of all normal goods. Assuming that leisure is a normal good, a rise in income would cause the individual to choose more leisure and thus spend less time working.

Both effects are ever present: either the substitution effect dominates the income effect (because of being stronger) and the rise in real wages causes the individual to choose more work (less leisure), or the income effect is dominant and a rise in real wages causes the individual to choose less work (more leisure), or they cancel each other out.

With this notion of income and substitution effects, the effects shown in Figures 2.4-2.6 must be reconsidered. A rise in real wages from w_1 to w_2 causes the individual to work more, as illustrated by the optimal choice moving from point A to point B. This is the section at which the substitution effect outweighs the income effect. When real wages rise from w_2 to w_3, the individual decides not to adjust the amount of work, keeping the same level of leisure. The section between points B and C corresponds to the region at which the effects exactly cancel each other out. Lastly, when wages rise from w_3 to w_4, the individual decides to work less, as shown by the optimal choice moving from point C to point D. So, this is the section at which the income effect outweighs the substitution effect (figure 2.7).

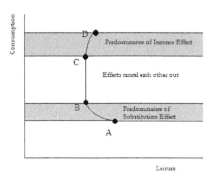

Figure 2.7: Sections at which the income and substitution effects dominate.

Dynamic structure of consumption-savings

When an individual makes his/her choice between consumption and leisure in the current period, he/she generally recognizes that a similar choice will be made in the future. This is formalized by a utility function $u(c_1, c_2, c_3, \ldots)$. Economists almost always simplify intertemporal problems assuming that preferences are additively separable, $u(c_1, c_2, c_3, \ldots) = u(c_1) + \beta u(c_2) + \beta^2 u(c_3) + \ldots$. The β parameter is called an intertemporal discount factor. Its value is less than 1 ($\beta < 1$) as it represents the fact that households are more concerned with present consumption than future consumption[5].

In this section, the aim is to assess individuals' intertemporal choices. For the sake of clarity, data regarding leisure will be ignored. It will be assumed that individuals live in two periods, the present (period 1) and the future (period 2). This division into two periods is enough to illustrate the basic principles of macroeconomic events that occur intertemporally in a structure with an infinite time horizon.

---

[5] $\beta = \frac{1}{1+\theta}$, where $\theta > 0$ is the subjective intertemporal preference rate. This parameter indicates the value of future utility in relation to present utility. The greater the value of β, the more patient the household is with regard to consumption.

In the intertemporal context, the two arguments that make up the utility function are period 1 consumption and period 2 consumption, which will be represented by c_1 and c_2, respectively. All the usual properties of the utility function are assumed: utility is always strictly increasing in both arguments; marginal utility always decreases in both arguments. The utility function will be written as $u(c1, c2)$, and can be represented by an indifference curve map.

In this model, individuals receive income twice during their lives - once in period 1 and once in period 2. They start off in period 1 with a certain amount of wealth, A_0. They choose consumption in period 1 (c_1) paying a price of P_1, and also decide how much wealth[6] they will carry forward to period 2, A_1. Thus, an individual's budget constraint in period 1 can be written as:

$$P_1 c_1 + A_1 = R A_0 + Y_1$$

where R is the gross nominal interest rate[7] that represents the returns on each monetary unit held as a financial asset from one period to another.

The same logic can be repeated for an individual's budget constraint in period 2:
$$P_2 c_2 + A_2 = R A_1 + Y_2$$

in which, owing to individuals living only for two periods, final wealth must be zero ($A_2 = 0$). The intertemporal representation of these events is shown as a timeline in figure 2.8.

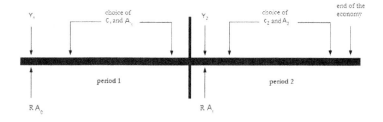

Figure 2.8: Intertemporal representation of the events of a two-period consumption structure.

[6]Note that A_0 and A_1 may take on negative values, indicating that an individual would be a borrower in these periods.

[7]A gross rate is defined as: $R = 1 + r$, where r is the net return for the period.

To continue the model, it is necessary to define a period's savings as the difference between total income and the total spent within said period:

$$S_1 = (R - 1)A_0 + Y_1 - P_1 c_1$$

Rearranging the period 1 budget constraint:

$$A_1 - A_0 = (R - 1)A_0 + Y_1 - P_1 c_1$$

Comparing the last two expressions, one can see that $S_1 = A_1 - A_0$. Thus, an individual's savings in period 1 is equal to the variation in his/her wealth within the period. Similarly, an individual's savings in period 2 is $S_2 = (R - 1)A_1 + Y_2 - P_2 c_2$ or $S_2 = A_2 - A_1$.

An approximation to general economic behavior is to suppose that individuals are rational during their life spans, in the sense that they save and/or borrow appropriately during their lives. Given this structure and taking the assumption of rationality into account, analysis of the model may begin. Thus, by combining the budget constraints of periods 1 and 2, we arrive at an individual's intertemporal budget constraint. Solving period 1's budget constraint for A_1:

$$A_1 = RA_0 + Y_1 - P_1 c_1$$

substituting this result in period 2's budget constraint,

$$P_2 c_2 = R[RA_0 + Y_1 - P_1 c_1] + Y_2$$

dividing both sides of the previous expression by R:

$$P_1 c_1 + \frac{P_2 c_2}{R} = Y_1 + \frac{Y_2}{R} + RA_0$$

The right-hand side of this last expression represents the discounted intertemporal resource, which considers the initial wealth and an individual's lifetime income (two periods in this model). The left-hand side represents discounted intertemporal consumption, which considers the consumption in all periods. The intertemporal budget constraint that an individual rationally uses to make his/her choices in time will be drawn in a locus $c_1 - c_2$. For the sake of simplicity, it will be assumed that initial wealth is zero ($A_0 = 0$).

Solving the previous expression for c_2:

$$c_2 = \left[\left(\frac{R}{P_2}\right)Y_1 + \frac{Y_2}{P_2}\right] - \left[\frac{P_1 R}{P_2}\right]c_1$$

Thus, the vertical intercept is $\left[\left(\frac{R}{P_2}\right)Y_1 + \frac{Y_2}{P_2}\right]$ and the slope is $\left[\frac{P_1 R}{P_2}\right]$. The graph representing an individual's intertemporal budget constraint is shown in figure 2.9.

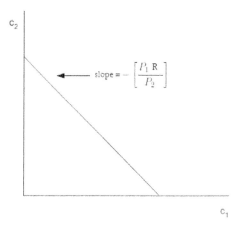

Figure 2.9: An individual's intertemporal budget constraint.

Optimal intertemporal choice

An individual's optimal intertemporal choice is an interaction between his/her indifference curve map and intertemporal budget constraints. In this model, an individual lives for two periods. In this case, his/her preferences can be reduced to:

$$u(c_1, c_2) = u(c_1) + \beta u(c_2)$$

Given that the individual will not consume in period 3, it can be assumed that keeping assets in the form of savings in period 2 would not be optimal ($A_2 = 0$). Thus, an individual's budget constraints in both periods are:

$$P_1 c_1 + A_1 = R A_0 + Y_1$$

$$P_2 c_2 = R A_1 + Y_2$$

The problem for the individual is to choose the levels of consumption for both periods, c_1 and c_2, and the level of wealth A_1 that maximizes his/her utility function, which is subject to budget constraints in both periods. The values of P and R are given. Thus, the problem of the individual can be written as:

$$\max_{c_1, c_2, A_1} u(c_1) + \beta u(c_2)$$

subject to,

$$P_1 c_1 + A_1 = R A_0 + Y_1$$
$$P_2 c_2 = R A_1 + Y_2$$

The Lagrangian for this problem is:

$$\mathscr{L} = u(c_1) + \beta u(c_2) - \lambda_1 [P_1 c_1 + A_1 - R A_0 - Y_1] - \lambda_2 [P_2 c_2 - R A_1 - Y_2]$$

The problem's first-order conditions are:

$$\frac{\partial \mathscr{L}}{\partial c_1} = \frac{\partial u}{\partial c_1} - \lambda_1 P_1 = 0$$

$$\frac{\partial \mathscr{L}}{\partial c_2} = \beta \frac{\partial u}{\partial c_2} - \lambda_2 P_2 = 0$$

$$\frac{\partial \mathscr{L}}{\partial A_1} = -\lambda_1 + \lambda_2 R = 0$$

Rewriting the first two first-order conditions, $\lambda_1 = \frac{\partial u / \partial c_1}{P_1}$ and $\lambda_2 = \beta \frac{\partial u / \partial c_2}{P_2}$, substituting these values in the third first-order condition and defining $\pi_2 = \frac{P_2}{P_1}$:

Theoretical result 2.1.2 (Euler Equation).

$$-\frac{\partial u/\partial c_1}{\beta\partial u/\partial c_2} = -\frac{R}{\pi_2}$$

$\underbrace{\qquad\qquad}_{MRS\ c_1\text{-}c_2}$ $\underbrace{\qquad}_{Relative\ price\ c_1\text{-}c_2}$

This is called a Euler Equation. It relates the marginal utility of consumption for both periods (MRS c_1-c_2) with the relative price of intertemporal consumption (the slopes of the indifference curves and budget constraint are equal). It is worth remembering that the indifference curve's slope measures the extra consumption that would be necessary in the following period to offset the loss of a unit of consumption in the current period. In contrast, the budget constraint's slope determines the premium, R, for saving more (Barro, 1997). It can be seen that high values for β (patient individuals) lead to indifference curves having low slopes.

A rise in R reduces the next period's cost of consumption, relative to current consumption, because of to households having the possibility of obtaining more future units of consumption for each previous unit of current consumption. It is this change in relative price that motivates households to increase future consumption in relation to present consumption. Economists call this mechanism the intertemporal substitution effect (Barro, 1997).

Figure 2.10 shows a graphical example, in which an individual's optimal choice is c_1^* in period 1 and c_2^* in period 2 (point E). It also shows an individual's income in both periods. What is actually shown is both periods' real income ($\frac{Y_1}{P_1}$ and $\frac{Y_2}{P_2}$) in which consumption levels are equal to income levels for the two periods (point D). Analyzing figure 2.10, optimal consumption in period (c_1^*) is greater than real income in the same period ($\frac{Y_1}{P_1}$), indicating that the individual is less patient in relation to current consumption. This individual is spending more than he/she earns, meaning that part of his/her wealth must be used to cover the period's excess consumption. Mathematically, rearranging period 1 budget constraint,

$$c_1 - \frac{Y_1}{P_1} = -\frac{A_1}{P_1}$$

it can be seen that if $c_1 > \frac{Y_1}{P_1}$ real wealth in period 1 will be negative, $-\frac{A_1}{P_1}$, indicating that this individual is a borrower. To see the consequences of this, period 2 budget constraint will be altered in the following way:

$$c_2 - \frac{Y_2}{P_2} = \frac{R A_1}{P_2}$$

as A_1 is negative (the individual is a borrower), the left-hand side of the previous expression should also be negative, $c_2 < \frac{Y_2}{P_2}$, indicating that consumption in period 2 should be lower than real income in this period. The reason for this occurrence lies in the fact that the individual has to pay off loan arranged in period 1. Thus, consumption higher than real income in period 1 must be balanced with real income higher than consumption in period 2.

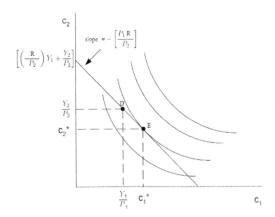

Figure 2.10: Interaction between the intertemporal budget constraint and an individual's preference to determine optimal intertemporal consumption.

Input markets

Firms represent the agents that acquire inputs, while households are those that supply them. Adjustments in input markets determine the amount of inputs and the aggregate product of an economy. In this section, we will explore how each input's price level is determined.

Definition of input markets

Generally speaking, it is assumed that inputs are physically equal. Households sell labor on the labor market and rent capital on the capital market. These markets establish unique price and wage (W) levels, and a unique return on capital (R) level, for the labor and capital markets, respectively. Thus, firms hire labor and capital paying W and R monetary units per hour, respectively. At the same time, the suppliers of inputs receive W and R monetary units for each hour of service supplied. It is assumed that firms and households take input price levels as a given.

Thus, L^s and L^d are the number of working hours households supply and the number of working hours firms demand in the labor market in each period. K^s and K^d are, respectively, the number of hours of rent of capital that households supply and that firms demand in the capital market in each period. All firms use inputs to produce goods using a production function:

$$Y = f(K^d, L^d)$$

This production function can be represented on a graph by an isoquant curve, a contour line showing the combinations of capital and labor that generate the same level of production. Plotting isoquant curves on a graph results in an isoquant map (figure 2.11).

Provided that the goods produced are being sold at price P, a firm's profit can be defined by:

$$\text{Profit} = PY - WL^d - RK^d$$

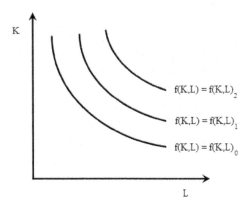

Figure 2.11: Isoquant map.

Demand for inputs

Firms define their demand for inputs aiming to maximize profits in each period.

$$\max_{K^d, L^d} PY - WL^d - RK^d$$

subject to the following technology:

$$Y = f(K^d, L^d)$$

The first-order conditions are:

$$P\frac{\partial Y}{\partial L^d} - W = 0$$

$$P\frac{\partial Y}{\partial K^d} - R = 0$$

Definition 2.1.5 (Problem of the firm). *A profit-maximizing firm chooses input and production levels with the sole objective of maximizing economic profit. That is, firms wish to obtain the largest possible difference between total revenue and total costs.*

The first-order conditions of the problem of the firm may be written in the following manner:

Theoretical result 2.1.3 (Demand for Inputs).

$$\underbrace{\frac{\partial Y}{\partial L^d}}$$

Marginal Productivity of Labor (MPL)

$$= \underbrace{\frac{W}{P}}$$

Real Marginal Cost of Labor (real MCL)

$$\underbrace{\frac{\partial Y}{\partial K^d}}$$

Marginal Productivity of Capital (MPK)

$$= \underbrace{\frac{R}{P}}$$

Real Marginal Cost of Capital (real MCK)

The theoretical result 2.1.3 states that firms choose input levels so that the marginal product of these inputs equals their real marginal costs. At this point, the last unit of an input contributes to the product enough to cover the extra cost of this unit of input in units of goods.

Combining the last two expressions:

Theoretical result 2.1.4 (Relative Demand for Inputs).

$$\underbrace{-\frac{\frac{\partial Y}{\partial L^d}}{\frac{\partial Y}{\partial K^d}}}_{\text{Marginal Rate of Technical Substitution (MRTS)}}$$

$$= \underbrace{-\frac{W}{R}}_{\text{Economic Rate of Substitution (ERS)}}$$

Definition 2.1.6 (Marginal Rate of Technical Substitution). *The negative slope of an isoquant curve consisting of two inputs, capital (K) and labor (L) is called the Marginal Rate of Technical Substitution (MRTS) at that point. That is,*

$$MRTS = -\frac{\partial K}{\partial L}\Big|_{f(K,L)=f(K,L)_i} = -\frac{PMgL}{PMgK}\Big|_{f(K,L)=f(K,L)_i}$$

where $|_{f(K,L)=f(K,L)_i}$ *indicates the slope is calculated along the isoquant* $f(K,L)_i$.

Intuitively, the marginal rate of technical substitution indicates how many additional units of capital should be employed to offset one less unit of labor.

Summarizing the results obtained in this section, theoretical results 2.1.1, 2.1.2, and 2.1.4 show the same features. Agents, when deciding upon their choices, use marginal rates of substitution between goods and their relative prices. First, households must face the consumption-leisure tradeoff analyzing the relative price between these goods (real wages). When the choice is intertemporal, the tradeoff is between consumption today and future consumption, and the relative price is the nominal interest rate. Firms must make the same type of decision when deciding the combination of units of labor and capital to be used, analyzing the relative prices of these inputs (W/R).

The model

In this section, the structural model of the economy proposed in this chapter is presented and solved, step by step. This begins with the presentation of the agents (households and firms), following which the equilibrium conditions are shown. Then, the steady state is found and the equations that make up the model's equilibrium are log-linearized.

Assumption 2.2.1. *The economy is closed, with no government or financial sector.*

Assumption 2.2.2. *This economy does not have a currency. That is, it is a barter economy.*

Assumption 2.2.3. *Adjustment costs do not exist.*

Households

Assumption 2.2.4. *The economy in this model is formed by a unitary set of households indexed by $j \in [0,1]$ whose problem is to maximize a particular intertemporal welfare function. To this end, a utility function is used, additively separable into consumption (C) and labor (L).*

It is to be expected that a rise in consumption brings utility (happiness) to households, while a rise in labor hours brings disutility. At this point in the book, this is not surprising, seeing as in the theoretical section, it was mentioned that leisure provides individuals with happiness and that the more time they spend working, the less time they will have for leisure.

Assumption 2.2.5. *Consumption is intertemporally additively separable (no habit formation).*

Assumption 2.2.6. *Population growth is ignored.*

Assumption 2.2.7. *The labor market structure is one of perfect competition (no wage rigidity).*

The representative household optimizes the following welfare function:

$$\max_{C_{j,t}, L_{j,t}, K_{j,t+1}} E_t \sum_{t=0}^{\infty} \beta^t \left(\frac{C_{j,t}^{1-\sigma}}{1-\sigma} - \frac{L_{j,t}^{1+\varphi}}{1+\varphi} \right) \tag{2.1}$$

where E_t is the expectations operator, β is the intertemporal discount factor, C is the consumption of goods, L is the number of hours worked, σ is the relative risk aversion coefficient, and φ is the marginal disutility in respect of labor supply.

As mentioned in the theoretical section, the utility function[8] must have certain characteristics: $U_C > 0$ and $U_L < 0$, this means that consumption and labor have positive and negative effects, respectively, on the utility of households. On the other hand, $U_{CC} < 0$ and $U_{LL} < 0$ indicate that the utility function is concave[9]. This represents the fact that, as consumption increases, so does utility, albeit at increasingly lower rates.

Households maximize their welfare function, which is subject to their intertemporal budget constraints, which indicates which resources are available and how they are allocated. Thus, it is assumed that households are the owners of the economy's factors of production (capital and labor). Households, providing labor and capital to firms, receive wages and returns on capital, respectively. They also own the firms, and therefore receive dividends. Thus, a household's intertemporal budget constraint can be written in the following way:

$$P_t(C_{j,t} + I_{j,t}) = W_t L_{j,t} + R_t K_{j,t} + \Pi_t \tag{2.2}$$

where P is the general price level, I is level of investment, W is the level of wages, K is the capital stock, R is the return on capital, and Π is the firms' profit (dividends).

---

[8]The most common utility function used to represent Household choices is the utility function with a constant relative risk aversion (CRRA) (Galí, 2008; Lim and McNelis, 2008; Clarida *et al.*, 2002; Galí and Monacelli, 2005; Christoffel and Kuester, 2008; Christoffel *et al.*, 2009; Ravenna and Walsh, 2006, among others). In the literature, other functions that represent utility do exist, for example: a logarithmic utility function, $U(C_t, L_t) = \ln C_t + \frac{L_t}{L_0} A \ln(1 - L_0)$ (Hansen, 1985); a utility function that is a combination of a logarithmic function and CRRA, $U(C_t, L_t) = \ln(C_t) - \frac{v}{1+\chi} L_t^{1+\chi}$ (Gertler and Karadi, 2011, among others).

[9]U_C and U_L are the first-order derivatives of the utility function in relation to consumption and labor, respectively, while, U_{CC} and U_{LL} are the second-order derivatives.

An additional equation that shows capital accumulation over time is required.

$$K_{j,t+1} = (1 - \delta)K_{j,t} + I_{j,t} \qquad (2.3)$$

where δ is the depreciation rate of physical capital.

The problem of the household is solved using the following Lagrangian formed by equations (2.1), (2.2) and (2.3):

$$\mathcal{L} = E_t \sum_{t=0}^{\infty} \beta^t \left\{ \left[\frac{C_{j,t}^{1-\sigma}}{1-\sigma} - \frac{L_{j,t}^{1+\varphi}}{1+\varphi} \right] \right.$$

$$\left. - \lambda_{j,t} \left[P_t C_{j,t} + P_t K_{j,t+1} - P_t(1-\delta)K_{j,t} - W_t L_{j,t} - R_t K_{j,t} - \Pi_t \right] \right\} \qquad (2.4)$$

where λ is the Lagrange multiplier.

Solving the previous problem, we arrive at the following first-order conditions:

$$\frac{\partial \mathcal{L}}{\partial C_{j,t}} = C_{j,t}^{-\sigma} - \lambda_{j,t} P_t = 0 \qquad (2.5)$$

$$\frac{\partial \mathcal{L}}{\partial L_{j,t}} = -L_{j,t}^{\varphi} + \lambda_{j,t} W_t = 0 \qquad (2.6)$$

$$\frac{\partial \mathcal{L}}{\partial K_{j,t+1}} = -\lambda_{j,t} P_t + \beta E_t \lambda_{j,t+1} [(1-\delta)E_t P_{t+1} + E_t R_{t+1}] = 0 \qquad (2.7)$$

Solving for λ_t equations (2.5) and (2.6), we arrive at the household's labor supply equation.

$$C_{j,t}^{\sigma} L_{j,t}^{\varphi} = \frac{W_t}{P_t} \qquad (2.8)$$

or,

$$\underbrace{-C_{j,t}^{\sigma} L_{j,t}^{\varphi}}_{\text{Consumption-leisure MRS}} = \underbrace{-\frac{W_t}{P_t}}_{\text{Consumption-leisure relative price}}$$

The labor supply equation states that the consumption-leisure relative price (real wage) must be equal to the leisure-consumption marginal rate of substitution (Theoretical Result 2.1.1). Thus, a rise in consumption, ceteris paribus, is only possible with a rise in the amount of labor hours (less leisure). In other words, there is a trade-off between working less (enjoying less leisure) and consuming more. On the other hand, higher real wages allow consumption to increase without there being a need to give up leisure[10].

Knowing that from equation (2.5) $\lambda_{j,t} = \frac{C_{j,t}^{-\sigma}}{P_t}$ e $\lambda_{j,t+1} = \frac{C_{j,t+1}^{-\sigma}}{P_{t+1}}$, and using these results in equation (2.7), the Euler equation is found:

$$-C_{j,t}^{-\sigma} + \beta E_t \left\{ \left(\frac{C_{j,t+1}^{-\sigma}}{P_{t+1}} \right) [(1-\delta)P_{t+1} + R_{t+1}] \right\} = 0$$

$$\left(\frac{E_t C_{j,t+1}}{C_{j,t}} \right)^{\sigma} = \beta \left[(1-\delta) + E_t \left(\frac{R_{t+1}}{P_{t+1}} \right) \right] \tag{2.9}$$

The previous equation determines the household's savings decision (in this model, savings is the acquisition of investment goods). Thus, when households decide their level of savings, they compare the utility rendered by consuming an additional amount today with the utility that would be rendered by consuming more in the future. Thus, if interest rate expectations rise, consuming "today" (at t) is more expensive and, ceteris paribus, future consumption (t+1) will rise.

One final remark concerning the Euler equation is worth being made. To simplify it, assume that $\beta = 1$ and $\delta = 1$,

$$\underbrace{-E_t \left[\frac{1}{\pi_{t+1}} \left(\frac{C_{j,t+1}}{C_{j,t}} \right)^{\sigma} \right]}_{\text{TMS } C_t\text{-}C_{t+1}} = \underbrace{-E_t \left(\frac{r_{t+1}}{\pi_{t+1}} \right)}_{\text{relative price } C_t\text{-}C_{t+1}}$$

where $E_t r_{t+1} = E_t \left(\frac{R_{t+1}}{P_{t+1}} \right)$ is the real rate of return on capital.

Thus, this last expression (Theoretical Result 2.1.2) states that the marginal rate of substitution of current consumption for future consumption is equal to the relative price of current consumption in terms of future consumption.

---

[10]With higher real wages, the consumption of goods will certainly be higher. On the other hand, the same cannot be said for leisure. If the income effect exceeds the substitution effect, leisure will increase, however, in the opposite case, leisure will decrease.

In short, the problem of the household boils down to two choices. The first is an intratemporal choice between acquiring consumption and leisure goods. The other is an intertemporal choice, in which the household must choose between present and future consumption.

Firms

The representative firm is the agent that produces the goods and services that will be either consumed or saved (and then transformed into capital) by households.

Assumption 2.2.8. *There is a continuum of firms indexed by j that maximize profit observing a structure of perfect competition, this means that their profits will be zero ($\Pi_t = 0$, for every t).*

To this end a Cobb-Douglas[11] production function is used:

$$Y_{j,t} = A_t K_{j,t}^{\alpha} L_{j,t}^{1-\alpha} \tag{2.10}$$

where A_t represents productivity, a variable that can be interpreted as the level of general knowledge about the "arts" of production available in an economy, Y_t is the product, and α is the elasticity of the level of production with respect to capital; α can also be thought of as the level of participation of capital in the productive process, whereas $(1 - \alpha)$ would be the level of participation of labor. Similarly to the household's utility function, the production function must have certain properties: it must be strictly increasing ($F_K > 0$ and $F_L > 0$), strictly concave ($F_{KK} < 0$ e $F_{LL} < 0$), and twice differentiable. It is also assumed that the production function has constant returns to scale, $F(zK_t, zL_t) = zY_t$. This function must also satisfy the Inada conditions: $\lim_{K \to 0} F_K = \infty$; $\lim_{K \to \infty} F_K = 0$; $\lim_{L \to 0} F_L = \infty$; and $\lim_{L \to \infty} F_L = 0$.

---

[11]Although many DSGE models use Cobb-Douglas technology, there are alternatives. Another very popular function in the literature is the CES (Constant Elasticity of Substitution) function,

$$F(K_t, L_t) = \left[\alpha K_t^{\rho} + (1 - \alpha) L_t^{\rho} \right]^{\frac{1}{\rho}}$$

where $\rho \in (-\infty, 1)$ is a parameter that determines the elasticity of substitution between two inputs.

The problem of the firm is solved by maximizing the Profit function, choosing the amounts of each input (L_t, K_t):

$$\max_{L_{j,t}, K_{j,t}} \Pi_{j,t} = A_t K_{j,t}^{\alpha} L_{j,t}^{1-\alpha} P_{j,t} - W_t L_{j,t} - R_t K_{j,t} \qquad (2.11)$$

Solving the previous problem, we arrive at the following first-order conditions:

$$\frac{\partial \Pi_{j,t}}{\partial K_{j,t}} = \alpha A_t K_{j,t}^{\alpha-1} L_{j,t}^{1-\alpha} P_{j,t} - R_t = 0 \qquad (2.12)$$

$$\frac{\partial \Pi_{j,t}}{\partial L_{j,t}} = (1-\alpha) A_t K_{j,t}^{\alpha} L_{j,t}^{-\alpha} P_{j,t} - W_t = 0 \qquad (2.13)$$

From equations (2.12) and (2.13):

$$\underbrace{\frac{R_t}{P_{j,t}}}_{\text{Real MCK}} = \alpha \underbrace{\frac{Y_{j,t}}{K_{j,t}}}_{\text{MPK}} \qquad (2.14)$$

$$\underbrace{\frac{W_t}{P_{j,t}}}_{\text{Real MCL}} = (1-\alpha) \underbrace{\frac{Y_{j,t}}{L_{j,t}}}_{\text{MPL}} \qquad (2.15)$$

Equations (2.14) and (2.15) represent the demand for capital and labor, respectively (Theoretical Result 2.1.3), in which marginal costs are equal to the marginal products[12].

Note that in equation (2.15) a reduction in real wages means higher demand for labor as, when the real cost of hiring workers reduces, firms increase their demand for labor until the marginal product of labor reduces to the same level as the fall in real wages[13] (Barro, 1997).

It is assumed that productivity shocks follow a first-order autoregressive process, such that:

$$\log A_t = (1 - \rho_A) \log A_{ss} + \rho_A \log A_{t-1} + \epsilon_t \qquad (2.16)$$

---

[12] Real MCK is the real marginal cost of capital; Real MCL is the real marginal cost of labor; MPK is the marginal product of capital; and MPL is the marginal product of labor.

[13] The same logic applies to capital (equation 2.14).

where A_{ss} is the value of productivity at the steady state, ρ_A is the autoregressive parameter of productivity, whose absolute value must be less than one ($|\rho_A| < 1$) to ensure the stationary nature of the process and $\epsilon_t \sim N(0, \sigma_A)$.

Assumption 2.2.9. *Productivity growth is ignored in this model.*

As the model follows the RBC approach, the price level must be equal to marginal cost. Thus, to obtain the marginal cost, the input demand equations must first be combined (equations (2.14) and (2.15)):

$$\underbrace{-\frac{W_t}{R_t}}_{\text{ERS}} = \underbrace{-\frac{(1-\alpha)K_{j,t}}{\alpha L_{j,t}}}_{\text{MRTS}}$$

Reminding the reader that this expression represents Theoretical Result 2.1.4. Its right-hand side is the marginal rate of technical substitution, which measures the rate at which labor can be replaced by capital while maintaining a constant level of production. The left-hand side is the economic rate of substitution, which measures the rate at which labor can be replaced by capital while maintaining the same cost.

Rearranging the previous expression,

$$L_{j,t} = \left(\frac{1-\alpha}{\alpha}\right)\frac{R_t}{W_t}K_{j,t} \tag{2.17}$$

and substituting equation (2.17) in the production function (equation (2.10)),

$$Y_{j,t} = A_t K_{j,t}^{\alpha} \left[\left(\frac{1-\alpha}{\alpha}\right)\frac{R_t}{W_t}K_{j,t}\right]^{1-\alpha}$$

$$K_{j,t} = \frac{Y_{j,t}}{A_t}\left[\left(\frac{\alpha}{1-\alpha}\right)\frac{W_t}{R_t}\right]^{1-\alpha} \tag{2.18}$$

Substituting equation (2.18) in (2.17),

$$L_{j,t} = \frac{Y_{j,t}}{A_t}\left(\frac{1-\alpha}{\alpha}\right)\frac{R_t}{W_t}\left[\left(\frac{\alpha}{1-\alpha}\right)\frac{W_t}{R_t}\right]^{1-\alpha}$$

$$\left(\frac{1-\alpha}{\alpha}\right)\frac{R_t}{W_t} = \left[\left(\frac{\alpha}{1-\alpha}\right)\frac{W_t}{R_t}\right]^{-1}$$

$$L_{j,t} = \frac{A_t}{Y_{j,t}}\left[\left(\frac{\alpha}{1-\alpha}\right)\frac{W_t}{R_t}\right]^{-\alpha} \qquad (2.19)$$

total cost (TC) is represented by:

$$TC_{j,t} = W_t L_{j,t} + R_t K_{j,t}$$

substituting equations (2.18) and (2.19) in the total cost function:

$$TC_t = W_t \frac{Y_{j,t}}{A_t}\left[\left(\frac{\alpha}{1-\alpha}\right)\frac{W_t}{R_t}\right]^{-\alpha} + R_t \frac{Y_{j,t}}{A_t}\left[\left(\frac{\alpha}{1-\alpha}\right)\frac{W_t}{R_t}\right]^{1-\alpha}$$

with a little algebraic massaging, we arrive at:

$$TC_{j,t} = \frac{Y_{j,t}}{A_t}\left(\frac{W_t}{1-\alpha}\right)^{1-\alpha}\left(\frac{R_t}{\alpha}\right)^{\alpha}$$

and the marginal cost is derived from the total cost[14]:

$$MC_{j,t} = \frac{1}{A_t}\left(\frac{W_t}{1-\alpha}\right)^{1-\alpha}\left(\frac{R_t}{\alpha}\right)^{\alpha} \qquad (2.20)$$

As the marginal cost depends solely on productivity and the prices of the factors of production, it will be the same for all firms ($MC_{j,t} = MC_t$). Knowing that $P_t = MC_t$, we arrive at the general price level,

$$P_t = \frac{1}{A_t}\left(\frac{W_t}{1-\alpha}\right)^{1-\alpha}\left(\frac{R_t}{\alpha}\right)^{\alpha} \qquad (2.21)$$

The model's equilibrium conditions

Now that each agent's behavior has been described, the interaction between them must be studied in order to determine macroeconomic equilibrium. Households decide how much to consume (C), how much to invest (I) and how much labor to supply (L), with the aim of maximizing utility, taking prices as given. On the other

---

[14] $MC_{j,t} = \frac{\partial TC_{j,t}}{\partial Y_{j,t}}$.

hand, firms decide how much to produce (Y) using available technology and choosing the factors of production (capital and labor), taking these prices as given.

Therefore, the model's equilibrium consists of the following blocks:

1. a price system, W_t, R_t and P_t;

2. an endowment of values for goods and inputs Y_t, C_t, I_t, L_t and K_t; and

3. a production-possibility frontier described by the following equilibrium condition of the goods market (aggregate supply = aggregate demand).

$$Y_t = C_t + I_t \tag{2.22}$$

Competitive equilibrium consists in finding a sequence of endogenous variables in the model such that the conditions that define equilibrium are satisfied. In short, this economy's model consists of the following equations from Table 2.1[15].

Steady state

After defining the economy's equilibrium, the steady state values must be defined. Indeed, the model presented is steady in the sense that there exists a value for the variables that is maintained over time: an endogenous variable x_t is at the steady state in each t, if $E_t x_{t+1} = x_t = x_{t-1} = x_{ss}$.

Some endogenous variables have their steady state values previously determined (exogenously). This is the case of productivity, which is the source of standard RBC models' shocks - at the steady state $E(\epsilon_t) = 0$. Thus, with equation (2.16) it is not possible to know the value of productivity at the steady state, the literature generally assigning $A_{ss} = 1$. The next step is to remove the variables' time indicators. Therefore, the structural model is:

---

[15] Because of the symmetry in the preferences of households and in the technology of firms, these two kinds of agents will be represented by representative agents (this eliminates the j subscript).

Table 2.1: Structure of the model.

Equation	(Definition)
$C_t^{\sigma} L_t^{\varphi} = \frac{W_t}{P_t}$	(Labor supply)
$\left(\frac{E_t C_{j,t+1}}{C_{j,t}}\right)^{\sigma} = \beta \left[(1-\delta) + E_t\left(\frac{R_{t+1}}{P_{t+1}}\right)\right]$	(Euler equation)
$K_{t+1} = (1-\delta)K_t + I_t$	(Law of motion of capital)
$Y_t = A_t K_t^{\alpha} L_t^{1-\alpha}$	(Production function)
$K_t = \alpha \frac{Y_t}{\frac{R_t}{P_t}}$	(Demand for capital)
$L_t = (1-\alpha) \frac{Y_t}{\frac{W_t}{P_t}}$	(Demand for labor)
$P_t = \frac{1}{A_t} \left(\frac{W_t}{1-\alpha}\right)^{1-\alpha} \left(\frac{R_t}{\alpha}\right)^{\alpha}$	(Price level)
$Y_t = C_t + I_t$	(Equilibrium condition)
$\log A_t = (1-\rho_A)\log A_{ss} + \rho_A \log A_{t-1} + \epsilon_t$	(Productivity shock)

Households

$$C_{ss}^{\sigma} L_{ss}^{\varphi} = \frac{W_{ss}}{P_{ss}} \tag{2.23}$$

$$1 = \beta\left(1 - \delta + \frac{R_{ss}}{P_{ss}}\right) \tag{2.24}$$

$$I_{ss} = \delta K_{ss} \tag{2.25}$$

Firms

$$K_{ss} = \alpha \frac{Y_{ss}}{\frac{R_{ss}}{P_{ss}}} \tag{2.26}$$

$$L_{ss} = (1-\alpha) \frac{Y_{ss}}{\frac{W_{ss}}{P_{ss}}} \tag{2.27}$$

$$Y_{ss} = K_{ss}^{\alpha} L_{ss}^{1-\alpha} \tag{2.28}$$

$$P_{ss} = \left(\frac{W_{ss}}{1-\alpha}\right)^{1-\alpha} \left(\frac{R_{ss}}{\alpha}\right)^{\alpha} \tag{2.29}$$

Equilibrium Condition

$$Y_{ss} = C_{ss} + I_{ss} \tag{2.30}$$

The system of equations formed by equations (2.23) to (2.30) will be used to determine the value of eight endogenous variables at the steady state (Y_{ss}, C_{ss}, I_{ss}, K_{ss}, L_{ss}, W_{ss}, R_{ss} and P_{ss}).

The first values that must be determined are the prices (W_{ss}, R_{ss} and P_{ss}). To this end, Walras' law must be taken into consideration.

Proposition 2.2.1 (Walras' Law). *For any price vector p, has $pz(p) \equiv 0$; i.e., the demand excess value is identically zero.*

Proof. In simple terms, the definition of excess demand is written and multiplied by $\mathbf{p}$:

$$\mathbf{pz}(\mathbf{p}) = \mathbf{p} \left[\sum_{i=1}^{n} \mathbf{x}_i(\mathbf{p}, \mathbf{p}\,\mathbf{w}_i) - \sum_{i=1}^{n} \mathbf{w}_i \right] = \sum_{i=1}^{n} \left[\mathbf{p}\,\mathbf{x}_i(\mathbf{p}, \mathbf{p}\,\mathbf{w}_i) - \mathbf{p}\,\mathbf{w}_i \right] = 0$$

since $\mathbf{x}_i(\mathbf{p}, \mathbf{p}\,\mathbf{w}_i)$ satisfies the budget constraint $\mathbf{p}\,\mathbf{x}_i = \mathbf{p}\,\mathbf{w}_i$ for each individual i=1,...,n. $\qquad\square$

In other words, Walras' law states that if each individual satisfies his/her budget constraint, the value of his/her excess demand is zero, therefore the sum of excess demand must also be zero. It is important to note that Walras' law states that the value of excess demand is identical to zero - the value of excess demand is zero for all prices (Varian, 1992).

Walras' Law implies the existence of k-1 independent equations in equilibrium with k goods. Thus, if demand is equal to supply in k-1 markets, they will also be equal in the kth market. Consequently, if there are k markets, only k-1 relative prices are required to determine equilibrium.

Provided that the excess aggregate demand function is homogeneous of degree zero, prices can be normalized and demands expressed in terms of relative price: $p_i = \frac{\hat{p}_i}{\sum_{j=1}^{k} \hat{p}_j}$. As a consequence, the sum of the normalized prices p_i must always be 1. Thus, attention can be directed to the price vector belonging to the unit simplex of dimension k-1: $S^{k-1} = \{\mathbf{p} \in R_+^k : \sum_{i=1}^{k} p_i = 1\}$. In short, taking Walras' Law into account, the economy's general price level can be normalized, $P_{ss} = 1$.

To find R_{ss}, equation (2.24) is used,

$$R_{ss} = P_{ss}\left[\left(\frac{1}{\beta}\right) - (1-\delta)\right] \qquad (2.31)$$

Note that equation (2.31) shows R_{ss} as a function of only the normalized general price level parameters[16], therefore its value is determined. It simply remains to find the steady state of the wage level (W_{ss}). Thus, from equation (2.29),

$$W_{ss}^{1-\alpha} = P_{ss}(1-\alpha)^{1-\alpha}\left(\frac{\alpha}{R_{ss}}\right)^{\alpha}$$

$$W_{ss} = (1-\alpha)P_{ss}^{\frac{1}{1-\alpha}}\left(\frac{\alpha}{R_{ss}}\right)^{\frac{\alpha}{1-\alpha}} \qquad (2.32)$$

The next step is to satisfy the equilibrium condition. To this end, the variables that make up aggregate demand (C_{ss} and I_{ss}) must be determined. The idea underlying the equilibrium condition is formed by the following proposition.

Proposition 2.2.2 (Market adjustment). *Given k markets, if demand is equal to supply in k-1 markets and $p_k > 0$, then demand must equal supply in the kth market.*

Proof. If not, Walras' Law is violated. □

Therefore, to meet the equilibrium condition, the input market conditions must be met. To this end, it is necessary to find the meeting point between the supplies (provided by households) and the demands (provided by firms) of the production inputs (labor and capital) (Figure 2.12).

First, equation (2.27) must be replaced in equation (2.23), solving for C_{ss},

$$C_{ss}^{\sigma}\left[(1-\alpha)\frac{Y_{ss}}{\frac{W_{ss}}{P_{ss}}}\right]^{\varphi} = \frac{W_{ss}}{P_{ss}}$$

---

[16]In the Dynare simulation, there is no need to substitute R_{ss} in the other equations. It should just be shown before the other steady states.

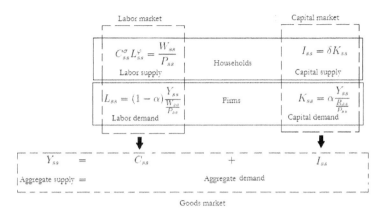

Figure 2.12: Steady state market adjustment structure. The dashed lines represent the labor, capital goods and consumer goods markets.

$$C_{ss} = \frac{1}{Y_{ss}^{\frac{\varphi}{\sigma}}} \left[\frac{W_{ss}}{P_{ss}} \left(\frac{\frac{W_{ss}}{P_{ss}}}{1-\alpha} \right)^{\varphi} \right]^{\frac{1}{\sigma}} \tag{2.33}$$

With the value C_{ss} known, I_{ss} still needs to be found. Consequently, equation (2.26) needs to be replaced in equation (2.25),

$$I_{ss} = \left(\frac{\delta \alpha}{R_{ss}} \right) Y_{ss} \tag{2.34}$$

Finally, Y_{ss} must be found. Substituting equations (2.33) and (2.34) in equation (2.30),

$$Y_{ss} = \frac{1}{Y_{ss}^{\frac{\varphi}{\sigma}}} \left[\frac{W_{ss}}{P_{ss}} \left(\frac{\frac{W_{ss}}{P_{ss}}}{1-\alpha} \right)^{\varphi} \right]^{\frac{1}{\sigma}} + \left(\frac{\delta \alpha}{R_{ss}} \right) Y_{ss}$$

$$\left(1 - \frac{\delta \alpha}{R_{ss}} \right) Y_{ss} = \frac{1}{Y_{ss}^{\frac{\varphi}{\sigma}}} \left[\frac{W_{ss}}{P_{ss}} \left(\frac{\frac{W_{ss}}{P_{ss}}}{1-\alpha} \right)^{\varphi} \right]^{\frac{1}{\sigma}}$$

$$Y_{ss} = \left(\frac{R_{ss}}{R_{ss} - \delta\alpha}\right)^{\frac{\sigma}{\sigma+\varphi}} \left[\frac{W_{ss}}{P_{ss}}\left(\frac{\frac{W_{ss}}{P_{ss}}}{1-\alpha}\right)^{\varphi}\right]^{\frac{1}{\sigma+\varphi}} \tag{2.35}$$

The previous procedures are summarized in the presentation of the steady state below:

$$A_{ss} = 1$$

$$P_{ss} = 1$$

$$R_{ss} = P_{ss}\left[\left(\frac{1}{\beta}\right) - (1-\delta)\right]$$

$$W_{ss} = (1-\alpha)P_{ss}^{\frac{1}{1-\alpha}}\left(\frac{\alpha}{R_{ss}}\right)^{\frac{\alpha}{1-\alpha}}$$

$$Y_{ss} = \left(\frac{R_{ss}}{R_{ss} - \delta\alpha}\right)^{\frac{\sigma}{\sigma+\varphi}} \left[\frac{W_{ss}}{P_{ss}}\left(\frac{\frac{W_{ss}}{P_{ss}}}{1-\alpha}\right)^{\varphi}\right]^{\frac{1}{\sigma+\varphi}}$$

$$I_{ss} = \left(\frac{\delta\alpha}{R_{ss}}\right)Y_{ss}$$

$$C_{ss} = \frac{1}{Y_{ss}^{\frac{\varphi}{\sigma}}}\left[(1-\alpha)^{-\varphi}\left(\frac{W_{ss}}{P_{ss}}\right)^{1+\varphi}\right]^{\frac{1}{\sigma}}$$

$$K_{ss} = \alpha\frac{Y_{ss}}{\frac{R_{ss}}{P_{ss}}}$$

$$L_{ss} = (1-\alpha)\frac{Y_{ss}}{\frac{W_{ss}}{P_{ss}}}$$

Using the previous sequence and the calibrated data shown in Table 2.2, we arrive at the steady state values for the variables (Table 2.3).

Table 2.2: Values of the structural model's parameters.

Parameter	Parameter meaning	Calibrated value
σ	Relative risk aversion coefficient	2
φ	Marginal disutility with regard to supply of labor	1.5
α	Elasticity of level of production in relation to capital	0.35
β	Discount factor	0.985
δ	Depreciation rate	0.025
ρ_A	Autoregressive parameter - productivity	0.95
σ_A	Standard deviation of productivity	0.01

Table 2.3: Values of variables at the steady state.

Variable	Steady state
A	1
R	0.040
W	2.084
Y	2.338
I	0.508
C	1.829
L	0.729
K	20.338

Log-linearization (Uhlig's method)

Handling and solving non-linear models is generally very arduous. When the model is very simple, it is possible to find an approximation of the policy function by recursively solving the value function. On the other hand, linear models are often easier to solve. The problem is converting a non-linear model to a sufficiently adequate linear approximation such that its solution helps in the understanding of the underlying non-linear system's behavior. Thus, a standard procedure is to log-linearize the model around its steady state (some methods use this approach in their solution procedures: Blanchard and Kahn, 1980; Uhlig, 1999; Sims, 2001; and Klein, 2000)[17][18].

Uhlig (1999) recommends a simple method of log-linearization of functions that does not require differentiation: simply replacing a variable X_t with $X_{ss}e^{\widetilde{X}_t}$, where $\widetilde{X}_t = \log X - \log X_{ss}$ represents the log of the variable's deviation in relation to its steady state. Uhlig further proposes the following solution tools:

$$e^{(\widetilde{X}_t + a\widetilde{Y}_t)} \approx 1 + \widetilde{X}_t + a\widetilde{Y}_t \qquad (2.36)$$

$$\widetilde{X}_t \widetilde{Y}_t \approx 0 \qquad (2.37)$$

$$E_t\left[ae^{\widetilde{X}_{t+1}}\right] \approx a + aE_t\left[\widetilde{X}_{t+1}\right] \qquad (2.38)$$

Labor supply

Beginning with the labor supply function,

$$C_t^{\sigma} L_t^{\varphi} = \frac{W_t}{P_t}$$

$X_t = X_{ss}e^{\widetilde{X}_t}$ is replaced in each variable of the previous equation.

$$C_{ss}^{\sigma} L_{ss}^{\varphi} e^{(\sigma\widetilde{C}_t + \varphi\widetilde{L}_t)} = \frac{W_{ss}}{P_{ss}} e^{(\widetilde{W}_t - \widetilde{P}_t)}$$

---

[17]For further information, see DeJong and Dave (2007) and Canova (2007).

[18]It is important to point out that the models can be solved directly using Dynare without the need of linearization

Then, the equation's Uhlig rule is used (2.36),

$$C_{ss}^{\sigma} L_{ss}^{\varphi}(1 + \sigma\widetilde{C}_t + \varphi\widetilde{L}_t) = \frac{W_{ss}}{P_{ss}}(1 + \widetilde{W}_t - \widetilde{P}_t)$$

given that at the steady state, $C_{ss}^{\sigma} L_{ss}^{\varphi} = \frac{W_{ss}}{P_{ss}}$, we arrive at:

$$\sigma\widetilde{C}_t + \varphi\widetilde{L}_t = \widetilde{W}_t - \widetilde{P}_t \qquad (2.39)$$

Euler equation for consumption

The same procedure will be used for the Euler equation.

$$\frac{1}{\beta} E_t \left(\frac{C_{t+1}}{C_t} \right)^{\sigma} = (1 - \delta) + E_t \left(\frac{R_{t+1}}{P_{t+1}} \right)$$

$X_t = X_{ss} e^{\widetilde{X}_t}$ is replaced in each variable of the previous equation.

$$\frac{1}{\beta} \left(\frac{C_{ss}^{\sigma}}{C_{ss}^{\sigma}} \right) e^{(\sigma E_t \widetilde{C}_{t+1} - \sigma\widetilde{C}_t)} = (1 - \delta) + \frac{R_{ss}}{P_{ss}} e^{[E_t(\widetilde{R}_{t+1} - \widetilde{P}_{t+1})]}$$

Then, the equation's Uhlig rule is used (2.36),

$$\frac{1}{\beta} \left[1 + \sigma(E_t \widetilde{C}_{t+1} - \widetilde{C}_t) \right] = (1 - \delta) + \frac{R_{ss}}{P_{ss}} \left[1 + E_t(\widetilde{R}_{t+1} - \widetilde{P}_{t+1}) \right]$$

given that at the steady state, $\frac{1}{\beta} = \frac{R_{ss}}{P_{ss}} + (1 - \delta)$, we arrive at:

$$\frac{\sigma}{\beta} (E_t \widetilde{C}_{t+1} - \widetilde{C}_t) = \frac{R_{ss}}{P_{ss}} E_t(\widetilde{R}_{t+1} - \widetilde{P}_{t+1}) \qquad (2.40)$$

Return on capital

Rewriting demand for capital,

$$R_t = \alpha \frac{Y_t}{K_t}$$

substituting $X_t = X_{ss} e^{\widetilde{X}_t}$ in each variable of the previous equation.

$$\frac{R_{ss}}{P_{ss}} e^{(\widetilde{R}_t - \widetilde{P}_t)} = \alpha \frac{Y_{ss}}{K_{ss}} e^{(\widetilde{Y}_t - \widetilde{K}_t)}$$

Now, the equation's Uhlig rule is used (2.36),

$$\frac{R_{ss}}{P_{ss}}(1 + \tilde{R}_t - \tilde{P}_t) = \alpha \frac{Y_{ss}}{K_{ss}}(1 + \tilde{Y}_t - \tilde{K}_t)$$

knowing that at the steady state, $\frac{R_{ss}}{P_{ss}} = \alpha \frac{Y_{ss}}{K_{ss}}$, we arrive at:

$$\tilde{R}_t - \tilde{P}_t = \tilde{Y}_t - \tilde{K}_t \qquad (2.41)$$

Wage levels

Demand for labor is:

$$\frac{W_t}{P_t} = (1 - \alpha)\frac{Y_t}{L_t}$$

Substituting $X_t = X_{ss}e^{\tilde{X}_t}$ in each variable of the previous equation:

$$\frac{W_{ss}}{P_{ss}}e^{(\tilde{W}_t - \tilde{P}_t)} = (1 - \alpha)\frac{Y_{ss}}{L_{ss}}e^{(\tilde{Y}_t - \tilde{L}_t)}$$

Now, the equation's Uhlig rule is used (2.36),

$$\frac{W_{ss}}{P_{ss}}(1 + \tilde{W}_t - \tilde{P}_t) = (1 - \alpha)\frac{Y_{ss}}{L_{ss}}(1 + \tilde{Y}_t - \tilde{L}_t)$$

Knowing that at the steady state, $\frac{W_{ss}}{P_{ss}} = (1 - \alpha)\frac{Y_{ss}}{L_{ss}}$, we get:

$$\tilde{W}_t - \tilde{P}_t = \tilde{Y}_t - \tilde{L}_t \qquad (2.42)$$

Production function

Using the same procedure as before for the production function:

$$Y_t = A_t K_t^\alpha L_t^{1-\alpha}$$

$$Y_{ss}e^{\tilde{Y}_t} = A_{ss}K_{ss}^\alpha L_{ss}^{1-\alpha}e^{(\tilde{A}_t + \alpha\tilde{K}_t + (1-\alpha)\tilde{L}_t)}$$

$$Y_{ss}(1 + \tilde{Y}_t) = A_{ss}K_{ss}^\alpha L_{ss}^{1-\alpha}(1 + \tilde{A}_t + \alpha\tilde{K}_t + (1-\alpha)\tilde{L}_t)$$

Knowing that at the steady state, $Y_{ss} = A_{ss} K_{ss}^\alpha L_{ss}^{1-\alpha}$:

$$\widetilde{Y}_t = \widetilde{A}_t + \alpha \widetilde{K}_t + (1-\alpha)\widetilde{L}_t \qquad (2.43)$$

Law of motion of capital

The law of motion of capital is:

$$K_{t+1} = (1-\delta)K_t + I_t$$

$$K_{ss}e^{\widetilde{K}_{t+1}} = (1-\delta)K_{ss}e^{\widetilde{K}_t} + I_{ss}e^{\widetilde{I}_t}$$

$$K_{ss}(1+\widetilde{K}_{t+1}) = (1-\delta)K_{ss}(1+\widetilde{K}_t) + I_{ss}(1+\widetilde{I}_t)$$

Dividing both sides of the previous equation by K_{ss},

$$(1+\widetilde{K}_{t+1}) = (1-\delta) + (1-\delta)\widetilde{K}_t + \frac{I_{ss}}{K_{ss}} + \frac{I_{ss}}{K_{ss}}\widetilde{I}_t$$

Knowing that at the steady state, $I_{ss} = \delta K_{ss}$:

$$\widetilde{K}_{t+1} = (1-\delta)\widetilde{K}_t + \delta\widetilde{I}_t \qquad (2.44)$$

Equilibrium condition

It simply remains to find the equilibrium condition's log-linear equation.

$$Y_t = C_t + I_t$$

$$Y_{ss}e^{\widetilde{Y}_t} = C_{ss}e^{\widetilde{C}_t} + I_{ss}e^{\widetilde{I}_t}$$

$$Y_{ss}(1+\widetilde{Y}_t) = C_{ss}(1+\widetilde{C}_t) + I_{ss}(1+\widetilde{I}_t)$$

Knowing that at the steady state, $Y_{ss} = C_{ss} + I_{ss}$:

$$Y_{ss}\widetilde{Y}_t = C_{ss}\widetilde{C}_t + I_{ss}\widetilde{I}_t \qquad (2.45)$$

Technological shock

The process of motion of productivity is:

$$\log A_t = (1 - \rho_A) \log A_{ss} + \rho_A \log A_{t-1} + \epsilon_t$$

Using a little algebra, we arrive at:

$$\widetilde{A}_t = \rho_A \widetilde{A}_{t-1} + \epsilon_t \tag{2.46}$$

Table 2.4 summarizes the log-linear model.

Table 2.4: Structure of the log-linear model.

Equation	(Definition)
$\sigma \widetilde{C}_t + \varphi \widetilde{L}_t = \widetilde{w}_t$	(Labor supply)
$\frac{\sigma}{\beta}(E_t \widetilde{C}_{t+1} - \widetilde{C}_t) = \frac{R_{ss}}{P_{ss}} E_t (\widetilde{R}_{t+1} - \widetilde{P}_{t+1})$	(Euler equation)
$\widetilde{K}_{t+1} = (1-\delta)\widetilde{K}_t + \delta \widetilde{I}_t$	(Law of motion capital)
$\widetilde{Y}_t = \widetilde{A}_t + \alpha \widetilde{K}_t + (1-\alpha)\widetilde{L}_t$	(Production function)
$\widetilde{K}_t = \widetilde{Y}_t - \widetilde{r}_t$	(Demand for capital)
$\widetilde{L}_t = \widetilde{Y}_t - \widetilde{w}_t$	(Demand for labor)
$Y_{ss}\widetilde{Y}_t = C_{ss}\widetilde{C}_t + I_{ss}\widetilde{I}_t$	(Equilibrium condition)
$\widetilde{A}_t = \rho_A \widetilde{A}_{t-1} + \epsilon_t$	(Productivity shock)

Here, we have $\widetilde{w}_t = \widetilde{W}_t - \widetilde{P}_t$ and $\widetilde{r}_t = \widetilde{R}_t - \widetilde{P}_t$, which represent wages and the real interest rate, respectively.

Productivity shock

In this section, the results of a productivity shock on the RBC economy in this chapter, will be analyzed. Firstly, the result of the productivity shock on the variables will be checked, following which we will seek to identify the theoretical standards presented at the start of the chapter in the simulation.

Figure 2.13 shows the effects of a positive disruption on the total productivity of the factors of production. The first evidence of this shock is the rise in the marginal productivities of labor and capital (equations (2.41) and (2.42)). Firms thus increase their demand for these inputs. This then affects the prices of the factors of production – wages (W) and return on capital (R) – increasing household income. With higher income, this agent responds by acquiring more consumer and investment goods (equation 2.45)). With regard to inputs, initially both labor and capital increase, but as wages decrease with time, households seek more leisure (labor supply reduces). On the other hand, with the rise in investments, the stock of capital shows a growing tendency until period 20 (equation 2.44)), forming a bell curve. In short, positive productivity shocks increase the consumption variables (C and I), demand for inputs (L and K) and the prices of these factors of production (W and R).

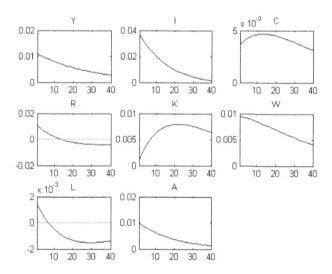

Figure 2.13: Effects of a productivity shock. Results of a Dynare simulation (impulse-response functions).

The aim of the group of figures in 2.14 to 2.17 is to understand how households "manage" their welfare given a positive productivity shock. Figure 2.14 shows the results of this shock on the leisure-

wages locus. It can be seen that the inflection point for the wage
level is 57% higher than its steady state level. Thus, increases that
are lower than this value cause households to seek more leisure (income effect). On the other hand, wage increases higher than the
inflection point cause the substitution effect to dominate – leisure
becomes more expensive. Figure 2.15 seeks to present a relationship with figure 2.7, its theoretical approach. We find that when
leisure is at relatively low levels (bottom left corner of Figure 2.15),
the preference of households is to increase leisure. This occurs until
the variable is 23% higher than the steady state (inflection point I).
From this point onwards, the substitution effect is dominant.

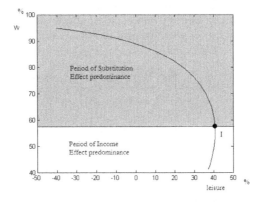

Figure 2.14: Leisure-wage locus. The x and y axes measure deviation in relation to the variable's steady state in percentage terms. Point I is the inflection
point between where the substitution effect and income effect dominate.

When the concern is the intertemporal tradeoff, figures 2.16 and
2.17 are used. In this first figure (present consumption versus future consumption), the inflection point is practically at the steady
state level of returns on capital. When the shock raises the value of
this variable, today's consumption becomes more expensive in relation to future consumption. Households thus reduce their acquisition of consumption goods in the current period (substitution effect). If, on the other hand, the return on capital reduces in relation
to its steady state, households are relatively poorer, causing them
to reduce present consumption (income effect). When the tradeoff
is intertemporal leisure (Figure 2.17), only the substitution effect is

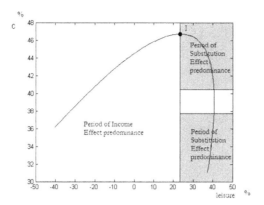

Figure 2.15: Leisure-consumption locus. The x and y axes measure deviations in relation to the variable's steady state in percentage terms. Point I is the inflection point between where the substitution effect and income effect dominate.

present. When R increases, future leisure becomes cheaper in relation to the current period. Therefore, a rise in the return on capital motivates households to work more today and less in the future.

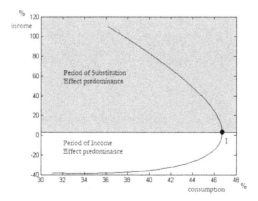

Figure 2.16: Consumption-income locus. The unit on the x and y axes measures percentage deviations in relation to the variable's steady state. Point I is the inflection point between which the substitution effect and income effect dominate.

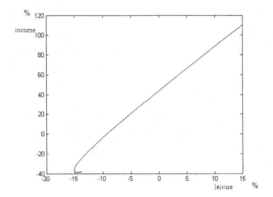

Figure 2.17: Leisure-income locus. The unit on the x and y axes measure, in percentage terms, deviations in relation to the variable's steady state. Point I is the inflection point between which the substitution effect and income effect dominate.

BOX 2.1 - Basic log-linear RBC model on Dynare

```
//RBC model - Chapter 2 (UNDERSTANDING DSGE MODELS)
//note: W and R are real in the simulation

var Y I C R K W L A ;
varexo e;
parameters sigma phi alpha beta delta rhoa;

sigma = 2;
phi = 1.5;
alpha = 0.35;
beta = 0.985;
delta = 0.025;
rhoa = 0.95;

model(linear);
#Pss = 1;
#Rss = Pss*((1/beta)-(1-delta));
#Wss = (1-alpha)*(Pss^(1/(1-alpha)))*((alpha/Rss)^(alpha/(1-alpha)));
#Yss = ((Rss/(Rss-delta*alpha))^(sigma/(sigma+phi)))
*(((1-alpha)^(-phi))*((Wss/Pss)^(1+phi)))^(1/(sigma+phi)));
#Kss = alpha*(Yss/Rss/Pss);
#Iss = delta*Kss;
#Css = Yss - Iss;
#Lss = (1-alpha)*(Yss/Wss/Pss);
//1-Labor supply
sigma*C + phi*L = W;
//2-Euler equation
(sigma/beta)*(C(+1)-C)=Rss*R(+1);
//3-Law of motion of capital
K = (1-delta)*K(-1)+delta*I;
//4-Production function
Y = A + alpha*K(-1) + (1-alpha)*L;
//5-Demand for capital
R = Y - K(-1);
//6-Demand for labor
W = Y - L;
//7-Equilibrium condition
Yss*Y = Css*C + Iss*I;
//8-Productivity shock
A = rhoa*A(-1) + e;
end;

steady;
check;
model_diagnostics;
model_info;

shocks;
var e;
stderr 0.01;
end;

stoch_simul;
```

Chapter 3
Basic New-Keynesian (NK) model

Modern macroeconomics is basically divided into two schools of economic thought. The first is Real Business Cycle (RBC) theory, that follows the classical tradition. The other, based on Keynesian principles, is New-Keynesian theory. The main difference between these two schools of thought is that RBC theory states that periodic expansions and recessions are natural and efficient responses to the technological state of an economy. Thus, a recession is not a terrible event for an economy, but rather a natural slowdown which is preceded by growth which will be followed by future expansion. Thus, RBC theory claims that the aggregate economy is in perfect competition on both the demand and supply sides. An important implication of RBC theory is that governments do not have an active role in the macroeconomy. In other words, neither fiscal nor monetary policy can be used to affect macroeconomic conditions. In contrast, New-Keynesian economics embraces the idea that economies are prone to market failures, which generate fluctuations. An important implication of this viewpoint is that governments can have a role in improving macroeconomic conditions.

The model developed in the previous chapter is based on the assumption of perfect competition in goods and inputs markets. It is this structure that sustains the classical convictions mentioned above. In the present chapter, the previous assumption is made more flexible with the introduction of imperfect competition, the "heart" of New-Keynesian models. This kind of model was initially developed by Rotemberg (1982), Blanchard and Kiyotaki (1987), Rotemberg and Woodford (1997), among others.

There will be no change to the structure of household behavior, but there will be significant alterations to the structure of the production sector. Now, the problem of the firm becomes more complex, requiring the inclusion of another two sectors: firms that produce final goods (retailers) and firms that produce intermediate goods (wholesalers). Imperfect competition occurs in the wholesale sector, which produces differentiated goods that are then sold and aggregated by retailers in an environment of perfect competition.

Brief theoretical review: New-Keynesians

This section seeks to present ideas regarding the structure of imperfect competition and price rigidity. It begins with a brief discussion on differentiated products and ways to aggregate them into one single good. Then, there is a brief commentary on the nature of price rigidity.

Differentiated Products and the Consumption Aggregator

In this study of representative consumers, which assumes the existence of only one product that consumers buy in order to gain utility, the use of a single consumption good is obviously a theoretical simplification. In reality, consumers buy a large number of goods and services that produce "utility". These products are actually interchangeable. Take, for example, the decision between going out for dinner and going to the cinema. Both options are forms of entertainment, but it is clear that they are not perfect substitutes for one another. Even if a consumer decides to go to the cinema, he/she will have to choose between the most recent comedy and an action movie clearly, these two movie genres are also imperfect substitutes. If it is believed that there is a large number of consumption options, each one being at least slightly different from another available option. One way to reconcile the use of a single consumption good is to assume that everything is made up of these many differentiated products. Specifically, it is assumed that the habitual notion of consumption is a function,

$$c = c(c_1, c_2, c_3, \ldots, c_N)$$

where c_1 is a type 1 consumer good (for example, a movie), c_2 is a type 2 consumer good (for example, dinner), etc. If there are N different products, the consumption of all things is a function of N different types of consumer good, formally known as a consumption aggregator function. In New-Keynesian models, the consumption function must generally satisfy the two following properties:

$$\frac{\partial c(.)}{\partial c_j} > 0$$

and,

$$\frac{\partial^2 c(.)}{\partial c_j^2} < 0$$

These two conditions mean, respectively, that total consumption is an increasing consumption function of a j type good, and that it increases at diminishing rates. These general properties apply to the representative consumer's utility function but not to the consumption aggregator function. The aggregate consumption function most commonly used in New-Keynesian models is[1]:

$$c(c_1, c_2, c_3, \ldots, c_N) = \left[(c_1)^{\frac{\psi-1}{\psi}} + (c_2)^{\frac{\psi-1}{\psi}} + (c_3)^{\frac{\psi-1}{\psi}} + \ldots + (c_N)^{\frac{\psi-1}{\psi}} \right]^{\frac{\psi}{\psi-1}}$$

where ψ is the elasticity of substitution between these differentiated goods, possessing great economic significance in New-Keynesian models. It determines to what degree, from a consumer's point of view, products differ from one another (figure 3.1). At one extreme is the value $\psi \rightarrow \infty$[2], which, when is substituted in the above expression, results in the simple linear sum $c_1 + c_2 + c_3 + \ldots + c_N$. Thus, each consumer good is as good as any other, from the viewpoint of the representative consumer, that is, the goods are perfect substitutes. With $\frac{\psi}{\psi-1} > 1$, however, the goods are only imperfect substitutes, which means that they are differentiated to some degree, depending on the exact value of ψ. Generally, New-Keynesian models assume $\frac{\psi}{\psi-1} > 1$.

---

[1] This function is a CES (Constant Elasticity of Substitution), and assuming only two goods, we get the following formula: $c(c_1, c_2) = \left[(c_1)^{\frac{\psi-1}{\psi}} + (c_2)^{\frac{\psi-1}{\psi}} \right]^{\frac{\psi}{\psi-1}}$.

[2] $\lim_{\psi \rightarrow \infty} \frac{\psi}{\psi-1} = 1$.

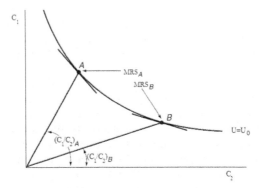

Figure 3.1: Graph describing the elasticity of substitution between two goods. Moving from point A to point B along the indifference curve ($U = U_0$), both the ratio (c_1/c_2) and the MRS will change. Elasticity of substitution ψ is defined as the ratio between these proportional changes. This parameter measures the curvature of an indifference curve.

Definition 3.1.1 (Elasticity of substitution between two goods).
For an aggregate function $c(c_1, c_2) = \left[(c_1)^{\frac{\psi-1}{\psi}} + (c_2)^{\frac{\psi-1}{\psi}} \right]^{\frac{\psi}{\psi-1}}$, *the elasticity of substitution* ψ *measures the proportional change in* c_1/c_2 *in relation to the proportional change in the Marginal Rate of Substitution (MRS) along an indifference curve. That is,*

$$\psi = \frac{\%\Delta(c_1/c_2)}{\%\Delta MRS} = \frac{\partial(c_1/c_2)}{\partial MRS} \cdot \frac{MRS}{(c_1/c_2)} = \frac{\partial \ln(c_1/c_2)}{\partial \ln MRS}$$

Firms in monopolistic competition

The fundamental idea of New-Keynesian models does not lie in the representative consumer, but in firms, each of the N differentiated products presumed to be produced by a distinct monopolistically competitive firm. In basic microeconomics, a fundamental characteristic of monopolistic competition is that goods are similar to each other, but not identical. Thus, a firm that produces a differentiated good has some degree of market power. This market power is demonstrated by the fact that firms are faced with negatively sloped demand curves and, therefore, marginal revenue curves strictly below their demand curves. This, in turn, implies that the characteristics of a firm's profit maximization choice will result in a price that is higher than marginal cost – algebraically, $P_j > MC_j$, where P_j and MC_j represent the nominal price and nominal marginal cost, respectively, in the profit maximization function of a firm that produces good j. These characteristics are summed up in Figure 3.2.

Definition 3.1.2 (Monopolistic competition). *A market is in monopolistic competition when it has many firms that produce very similar, but not identical products, and when new firms can freely enter the market. The causes of differentiation between products can be many and varied: products' intrinsic qualities, location of firms, additional services provided by firms etc.*

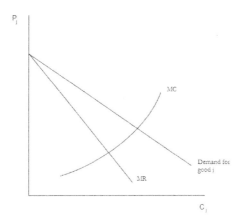

Figure 3.2: A firm in monopolistic competition faces a negatively sloped demand curve for its product. The marginal revenue (MR) curve is below the demand curve, and a profit-maximizing firm's choice of production occurs when MR=MC. At this point, price exceeds marginal cost (MC).

Recall the previous consumption aggregator expression where $\psi \to \infty$ implies that goods are perfect substitutes. This means that firms have no market power (and thus face a perfectly elastic demand curve). Therefore, defining $\psi \to \infty$ is a way of "turning off" the elements that New-Keynesian models use to include monopolistic competition.

In perfect competition, it does not make sense for firms to have the power to decide the prices of their goods. Furthermore, because of to the perfect substitutability among all products, all firms are price-takers. Therefore, the idea of a price-taking firm is incompatible with what will be presented in the following section: firms often define the prices of their goods.

The concept of monopolistic competition provides an intermediate theoretical basis between pure monopoly and perfect competition. Modern New-Keynesian models are based on the viewpoint of monopolistic competition, in the goods market, in contrast with the RBC structure of perfect competition. The basic economic idea that underlies the monopolistic competition view is that all goods are, to some degree, imperfect substitutes for one another.

Price stickiness

Perhaps the main task of New-Keynesian theoreticians is demonstrating that wage and price stickiness can derive from the behavior of the optimizing agents. One feature of this school of thought is its diversity of approach; however, the following elements are common to all of them:

- In New-Keynesian models, there is imperfect competition in the market for products. The previous Keynesian models assumed perfect competition.

- While previous Keynesian models consider nominal stickiness in monetary wages, New-Keynesian models also focus on the stickiness of the prices of products.

- Besides the factors that cause stickiness in nominal variables, New-Keynesian models introduce real stickiness.

Definition 3.1.3 (Price stickiness). *This refers to a situation in which the price of a good does not change immediately to a new equilibrium price when demand and/or supply curves are altered. Therefore, it is a failure of buyers and sellers to adapt to new market conditions and arrive at an equilibrium price.*

Generally, the stylized facts about alterations in prices and wages are:

- Prices and wages are temporarily rigid.

- Prices and wages are readjusted on average two or three times a year.

- Prices and wages being adjusted frequently are the main factor responsible for high inflation.

- Prices and wages are not readjusted simultaneously.

- Changes in prices of tradable goods are more frequent than with non-tradable goods.

One of the tasks of this school of thought is to seek evidence (explanations) for price stickiness, considering that the main structure of any modern theory of price stickiness assumes that firms, when changing the prices of their goods, would be faced with some form of cost. The classic example of a cost of this kind is the cost faced by a restaurant that needs to reprint its menu to update the prices of its options. This is why the cost of changing prices is called a "menu cost". If we wish to find a concrete example, suppose that demand conditions indicate that a restaurant could increase the price of its dinner with a rise in revenue of $1,000. However, to implement this change, the restaurant would need to print new menus. Supposing that this reprinting cost is $2,000, it is evident that changing the price of dinner is not an advantage for the restaurant, thus the price of dinner remains the same.

The model

This chapter develops the model addressed in the previous chapter, introducing price stickiness and monopolistic competition, which are at the core of New-Keynesian models. The RBC model's general assumptions (2.2.1-2.2.3) remain valid.

Households

As households follow the same optimizing behavior as the RBC model (assumptions 2.2.4-2.2.7 remain valid), there is no need to repeat the problem in this chapter. Thus, the equations that maximize utility will be taken from the previous chapter:

Equation (2.3),

$$K_{j,t+1} = (1 - \delta)K_{j,t} + I_{j,t} \tag{3.1}$$

Equation (2.8),

$$C_{j,t}^{\sigma} L_{j,t}^{\varphi} = \frac{W_t}{P_t} \tag{3.2}$$

And equation (2.9),

$$\left(\frac{E_t C_{j,t+1}}{C_{j,t}}\right)^{\sigma} = \beta \left[(1 - \delta) + E_t\left(\frac{R_{t+1}}{P_{t+1}}\right)\right] \tag{3.3}$$

Firms

As for the problem of the firm, assumption 2.2.9 remains valid. Assumption 2.2.8, on the other hand, ceases to be so in this model. Thus,

Assumption 3.2.1. *It is assumed that the market structure is one of monopolistic competition.*

The economy's producing sector is thus divided into two parts: an intermediate goods sector (wholesale firms) and a final goods sector (retail firms). The intermediate goods sector consists of a large number of companies, each one producing differentiable goods. These companies must decide the quantity of factors of production to be used and the prices of their goods using a production function. In the final goods sector, there is a single firm that, using a specific, pertinent technology, aggregates intermediate goods into one single good that will be consumed by economic agents.

Firms that produce final goods (retail firms)

From an aggregate perspective, monopolistic competition, among other factors, compels us to recognize the fact that consumers buy a large variety of goods, there being a need, therefore, for models that assume that consumers buy only one kind of good (an aggregate bundle with all goods), as in the previous chapter's RBC model.

Assumption 3.2.2. *This aggregate good (bundle of goods) is sold by a retail firm within a structure of perfect competition. That is, it is assumed that a given retail firm is completely identical to any other.*

The theoretical implication of assumption 3.2.2 is that a representative retail firm exists. Because of to this assumption that retailers sell their products in a market that is in perfect competition, there is nothing here that is very different from the idea presented in the RBC model.

With the aim of producing an aggregate good, a retailer must buy a large quantity of goods from the wholesale sector. That is, these are the inputs used in a retail firm's production process. Thus, a retailer buys a large variety of wholesale goods (clothes, electronic products, etc.,) and transforms them into an aggregate good (a bundle of goods) that will be sold to the final agent.

How much is a "large variety of goods"? If on the one hand consumers do not face a literally infinite number of consumption possibilities, on the other, they may buy a large variety of goods that vary in size, color, style etc. For this reason and for mathematical convenience, in this kind of model, "many" is treated as "infinite". It is assumed that there is a continuum of wholesale goods and that each good is indexed within the unit interval $[0,1]$. Thus, a continuous number of wholesale goods is taken into account rather than a discrete number.

In order to make things clearer, it is assumed that it is possible to represent a particular wholesale good at any point within the unit interval $[0,1]$. Each of these goods is imperceptible infinitesimally small when compared to the total amount of available goods.

Therefore, it is assumed that each good belonging to the unit interval is produced by a single wholesaler and is imperfectly substitutable by any other good. Thus, these goods are differentiated products, which allows for the possibility of some degree of monopoly power.

To represent the problem that a retail firm faces, its production technology and maximization problem must be described. Since the incorporation of the idea of monopolistic competition in mainstream macroeconomics in the eighties and nineties, the most widely applied functional form for aggregation technology is the Dixit-Stiglitz aggregator (Dixit and Stiglitz, 1977):

$$Y_t = \left(\int_0^1 Y_{j,t}^{\frac{\psi-1}{\psi}} \, dj \right)^{\frac{\psi}{\psi-1}} \tag{3.4}$$

where Y_t is the product of retailers in period t, and $Y_{j,t}$ for $j \in [0,1]$ is wholesale good j, and $\psi > 1$ is the elasticity of substitution between wholesale goods[3].

With P_t as the nominal price of a retail product and $P_{j,t}$ as the nominal price of wholesale good j, the price of each wholesale good is taken as a given by retail firms. Therefore, the problem of the representative retail firm is maximizing its profit function:

$$\max_{Y_{j,t}} P_t Y_t - \int_0^1 P_{j,t} Y_{j,t} dj \tag{3.5}$$

Substituting the aggregator technology in the last expression (Equation (3.4) in equation (3.5)), we get:

$$\max_{Y_{j,t}} P_t \left(\int_0^1 Y_{j,t}^{\frac{\psi-1}{\psi}} \, dj \right)^{\frac{\psi}{\psi-1}} - P_{j,t} \int_0^1 Y_{j,t} dj \tag{3.6}$$

Taking the first-order condition for the above problem,

$$\frac{\psi}{\psi-1} P_t \left(\int_0^1 Y_{j,t}^{\frac{\psi-1}{\psi}} \, dj \right)^{\frac{\psi}{\psi-1}-1} \frac{\psi-1}{\psi} Y_{j,t}^{\frac{\psi-1}{\psi}-1} - P_{j,t} = 0$$

---

[3]Smets and Wouters (2007) assume that the elasticity of substitution between intermediate goods is stochastic: $\psi_t = \psi + v_t$, with $v_t \sim N(0, \sigma_v)$.

or,

$$P_t \left(\int_0^1 Y_{j,t}^{\frac{\psi-1}{\psi}} dj \right)^{\frac{1}{\psi-1}} Y_{j,t}^{\frac{-1}{\psi}} - P_{j,t} = 0$$

Remember that the aggregator (equation 3.4) may also be written as,

$$Y_t^{\frac{1}{\psi}} = \left(\int_0^1 Y_{j,t}^{\frac{\psi-1}{\psi}} dj \right)^{\frac{1}{\psi-1}}$$

The right-hand side of this last equation is the term that should be eliminated from the first-order condition, thus:

$$P_t Y_t^{\frac{1}{\psi}} Y_{j,t}^{\frac{-1}{\psi}} - P_{j,t} = 0$$

Raising the previous expression to the power of $-\psi$ and with some algebraic manipulation, we get:

$$Y_{j,t} = Y_t \left(\frac{P_t}{P_{j,t}} \right)^{\psi} \tag{3.7}$$

This expression is the demand function for wholesale good j, which is directly proportional to aggregate demand (Y_t) and inversely proportional to its relative price level $\left(\frac{1}{\frac{P_{j,t}}{P_t}} \right)$.

Substituting equation (3.7) in equation (3.4),

$$Y_t = \left\{ \int_0^1 \left[Y_t \left(\frac{P_t}{P_{j,t}} \right)^{\psi} \right]^{\frac{\psi-1}{\psi}} dj \right\}^{\frac{\psi}{\psi-1}}$$

$$Y_t = Y_t P_t^{\psi} \left\{ \int_0^1 \left[\left(\frac{1}{P_{j,t}} \right)^{\psi} \right]^{\frac{\psi-1}{\psi}} dj \right\}^{\frac{\psi}{\psi-1}}$$

$$P_t^{\psi} = \left[\int_0^1 \left(P_{j,t}^{\psi} \right)^{\frac{\psi-1}{\psi}} dj \right]^{\frac{\psi}{\psi-1}}$$

$$P_t = \left[\int_0^1 P_{j,t}^{1-\psi} dj \right]^{\frac{1}{1-\psi}} \tag{3.8}$$

Equation (3.8) is the pricing rule for final (retail) goods.

Firms that produce intermediate goods (wholesale firms)

As already described, wholesale firms sell their differentiated products to retail firms.

Assumption 3.2.3. *Owing to the differentiated nature of wholesale goods, wholesale firms have some degree of market power and are thus price setters (market structure of monopolistic competition).*

Assumption 3.2.4. *It is assumed that fixed production costs do not exist. This means that average variable cost is equal to average total cost.*

Assumption 3.2.5. *It is assumed that the per unit production cost of a wholesale product is always the same regardless of the scale of production. This means that it is being assumed that wholesale firms have constant returns to scale, resulting in a marginal production cost, regardless of the quantity produced.*

These two assumptions lead to an opportune mathematical consequence where the marginal cost function coincides with the average total cost function. This, in turn, means that total cost may be expressed simply by multiplying the quantity produced and the marginal cost.

The retail firm solves its problem in two stages. First, the firm takes the prices of the factors of production (return on capital and wages) and determines the amount of capital and labor that it will use to minimize its total production cost:

$$\min_{L_{j,t}, K_{j,t}} W_t L_{j,t} + R_t K_{j,t} \tag{3.9}$$

subject to the following technology,

$$Y_{j,t} = A_t K_{j,t}^{\alpha} L_{j,t}^{1-\alpha} \tag{3.10}$$

with the law of motion of productivity,

$$\log A_t = (1 - \rho_A)\log A_{ss} + \rho_A \log A_{t-1} + \varepsilon_t \tag{3.11}$$

where A_{ss} is the value of productivity at the steady state, ρ_A is the autoregressive parameter of productivity, whose absolute value must be less than 1, $|\rho_A| < 1$, to ensure the steadiness of the process, and $\varepsilon_t \sim N(0, \sigma_A)$.

Using the Lagrangian to solve the problem of the wholesale firm,

$$\mathcal{L} = W_t L_{j,t} + R_t K_{j,t} + \mu_{j,t}\left(Y_{j,t} - A_t K_{j,t}^{\alpha} L_{j,t}^{1-\alpha}\right) \tag{3.12}$$

The first-order conditions for the previous problem are:

$$\frac{\partial \mathcal{L}}{\partial L_{j,t}} = W_t - (1-\alpha)\mu_{j,t} A_t K_{j,t}^{\alpha} L_{j,t}^{\alpha} = 0 \tag{3.13}$$

$$\frac{\partial \mathcal{L}}{\partial K_{j,t}} = R_t - \alpha \mu_{j,t} A_t K_{j,t}^{\alpha-1} L_{j,t}^{1-\alpha} = 0 \tag{3.14}$$

With $\mu_{j,t} = MC_{j,t}$ (MC - Marginal Cost), equations (3.13) and (3.14), become:

$$L_{j,t} = (1-\alpha)MC_{j,t}\frac{Y_{j,t}}{W_t} \tag{3.15}$$

$$K_{j,t} = \alpha MC_{j,t}\frac{Y_{j,t}}{R_t} \tag{3.16}$$

These two equations represent the demand of a wholesale firm j for labor and capital, respectively.

Since production technology is the same as in the previous chapter's model, there is no need to work out again the total and marginal cost functions. To this end, it is sufficient to use equation (2.20):

$$MC_{j,t} = \frac{1}{A_t}\left(\frac{W_t}{1-\alpha}\right)^{1-\alpha}\left(\frac{R_t}{\alpha}\right)^{\alpha} \tag{3.17}$$

Note that equation (3.17) meets the result of assumptions 3.2.4 and 3.2.5 that $MC_{j,t} = \frac{CT_{j,t}}{Y_{j,t}}$.

Calvo pricing

The second stage of the problem of the wholesale firm is defining the price of its goods. This firm decides how much to produce in each period according to the Calvo rule (Calvo, 1983).

Thus, the wholesale firm has a θ probability of keeping the price of its good fixed in the next period and a $1 - \theta$ probability of optimally defining its price. For this second type of firm, having defined the price of its good in t, there is a θ probability that this price remains fixed in t+1, a θ^2 probability that it remains fixed in t+2, and so on. Consequently, the firm must consider these probabilities when defining the price of its good in t.

> **Definition 3.2.1** (Calvo's rule). *Establishes that in each period t, a fraction $0 < \theta < 1$ of firms is randomly selected and allowed to define the prices of its goods for the period. The rest of the firms (the θ fraction) keeps the prices of its goods defined by a stickiness rule which, in the literature, may follow one of the three possibilities below:*
>
> 1. *Maintain the previous period's price*
>
> $$P_{j,t} = P_{j,t-1}$$
>
> 2. *Update the price using the steady state gross inflation rate* (π_{ss})
>
> $$P_{j,t} = \pi_{ss}P_{j,t-1}$$
>
> 3. *Update the price using the previous period's gross inflation rate* (π_{t-1})
>
> $$P_{j,t} = \pi_{t-1}P_{j,t-1}$$

Assumption 3.2.6. *In this book, the first rule will be used to determine price stickiness,* $P_{j,t} = P_{j,t-1}$.

Therefore, the problem of the wholesale firm that is capable of readjusting the price of its good is:

$$\max_{P_{j,t}^*} E_t \sum_{i=0}^{\infty} (\beta\theta)^i (P_{j,t}^* Y_{j,t+i} - TC_{j,t+i}) \qquad (3.18)$$

Substituting equation (3.7) in equation (3.18),

$$\max_{P_{j,t}^*} E_t \sum_{i=0}^{\infty} (\beta\theta)^i \left[P_{j,t}^* Y_{t+i} \left(\frac{P_{t+i}}{P_{j,t}^*} \right)^{\psi} - Y_{t+i} \left(\frac{P_{t+i}}{P_{j,t}^*} \right)^{\psi} MC_{j,t+i} \right] \qquad (3.19)$$

Taking the previous problem's first-order condition,

$$0 = E_t \sum_{i=0}^{\infty} (\beta\theta)^i \left[(1-\psi) Y_{j,t+i} + \psi \frac{Y_{j,t+i}}{P_{j,t}^*} MC_{j,t+i} \right]$$

$$P_{j,t}^* = \left(\frac{\psi}{\psi - 1} \right) E_t \sum_{i=0}^{\infty} (\beta\theta)^i MC_{j,t+i} \qquad (3.20)$$

Note that all wholesale firms that fix their prices have the same markup on the same marginal cost. Thus, in all periods, $P_{j,t}^*$ is the same price for all the $1 - \theta$ firms that set their prices. Combining equation (3.8)'s pricing rule and the fact that firms within their respective groups firms that define their prices and firms subject to stickiness use the same prices (as they are subject to the same level of technology), the aggregate price level is obtained thus:

$$P_t^{1-\psi} = \int_0^{\theta} P_{t-1}^{1-\psi} dj + \int_{\theta}^1 P_t^{*1-\psi} dj$$

$$P_t^{1-\psi} = \left[j P_{t-1}^{1-\psi} \right]_0^{\theta} + \left[j P_t^{*1-\psi} \right]_{\theta}^1$$

$$P_t^{1-\psi} = \theta P_{t-1}^{1-\psi} + (1-\theta) P_t^{*1-\psi}$$

$$P_t = \left[\theta P_{t-1}^{1-\psi} + (1-\theta) P_t^{*1-\psi} \right]^{\frac{1}{1-\psi}} \qquad (3.21)$$

It is important to remember that there is a continuum of firms, and the group that can alter its price (and the group that cannot) is chosen randomly, regardless of when each firm last altered its price. This means that the distribution of prices among firms does not change between periods.

The model's equilibrium condition

It is still necessary to establish an equilibrium condition in the goods market.

$$Y_t = C_t + I_t \tag{3.22}$$

In short, this economy's model consists of the following equations in Table 3.1.

Table 3.1: Model structure.

Equation	(Definition)
$C_t^\sigma L_t^\varphi = \frac{W_t}{P_t}$	(Labor supply)
$\left(\frac{E_t C_{t+1}}{C_t}\right)^\sigma = \beta \left[(1-\delta) + E_t \left(\frac{R_{t+1}}{P_{t+1}}\right)\right]$	(Euler Equation)
$K_{t+1} = (1-\delta)K_t + I_t$	(Law of motion of capital)
$Y_t = A_t K_t^\alpha L_t^{1-\alpha}$	(Production function)
$K_t = \alpha MC_t \frac{Y_t}{R_t}$	(Demand for capital)
$L_t = (1-\alpha) MC_t \frac{Y_t}{W_t}$	(Demand for labor)
$MC_t = \frac{1}{A_t} \left(\frac{W_t}{1-\alpha}\right)^{1-\alpha} \left(\frac{R_t}{\alpha}\right)^\alpha$	(Marginal cost)
$P_t^* = \left(\frac{\psi}{\psi-1}\right) E_t \sum_{i=0}^{\infty} (\beta\theta)^i MC_{t+i}$	(Optimal price level)
$P_t = \left[\theta P_{t-1}^{1-\psi} + (1-\theta)P_t^{*\,1-\psi}\right]^{\frac{1}{1-\psi}}$	(General price level)
$\pi_t = \frac{P_t}{P_{t-1}}$	(Gross inflation rate)
$Y_t = C_t + I_t$	(Equilibrium condition)
$\log A_t = (1-\rho_A) \log A_{ss} + \rho_A \log A_{t-1} + \epsilon_t$	(Productivity shock)

Steady state

As in the previous chapter, armed with the model's solution, the next step is finding the steady state, the point of origin of the simulations that will be performed and the point of reference for log-linearization. The idea that an endogenous variable x_t is at the steady state in each period t, if $E_t x_{t+1} = x_t = x_{t-1} = x_{ss}$, remains valid. The first step is to write the model's steady state.

Households

$$C_{ss}^{\sigma} L_{ss}^{\varphi} = \frac{W_{ss}}{P_{ss}} \tag{3.23}$$

$$1 = \beta \left(1 - \delta + \frac{R_{ss}}{P_{ss}} \right) \tag{3.24}$$

$$\delta K_{ss} = I_{ss} \tag{3.25}$$

Firms

$$L_{ss} = (1 - \alpha) MC_{ss} \frac{Y_{ss}}{W_{ss}} \tag{3.26}$$

$$K_{ss} = \alpha MC_{ss} \frac{Y_{ss}}{R_{ss}} \tag{3.27}$$

$$Y_{ss} = K_{ss}^{\alpha} L_{ss}^{1-\alpha} \tag{3.28}$$

$$MC_{ss} = \left(\frac{W_{ss}}{1 - \alpha} \right)^{1-\alpha} \left(\frac{R_{ss}}{\alpha} \right)^{\alpha} \tag{3.29}$$

$$P_{ss} = \left(\frac{\psi}{\psi - 1} \right) \left(\frac{1}{1 - \beta \theta} \right) MC_{ss} \tag{3.30}$$

where: $\sum_{i=0}^{\infty} (\beta \theta)^i = \frac{1}{1 - \beta \theta}$ [4].

---

[4]The sum of the infinite terms of a geometric progression is called a geometric series, and the sum is:

$$S_{\infty} = \sum_{n=0}^{\infty} a_1 q^n = \frac{a_1}{1 - q}$$

Equilibrium condition

$$Y_{ss} = C_{ss} + I_{ss} \tag{3.31}$$

Initially, the values of prices P_{ss}, R_{ss}, W_{ss} and MC_{ss} must be determined. For the same reasons as described in the previous chapter, the general price level will be normalized ($P_{ss} = 1$), The values of R_{ss} and MC_{ss} are thus also known,

so, from equation (3.24),

$$R_{ss} = P_{ss} \left[\frac{1}{\beta} - (1 - \delta) \right] \tag{3.32}$$

and from equation (3.30),

$$MC_{ss} = \left(\frac{\psi - 1}{\psi} \right)(1 - \beta\theta)P_{ss} \tag{3.33}$$

With R_{ss} and MC_{ss}, known, the value of W_{ss} is also known, and from equation (3.29),

$$W_{ss}^{1-\alpha} = MC_{ss}(1 - \alpha)^{1-\alpha} \left(\frac{\alpha}{R_{ss}} \right)^{\alpha}$$

$$W_{ss} = (1 - \alpha)MC_{ss}^{\frac{1}{1-\alpha}} \left(\frac{\alpha}{R_{ss}} \right)^{\frac{\alpha}{1-\alpha}} \tag{3.34}$$

Having determined the values of the prices, the next step is to determine equilibrium in the inputs markets with the aim of obtaining the variables that make up aggregate demand (C_{ss} and I_{ss}). Thus, substituting equation (3.27) in equation (3.25),

$$I_{ss} = \left(\frac{\delta\alpha MC_{ss}}{R_{ss}} \right) Y_{ss} \tag{3.35}$$

and substituting equation (3.26) in equation (3.23),

$$C_{ss}^{\sigma} \left[(1 - \alpha)MC_{ss} \frac{Y_{ss}}{W_{ss}} \right]^{\varphi} = \frac{W_{ss}}{P_{ss}}$$

$$C_{ss} = \frac{1}{Y_{ss}^{\frac{\varphi}{\sigma}}} \left\{ \frac{W_{ss}}{P_{ss}} \left[\frac{W_{ss}}{(1 - \alpha)MC_{ss}} \right]^{\varphi} \right\}^{\frac{1}{\sigma}} \tag{3.36}$$

the expressions for investment and consumption are obtained. Lastly, in order to determine the steady-state output (Y_{ss}), it is necessary to meet the equilibrium condition of the goods market (equation (3.31)) with equations (3.35) and (3.36),

$$Y_{ss} = \left(\frac{\delta \alpha MC_{ss}}{R_{ss}}\right) Y_{ss} + \frac{1}{Y_{ss}^{\frac{\varphi}{\sigma}}} \left\{ \frac{W_{ss}}{P_{ss}} \left[\frac{W_{ss}}{(1-\alpha)MC_{ss}} \right]^{\varphi} \right\}^{\frac{1}{\sigma}}$$

$$\left(1 - \frac{\delta \alpha MC_{ss}}{R_{ss}}\right) Y_{ss} = \frac{1}{Y_{ss}^{\frac{\varphi}{\sigma}}} \left\{ \frac{W_{ss}}{P_{ss}} \left[\frac{W_{ss}}{(1-\alpha)MC_{ss}} \right]^{\varphi} \right\}^{\frac{1}{\sigma}}$$

$$Y_{ss}^{1+\frac{\varphi}{\sigma}} = \left(\frac{R_{ss}}{R_{ss} - \delta \alpha MC_{ss}}\right) \left\{ \frac{W_{ss}}{P_{ss}} \left[\frac{W_{ss}}{(1-\alpha)MC_{ss}} \right]^{\varphi} \right\}^{\frac{1}{\sigma}}$$

$$Y_{ss} = \left(\frac{R_{ss}}{R_{ss} - \delta \alpha MC_{ss}}\right)^{\frac{\sigma}{\sigma+\varphi}} \left\{ \frac{W_{ss}}{P_{ss}} \left[\frac{W_{ss}}{(1-\alpha)MC_{ss}} \right]^{\varphi} \right\}^{\frac{1}{\sigma+\varphi}} \qquad (3.37)$$

The previous procedures are summed up in the presentation of the steady state below:

$$A_{ss} = 1$$

$$P_{ss} = 1$$

$$R_{ss} = P_{ss} \left[\frac{1}{\beta} - (1-\delta) \right]$$

$$MC_{ss} = \left(\frac{\psi - 1}{\psi}\right)(1 - \beta\theta)P_{ss}$$

$$W_{ss} = (1-\alpha)MC_{ss}^{\frac{1}{1-\alpha}} \left(\frac{\alpha}{R_{ss}}\right)^{\frac{\alpha}{1-\alpha}}$$

$$Y_{ss} = \left(\frac{R_{ss}}{R_{ss} - \delta \alpha MC_{ss}}\right)^{\frac{\sigma}{\sigma+\varphi}} \left\{ \frac{W_{ss}}{P_{ss}} \left[\frac{W_{ss}}{(1-\alpha)MC_{ss}} \right]^{\varphi} \right\}^{\frac{1}{\sigma+\varphi}}$$

$$I_{ss} = \left(\frac{\delta \alpha MC_{ss}}{R_{ss}}\right) Y_{ss}$$

$$C_{ss} = \frac{1}{Y_{ss}^{\frac{\varphi}{\sigma}}} \left\{ \frac{W_{ss}}{P_{ss}} \left[\frac{W_{ss}}{(1-\alpha)MC_{ss}} \right]^{\varphi} \right\}^{\frac{1}{\sigma}}$$

$$L_{ss} = (1-\alpha)MC_{ss}\frac{Y_{ss}}{W_{ss}}$$

$$K_{ss} = \alpha MC_{ss}\frac{Y_{ss}}{R_{ss}}$$

Table 3.2 shows the calibrated values that will be used in the NK model's simulation. Table 3.3 shows the steady state numerically.

Table 3.2: Values of the structural model's parameters.

Parameter	Meaning of the parameter	Calibrated
σ	Relative risk aversion coefficient	2
φ	Marginal disutility with respect to labor supply	1.5
α	Elasticity of output with respect to capital	0.35
β	Discount factor	0.985
δ	Depreciation rate	0.025
ρ_A	Autoregressive parameter of productivity	0.95
σ_A	Standard deviation of productivity	0.01
θ	Price stickiness parameter	0.75
ψ	Elasticity of substitution between intermediate goods	8

Table 3.3: Values of variables at the steady state.

Variable	Steady state
A	1
R	0.040
MC	0.2286
W	0.2152
Y	0.778
I	0.039
C	0.739
L	0.537
K	1.547

Log-linearization (Uhlig's method)

In this section, the "trick" developed by Uhlig (1999) will continue to be used in the log-linearization procedure. Some of the NK model's equations have already been log-linearized in the previous chapter. To avoid unnecessary superposition, these equations will simply be reproduced. Efforts will be focused on obtaining the "New-Keynesian Phillips Equation", which will be developed step by step.

Thus, using the previous chapter's equations:

$$\sigma \tilde{C}_t + \varphi \tilde{L}_t = \widetilde{W}_t - \tilde{P}_t \tag{3.38}$$

$$\frac{\sigma}{\beta}(E_t \tilde{C}_{t+1} - \tilde{C}_t) = \frac{R_{ss}}{P_{ss}} E_t(\tilde{R}_{t+1} - \tilde{P}_{t+1}) \tag{3.39}$$

$$\tilde{R}_t = \widetilde{MC}_t + \tilde{Y}_t - \tilde{K}_t \tag{3.40}$$

$$\widetilde{W}_t = \widetilde{MC}_t + \tilde{Y}_t - \tilde{L}_t \tag{3.41}$$

$$\tilde{Y}_t = \tilde{A}_t + \alpha \tilde{K}_t + (1 - \alpha)\tilde{L}_t \tag{3.42}$$

$$\tilde{K}_{t+1} = (1 - \delta)\tilde{K}_t + \delta \tilde{I}_t \tag{3.43}$$

$$Y_{ss}\tilde{Y}_t = C_{ss}\tilde{C}_t + I_{ss}\tilde{I}_t \tag{3.44}$$

$$\tilde{A}_t = \rho_A \tilde{A}_{t-1} + \epsilon_t \qquad (3.45)$$

Marginal cost

The marginal cost equation is a new element in this chapter, but its log-linearization is similar to that demonstrated in the previous chapter:

From equation (3.17),

$$MC_{ss}(1 + \widetilde{MC}_t) = \left(\frac{W_{ss}}{1-\alpha}\right)^{1-\alpha}\left(\frac{R_{ss}}{\alpha}\right)^{\alpha}[1 - \tilde{A}_t + (1-\alpha)\widetilde{W}_t + \alpha\tilde{R}_t]$$

with,

$$MC_{ss} = \left(\frac{W_{ss}}{1-\alpha}\right)^{1-\alpha}\left(\frac{R_{ss}}{\alpha}\right)^{\alpha}$$

therefore,

$$\widetilde{MC}_t = (1-\alpha)\widetilde{W}_t + \alpha\tilde{R}_t - \tilde{A}_t \qquad (3.46)$$

Determining the New-Keynesian Phillips curve

Beginning with the log-linearization of the equation that defines the optimal price level, equation (3.20),

$$P_{ss}(1 + \tilde{P}_t^*) = \left(\frac{\psi}{\psi-1}\right)\left(\frac{1-\beta\theta}{1-\beta\theta}\right)MC_{ss}E_t\sum_{i=0}^{\infty}(\beta\theta)^i(1 + \widetilde{MC}_{t+i})$$

with,

$$P_{ss} = \left(\frac{\psi}{\psi-1}\right)\left(\frac{1}{1-\beta\theta}\right)MC_{ss}$$

we arrive at,

$$1 + \tilde{P}_t^* = 1 + (1-\beta\theta)E_t\sum_{i=0}^{\infty}(\beta\theta)^i\widetilde{MC}_{t+i}$$

$$\tilde{P}_t^* = (1-\beta\theta)E_t\sum_{i=0}^{\infty}(\beta\theta)^i\widetilde{MC}_{t+i} \qquad (3.47)$$

The next step is log-linearizing the final goods' markup rule. From equation (3.21),

$$P_{ss}^{1-\psi}[1+(1-\psi)\widetilde{P}_t] = \theta P_{ss}^{1-\psi}[1+(1-\psi)\widetilde{P}_{t-1}]+(1-\theta)P_{ss}^{1-\psi}[1+(1-\psi)\widetilde{P}_t^*]$$

$$1+\widetilde{P}_t = \theta + \theta\widetilde{P}_{t-1}+1-\theta+(1-\theta)\widetilde{P}_t^*$$

$$\widetilde{P}_t = \theta\widetilde{P}_{t-1}+(1-\theta)\widetilde{P}_t^* \qquad (3.48)$$

Equation (3.47) must then be substituted in equation (3.48),

$$\widetilde{P}_t = \theta\widetilde{P}_{t-1}+(1-\theta)(1-\beta\theta)E_t\sum_{i=0}^{\infty}(\beta\theta)^i\widetilde{MC}_{t+i} \qquad (3.49)$$

The second element of the right-hand side of equation (3.49) possesses an infinite sum of the future nominal marginal cost. Therefore, it is necessary to find a way to remove this term. To this end, a technique known as "quasi-differencing" can be used. Both sides of equation (3.49) must be multiplied by the lag operator $(1-\beta\theta L^{-1})$. This lag operator, applied to a variable X_t, will result in $L^{-1}X_t = X_{t+1}$.

Therefore, multiplying equation (3.49) by $(1-\beta\theta L^{-1})$:

$$\widetilde{P}_t - \beta\theta E_t\widetilde{P}_{t+1} = \theta\widetilde{P}_{t-1}+(1-\theta)(1-\beta\theta)E_t\sum_{i=0}^{\infty}(\beta\theta)^i\widetilde{MC}_{t+i}-\beta\theta\theta\widetilde{P}_t$$

$$-\beta\theta(1-\theta)(1-\beta\theta)E_t\sum_{i=0}^{\infty}(\beta\theta)^i\widetilde{MC}_{t+1+i}$$

As quasi-differencing is applied in order to cancel out the t+1 terms, the previous equation results in:

$$\widetilde{P}_t - \beta\theta E_t\widetilde{P}_{t+1} = \theta\widetilde{P}_{t-1}-\beta\theta\theta\widetilde{P}_t+(1-\theta)(1-\beta\theta)\widetilde{MC}_t$$

Then, P_t must be deducted from the nominal marginal cost,

$$\widetilde{P}_t-\beta\theta E_t\widetilde{P}_{t+1} = \theta\widetilde{P}_{t-1}-\beta\theta\theta\widetilde{P}_t+(1-\theta)(1-\beta\theta)\widetilde{P}_t+(1-\theta)(1-\beta\theta)(\widetilde{MC}_t-\widetilde{P}_t)$$

$$\widetilde{P}_t - \beta\theta E_t\widetilde{P}_{t+1} = \theta\widetilde{P}_{t-1}-\beta\theta\theta\widetilde{P}_t+\widetilde{P}_t-\beta\theta\widetilde{P}_t-\theta\widetilde{P}_t+\beta\theta\theta\widetilde{P}_t$$

$$+(1-\theta)(1-\beta\theta)(\widetilde{MC}_t-\widetilde{P}_t)$$

$$\theta(\widetilde{P}_t - \widetilde{P}_{t-1}) = \beta\theta(E_t\widetilde{P}_{t+1} - \widetilde{P}_t) + (1-\theta)(1-\beta\theta)(\widetilde{MC}_t - \widetilde{P}_t)$$

Lastly, both sides of the previous equation must be divided by θ, With the gross inflation rates in t and t+1 being : $\tilde{\pi}_t = \widetilde{P}_t - \widetilde{P}_{t-1}$; and $E_t\tilde{\pi}_{t+1} = E_t\widetilde{P}_{t+1} - \widetilde{P}_t$, we arrive at the New-Keynesian Phillips equation:

$$\tilde{\pi}_t = \beta E_t\tilde{\pi}_{t+1} + \left[\frac{(1-\theta)(1-\beta\theta)}{\theta}\right](\widetilde{MC}_t - \widetilde{P}_t) \tag{3.50}$$

Table 3.4 sums up the log-linear model.

Table 3.4: Structure of the log-linear model.

Equation	(Definition)
$\sigma\widetilde{C}_t + \varphi\widetilde{L}_t = \widetilde{W}_t - \widetilde{P}_t$	(Labor supply)
$\frac{\sigma}{\beta}(E_t\widetilde{C}_{t+1} - \widetilde{C}_t) = \frac{R_{ss}}{P_{ss}}E_t(\widetilde{R}_{t+1} - \widetilde{P}_{t+1})$	(Euler Equation)
$\widetilde{K}_{t+1} = (1-\delta)\widetilde{K}_t + \delta\widetilde{I}_t$	(Law of motion of capital)
$\widetilde{Y}_t = \widetilde{A}_t + \alpha\widetilde{K}_t + (1-\alpha)\widetilde{L}_t$	(Production function)
$\widetilde{K}_t = \widetilde{MC}_t + \widetilde{Y}_t - \widetilde{R}_t$	(Demand for labor)
$\widetilde{L}_t = \widetilde{MC}_t + \widetilde{Y}_t - \widetilde{W}_t$	(Demanda por trabalho)
$\widetilde{MC}_t = [(1-\alpha)\widetilde{W}_t + \alpha\widetilde{R}_t - \widetilde{A}_t]$	(Marginal cost)
$\tilde{\pi}_t = \beta E_t\tilde{\pi}_{t+1} + \left[\frac{(1-\theta)(1-\beta\theta)}{\theta}\right](\widetilde{MC}_t - \widetilde{P}_t)$	(Phillips equation)
$\tilde{\pi}_t = \widetilde{P}_t - \widetilde{P}_{t-1}$	(Gross inflation rate)
$Y_{ss}\widetilde{Y}_t = C_{ss}\widetilde{C}_t + I_{ss}\widetilde{I}_t$	(Equilibrium condition)
$\widetilde{A}_t = \rho_A\widetilde{A}_{t-1} + \epsilon_t$	(Productivity shock)

Productivity shock

In this section, the results of a positive productivity shock on the model's variables will be discussed. First, the NK model's impulse-response functions will be analyzed (figure 3.3), following which the differences between the two models' results (RBC vs NK) will be discussed (figures 3.4 and 3.5).

The productivity shock in question caused the values of the marginal products of labor and capital to rise. Consequently, firms increased their demand for inputs (labor and capital). The prices of these inputs thus responded positively to this greater level of demand. Bearing in mind that higher wages increase the income of households, if, on the one hand, this higher level of income increases the acquisition of goods (I and C), on the other, it increases the demand for another "good", leisure (income effect). This fall in labor supply explains the higher resistance of wages returning to the steady state, while returns on capital fell below even their initial level (steady state) in period 10. With the growth in aggregate supply, the elements that make up aggregate demand increase, most notably investments, whose result is 10 times greater than that of consumption goods. This higher capital supply (strong growth in investments) explains the returns on capital's swifter return to the steady state.

In short, higher productivity increased the spending variables (consumption and investment) and input prices, with wages showing greater persistence when returning to the steady state. With regard to the factors of production, capital widened, exhibiting a bell-shaped curve with an inflection point in period 20. However, labor supply decreased because of to a strong predominance of the income effect.

After the NK model is analyzed individually, it becomes important to understand the effects of price stickiness on macroeconomic variables. Figure 3.4 shows the results of the IRFs for the RBC and NK models. It can be said that the effects on product, investments, capital stock and real prices of inputs ($W/P, R/P$) were not significantly different. On the other hand, the effects on the acquisition of consumer goods (an element of demand) and on labor supply (an element of supply) were essentially different. In the NK model, the productivity shock led to a significant rise in consumption compared to the results of the RBC model. In the latter, the effects on labor supply were greater compared to the former. In short, the productivity shock affected product via aggregate demand in the NK model, while in the RBC model product was affected via aggregate supply.

This difference in the behavior of households regarding the acquisition of "goods" is explained in figure 3.5. Greater price stickiness causes real wages, at the inflection point between the periods in which the income and substitution effects dominate, to practically double in value. In the RBC model, this point indicated a value of 57% in relation to the steady state, while in the NK model it reached 98%. Thus, with price stickiness (price levels adjusting more slowly to the equilibrium level), productivity had less effect on the components of household income ($W/P, R/P$).

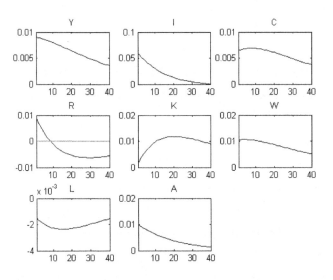

Figure 3.3: Effects of a productivity shock.   Dynare simulation results (Impulse-response functions).

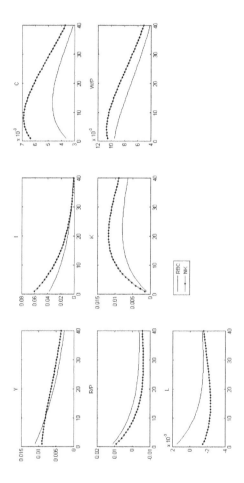

Figure 3.4: Comparison between impulse-response functions in the RBC and
NK models.

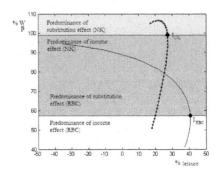

Figure 3.5: Leisure-wages locus. The x and y axes measure the variable's deviation in relation to the steady state in percentage terms. Point I is the inflection
point between which the substitution effect and income effect dominate.

BOX 3.1 - Basic log-linear NK model on Dynare.

```
//NK model - Chapter 3 (UNDERSTANDING DSGE MODELS)
var Y I C R K W L MC P PI A;
varexo e;
parameters sigma phi alpha beta delta rhoa psi theta;

sigma = 2;
phi = 1.5;
alpha = 0.35;
beta = 0.985;
delta = 0.025;
rhoa = 0.95;
psi = 8;
theta = 0.75;

model(linear);
#Pss = 1;
#Rss = Pss*((1/beta)-(1-delta));
#MCss = ((psi-1)/psi)*(1-beta*theta)*Pss;
#Wss = (1-alpha)*(MCss^(1/(1-alpha)))*((alpha/Rss)^(alpha/(1-alpha)));
#Yss = ((Rss/(Rss-delta*alpha*MCss))^(sigma/(sigma+phi)))
*((Wss/Pss)*(Wss/((1-alpha)*MCss))^phi)^(1/(sigma+phi)));
#Kss = alpha*MCss*(Yss/Rss);
#Iss = delta*Kss;
#Css = Yss - Iss;
#Lss = (1-alpha)*MCss*(Yss/Wss);
//1-Labor supply
sigma*C + phi*L = W - P;
//2-Euler equation
(sigma/beta)*(C(+1)-C)=(Rss/Pss)*(R(+1)-P(+1));
//3-Law of motion of capital
K = (1-delta)*K(-1) + delta*I;
//4-Production function
Y = A + alpha*K(-1) + (1-alpha)*L;
//5-Demand for capital
K(-1) = Y - R;
//6-Demand for labor
L = Y - W;
//7-Marginal cost
MC = (1-alpha)*W + alpha*R - A;
//8-Phillips equation
PI = beta*PI(+1)+((1-theta)*(1-beta*theta)/theta)*(MC-P);
//9-Gross inflation rate
PI = P - P(-1);
//10-Goods market equilibrium condition
Yss*Y = Css*C + Iss*I;
//11-Productivity shock
A = rhoa*A(-1) + e;
end;

steady;
check(qz_zero_threshold=1e-20);

shocks;
var e;
stderr 0.01;
```

```
end;

stoch_simul(nograph,qz_zero_threshold=1e-20) Y I C R K W L PI A;
```

Chapter 4

New-Keynesian model with wage stickiness

An irrefutable criticism leveled at Keynesians by classical theorists in the seventies was that the former simply assumed that wages were rigid, without presenting a good economic explanation for the cause of this phenomenon. New-Keynesian researchers thus made efforts to develop an explanation of wage stickiness in terms consistent with economic rationality.

Following the Keynesian tradition, in this chapter a model with wage stickiness will be analyzed the same way as with price stickiness in the previous chapter. Here, households provide differentiated labor and independent firms in perfect competition aggregate this labor into a single kind of labor that will be used by firms that produce intermediate goods. This method of aggregating labor means that workers possess some degree of monopoly power and define their wages, when allowed to do so, based on a consumption-leisure marginal rate of substitution. Thus, as in the pricing model, there is a Calvo's rule to define wages, and in each period, $1 - \theta_W$ workers are chosen randomly to define their wages.

Brief theoretical review: wage stickiness

Keynesians argue that, in the short term, nominal wages (W) are imperfectly flexible. The idea is that there exists institutional stickiness in respect of the way in which wages are defined. For example, it is costly for workers and firms to negotiate contracts, so wages are generally fixed to remain in effect for one year or more. Some contracts possess an indexation clause. Indexing in relation to the inflation rate is relatively simple, because there is an observed inflation measurement that is known to both workers and firms, such as the consumer price index, which can be used for this purpose. Although the idea is simple and low cost, it is seldom used, as it is difficult to include other contingencies in labor contracts. Suppose that a firm wishes to pay workers according to their respective levels of productivity; more productive workers would receive higher wages, and less productive workers would receive lower wages. However, it may be difficult for workers and firms to measure individual productivity in the firm's product.

If workers and firms negotiate contracts in nominal terms, it is possible to think of this variable as fixed, at least in the short term. Although nominal wages do not respond to the factors that affect the labor market, in the long term they are flexible. Thus, given that nominal wages are fixed in the short term, a situation such as that described in Figure 4.1 may arise, where the market equilibrium wage ($\frac{W}{P}e$) is below the contractual wage ($\frac{W^*}{P}$). Consider the following situation: at moment in time 1, labor market conditions (labor supply and demand) define wages $\frac{W^*}{P}$. In the short term, it is possible for demand conditions to change, causing the curve to shift to the left. At this point, workers wish to work L'', but firms will only hire L'. In the long term, these contracts will be negotiated and nominal wages will be equal to market equilibrium wages ($\frac{W^*}{P} = \frac{W}{P}e$). Therefore, in models with wage stickiness, the amount of labor is always determined by the amount that the representative firm wishes to hire, or in other words, by the labor demand curve.

Definition 4.1.1 (Wage stickiness). *The general difficulty that a firm faces when trying to reduce wages, owing to either labor agreements or fear of a fall in the productivity of employees, or another reason that conveys the same idea.*

Why would wages be rigid in the short term?

Some reasons why a company may pay higher real wages than what it "needs" to, are: it would discourage absence from work (since the cost of leisure is higher); it would reduce employee turnover (reducing hiring and training costs); and it would increase worker productivity, as workers would be "happier". Following this idea, Henry

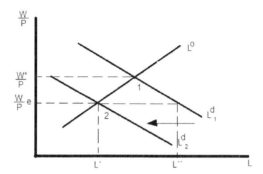

Figure 4.1: An example of contractual wages being higher than market equilibrium wages.

Ford, at the beginning of the 20th century, established wages for his employees that were above market value. Efficiency wage models follow this premise[1].

The main idea of this approach can be formalized by defining a worker productivity index, which would be a positive function of real wages:

$$\epsilon = \epsilon\left(\frac{W}{P}\right)$$

Thus, a production function that considers this level of productivity can be conceived:

$$Y = f(\overline{K}, \epsilon L)$$

Assuming that capital is fixed, product increases when the amount of labor increases ($L\uparrow$) or when worker productivity improves ($\epsilon\uparrow$). In this context, a firm must establish real wages so that the cost of one unit of labor productivity is minimized, or in other words, it must maximize the number of units of labor productivity that can be bought with each monetary unit spent on the payroll. This is

---

[1]For further information on efficiency-wages, see: Raff and Summers (1987); Akerlof and Yellen (1990).

done by increasing real wages to the point at which the elasticity of the index of efficiency [$\epsilon\left(\frac{W}{P}\right)$] in relation to real wages, equals one[2].

In other words, if the productivity index's elasticity is greater than one, a rise in real wages will show results superior to the additional cost of this rise. Thus, wages should be increased to the point at which the return of efficiency equals the additional cost to the payroll.

Efficiency-wages are not the only explanation for wage stickiness. The high and persistent levels of unemployment in Europe are related to hysteresis[3]. While it is known that a series of explanations for this phenomenon exists, to present the idea, the insider-outsider model shall be described.

In this model, both the product market and labor market are considered to be in imperfect competition. The basic idea is that members of a union (the insiders) have the power to negotiate with employees, as it is expensive to replace them with non-union workers (the outsiders). The cost of replacing an insider with an outsider involves the latter's recruitment and training. It is also considered that insiders use their bargaining power to keep real wages higher than market equilibrium wages, resulting in a group of unemployed outsiders. Hysteresis arises in moments of recession, when some insider workers become outsiders – figure 4.1 helps in this understanding. The recession causes the labor demand curve to shift to the left, causing unemployment, represented by the distance between L" and L'. For the study of this chapter, more important than the idea of hysteresis is the power of unions to determine a real wage level higher than the market equilibrium level.

2

$$\frac{\left(\frac{W_t}{P_t}\right)}{\epsilon}\frac{\partial\epsilon}{\partial\left(\frac{W_t}{P_t}\right)} = 1$$

[3]A variable demonstrates hysteresis if, after moving away from its initial point because of to a shock, it does not show any tendency of returning to this initial point.

The model

This model is similar to the NK model presented in the previous chapter, with the exception of the labor supply equation, which was defined by the optimization of the utility function in relation to the amount of work hours. This equation stated that real wages should be equal to the consumption-leisure marginal rate of substitution. In the model with Calvo wage stickiness, the optimal wage equation of those households capable of defining their own wages, states that this wage will be a markup (a function of the elasticity of substitution of differentiated labor) on the future discounted consumption-leisure marginal rate of substitution multiplied by the general price level.

The overall assumptions of the model in chapter 2 (2.2.1-2.2.3) remain valid in this chapter.

Households

The preferences of households are the same as in the RBC and basic NK models (assumptions 2.2.4-2.2.6 remain valid). Therefore, the equations that define the law of motion of capital and intertemporal consumption (Euler equation) will be taken from chapter 2.

Equation (2.3),

$$K_{t+1} = (1 - \delta)K_t + I_t \qquad (4.1)$$

And equation (2.9),

$$\left(\frac{E_t C_{t+1}}{C_t} \right)^{\sigma} = \beta \left[(1 - \delta) + E_t \left(\frac{R_{t+1}}{P_{t+1}} \right) \right] \qquad (4.2)$$

Definition of wages

Assumption 2.2.7 – the structure in which households define wages - is no longer valid in this chapter.

Assumption 4.2.1. *Households defining wages involves the assumption that they supply differentiated labor in a market structure of monopolistic competition. This service is sold to a representative firm that aggregates these different types of labor (L_j) into a single labor input (L).*

To satisfy the aim of assumption 4.2.1, the labor-aggregating firm uses the following technology:

$$L_t = \left(\int_0^1 L_{j,t}^{\frac{\psi_W - 1}{\psi_W}} dj \right)^{\frac{\psi_W}{\psi_W - 1}} \tag{4.3}$$

where φ_W is the elasticity of substitution between differentiated jobs and $L_{j,t}$ is the amount of differentiated labor supplied by household j. Each type of labor j is paid for with a wage $W_{j,t}$.

The problem of the labor-aggregating firm is maximizing its profit:

$$\max_{L_{j,t}} W_t L_t - \int_0^1 W_{j,t} L_{j,t} dj \tag{4.4}$$

Substituting equation (4.3) in equation (4.4),

$$\max_{L_{j,t}} W_t \left(\int_0^1 L_{j,t}^{\frac{\psi_W - 1}{\psi_W}} dj \right)^{\frac{\psi_W}{\psi_W - 1}} - W_{j,t} \int_0^1 L_{j,t} dj \tag{4.5}$$

The first-order condition for the previous problem is:

$$W_t \left(\frac{\psi_W}{\psi_W - 1} \right) \left(\int_0^1 L_{j,t}^{\frac{\psi_W - 1}{\psi_W}} dj \right)^{\frac{\psi_W}{\psi_W - 1} - 1} \left(\frac{\psi_W - 1}{\psi_W} \right) L_{j,t}^{\frac{\psi_W - 1}{\psi_W} - 1} - W_{j,t} = 0$$

or,

$$W_t \left(\int_0^1 L_{j,t}^{\frac{\psi_W - 1}{\psi_W}} dj \right)^{\frac{1}{\psi_W - 1}} L_{j,t}^{-\frac{1}{\psi_W}} - W_{j,t} = 0$$

Given that equation (4.3) can be written in the following way:

$$L_t^{\frac{1}{\psi_W}} = \left(\int_0^1 L_{j,t}^{\frac{\psi_W - 1}{\psi_W}} dj \right)^{\frac{1}{\psi_W - 1}}$$

Note that the previous expression is part of the first-order condition, and must thus be replaced in that equation,

$$W_t L_t^{\frac{1}{\psi_W}} L_{j,t}^{\frac{-1}{\psi_W}} - W_{j,t} = 0$$

With a little algebraic manipulation, we arrive at the demand equation for differentiated labor j:

$$L_{j,t} = L_t \left(\frac{W_t}{W_{j,t}} \right)^{\psi_W} \tag{4.6}$$

Substituting equation (4.6) in equation (4.3):

$$L_t = \left\{ \int_0^1 \left[L_t \left(\frac{W_t}{W_{j,t}} \right)^{\psi_W} \right]^{\frac{\psi_W - 1}{\psi_W}} dj \right\}^{\frac{\psi_W}{\psi_W - 1}}$$

$$L_t = L_t W_t^{\psi_W} \left\{ \int_0^1 \left[\left(\frac{1}{W_{j,t}} \right)^{\psi_W} \right]^{\frac{\psi_W - 1}{\psi_W}} dj \right\}^{\frac{\psi_W}{\psi_W - 1}}$$

$$W_t^{\psi_W} = \left[\int_0^1 (W_{j,t})^{\psi_W - 1} dj \right]^{\frac{\psi_W}{\psi_W - 1}}$$

It is easy to see that the aggregate wage level is:

$$W_t = \left(\int_0^1 W_{j,t}^{1-\psi_W} dj \right)^{\frac{1}{1-\psi_W}} \tag{4.7}$$

In each period, $1-\theta_W$ households, chosen independently and at random, optimally define their wages. The remaining households, θ_W, follow a wage stickiness rule (the Calvo rule, Definition 3.2.1). In the literature, one of the following three possibilities is often used as a wage stickiness rule:

1. Keeping the same wage level as the previous period

$$W_{j,t} = W_{j,t-1}$$

2. Updating wages using the steady state gross inflation rate (π_{ss})

$$W_{j,t} = \pi_{ss} W_{j,t-1}$$

3. Updating wages using the previous period's gross inflation rate (π_{t-1})

$$W_{j,t} = \pi_{t-1} W_{j,t-1}$$

Assumption 4.2.2. *This study will assume the first rule of wage stickiness,* $W_{j,t} = W_{j,t-1}$.

The $1-\theta_W$ fraction of households that can choose wage levels in period t knows that, even choosing optimal wage $W_{j,t}^*$ for the period, it faces a $\theta_W{}^N$ probability of these wages remaining fixed for N future periods. When household j chooses wage $W_{j,t}^*$, it must seek to solve the following problem[4]:

$$\max_{W_{j,t}^*} E_t \sum_{i=0}^{\infty} (\beta\theta_W)^i \left\{ -\frac{L_{j,t+i}^{1+\varphi}}{1+\varphi} - \lambda_{t+i}\left[-W_{j,t}^* L_{j,t+i}\right] \right\} \qquad (4.8)$$

Substituting equation (4.6) in equation (4.8),

$$\max_{W_{j,t}^*} E_t \sum_{i=0}^{\infty} (\beta\theta_W)^i \left\{ -\frac{1}{1+\varphi}\left[L_{t+i}\left(\frac{W_{t+i}}{W_{j,t}^*}\right)^{\psi_W} \right]^{1+\varphi} \right.$$

$$\left. + \lambda_{t+i}\left[W_{j,t}^* L_{t+i}\left(\frac{W_{t+i}}{W_{j,t}^*}\right)^{\psi_W} \right] \right\} \qquad (4.9)$$

resulting in the following first-order condition:

$$0 = E_t \sum_{i=0}^{\infty} (\beta\theta_W)^i \left\{ \psi_W \left[L_{t+i}\left(\frac{W_{t+i}}{W_{j,t}^*}\right)^{\psi_W} \right]^{\varphi} L_{t+i}\left(\frac{W_{t+i}}{W_{j,t}^*}\right)^{\psi_W} \frac{1}{W_{j,t}^*} \right.$$

$$\left. +(1-\psi_W)\lambda_{t+i}L_{t+i}\left(\frac{W_{t+i}}{W_{j,t}^*}\right)^{\psi_W} \right\}$$

or,

$$0 = E_t \sum_{i=0}^{\infty} (\beta\theta_W)^i \left\{ \psi_W L_{j,t+i}^{\varphi} \frac{1}{W_{j,t}^*} + (1-\psi_W)\lambda_{t+i} \right\}$$

---

[4]Only the parts related to the utility function's choice of labor and budget constraints of households are used in the wage definition problem.

With some manipulation, and knowing that $\lambda_{t+i} = \frac{C_{j,t+i}^{-\sigma}}{P_{t+i}}$ (Equation (2.5) from chapter 2), we arrive at the optimal wage equation defined by the households chosen for this purpose:

$$W_{j,t}^* = \left(\frac{\psi_W}{\psi_W - 1} \right) E_t \sum_{i=0}^{\infty} (\beta \theta_W)^i C_{j,t+i}^{\sigma} L_{j,t+i}^{\varphi} P_{t+i} \qquad (4.10)$$

As $1 - \theta_W$ fraction of households chooses the same nominal wages, $W_{j,t}^* = W_t^*$, and the remaining households (θ_W) remain with the same wages as the previous period, the aggregate nominal wage results in:

$$W_t^{1-\psi_W} = \int_0^{\theta_W} W_{t-1}^{1-\psi_W} \, dj + \int_{\theta_W}^1 W_t^{*\,1-\psi_W} \, dj$$

$$W_t^{1-\psi_W} = \left[j W_{t-1}^{1-\psi_W} \right]_0^{\theta_W} + \left[j W_t^{*\,1-\psi_W} \right]_{\theta_W}^1$$

$$W_t^{1-\psi_W} = \theta_W W_{t-1}^{1-\psi_W} + (1 - \theta_W) W_t^{*\,1-\psi_W}$$

Lastly, we arrive at the aggregate nominal wage rule:

$$W_t = \left[\theta_W W_{t-1}^{1-\psi_W} + (1 - \theta_W) W_t^{*\,1-\psi_W} \right]^{\frac{1}{1-\psi_W}} \qquad (4.11)$$

Firms

The assumptions of the firms group (assumptions 3.2.2-3.2.6) remain the same in this chapter. Thus, the equations resulting from this agent's optimization problems will be used here:

Equation (3.10),

$$Y_{j,t} = A_t K_{j,t}^{\alpha} L_{j,t}^{1-\alpha} \qquad (4.12)$$

$$\log A_t = (1 - \rho_A) \log A_{ss} + \rho_A \log A_{t-1} + \varepsilon_t \qquad (4.13)$$

Equation (3.15),

$$L_{j,t} = (1 - \alpha) M C_{j,t} \frac{Y_{j,t}}{W_t} \qquad (4.14)$$

Equation (3.16),

$$K_{j,t} = \alpha MC_{j,t} \frac{Y_{j,t}}{R_t} \tag{4.15}$$

Equation (3.22),

$$MC_{j,t} = \frac{1}{A_t}\left(\frac{W_t}{1-\alpha}\right)^{1-\alpha}\left(\frac{R_t}{\alpha}\right)^{\alpha} \tag{4.16}$$

Equation (3.25),

$$P_{j,t}^* = \left(\frac{\psi}{\psi-1}\right) E_t \sum_{i=0}^{\infty} (\beta\theta)^i CM_{j,t+i} \tag{4.17}$$

Equation (3.26),

$$P_t = \left[\theta P_{t-1}^{1-\psi} + (1-\theta)P_t^{*\,1-\psi}\right]^{\frac{1}{1-\psi}} \tag{4.18}$$

The model's equilibrium condition

The equilibrium condition in the goods market is the same as in previous chapters:

$$Y_t = C_t + I_t \tag{4.19}$$

The equilibrium structure of this economy's model comprises the equations in Table 4.1.

Steady state

This section maintains the procedure adopted in previous chapters for solving the steady state. To this end, the system of equations that form the economy at the steady state must first be written:

Households

$$W_{ss} = \left(\frac{\psi_W}{\psi_W - 1}\right)\left(\frac{C_{ss}^{\sigma} L_{ss}^{\varphi} P_{ss}}{1 - \beta\theta_W}\right) \tag{4.20}$$

where: $\sum_{i=0}^{\infty}(\beta\theta_W)^i = \frac{1}{1-\beta\theta_W}$

$$1 = \beta\left(1 - \delta + \frac{R_{ss}}{P_{ss}}\right) \tag{4.21}$$

$$\delta K_{ss} = I_{ss} \tag{4.22}$$

Table 4.1: Structure of the model.

Equation	(Definition)
$W_{j,t}^* =$ $\left(\frac{\psi_W}{\psi_W-1}\right) E_t \sum_{i=0}^{\infty}(\beta\theta_W)^i C_{j,t+i}^\sigma L_{j,t+i}^\varphi P_{t+i}$	(Definition of optimal wages)
$W_t =$ $\left[\theta_W W_{t-1}^{1-\varphi_W} + (1-\theta_W)W_t^{*\,1-\varphi_W}\right]^{\frac{1}{1-\varphi_W}}$	(Level of aggregate wages)
$\pi_{W,t} = W_t/W_{t-1}$	(Gross wage inflation rate)
$\left(\frac{E_t C_{t+1}}{C_t}\right)^\sigma = \beta\left[(1-\delta)+\left(\frac{E_t R_{t+1}}{E_t P_{t+1}}\right)\right]$	(Euler equation)
$K_{t+1} = (1-\delta)K_t + I_t$	(Law of motion of capital)
$Y_t = A_t K_t^\alpha L_t^{1-\alpha}$	(Production function)
$K_t = \alpha MC_t \frac{Y_t}{R_t}$	(Demand for capital)
$L_t = (1-\alpha)MC_t \frac{Y_t}{W_t}$	(Demand for labor)
$MC_t = \frac{1}{A_t}\left(\frac{W_t}{1-\alpha}\right)^{1-\alpha}\left(\frac{R_t}{\alpha}\right)^\alpha$	(Marginal cost)
$P_t^* = \left(\frac{\psi}{\psi-1}\right)E_t \sum_{i=0}^{\infty}(\beta\theta)^i CM_{t+i}$	(Optimal price level)
$P_t = \left[\theta P_{t-1}^{1-\psi} + (1-\theta)P_t^{*\,1-\psi}\right]^{\frac{1}{1-\psi}}$	(General price level)
$\pi_t = P_t/P_{t-1}$	(Gross inflation rate)
$Y_t = C_t + I_t$	(Equilibrium condition)
$\log A_t = (1-\rho_A)\log A_{ss} + \rho_A \log A_{t-1} + \epsilon_t$	(Productivity shock)

Firms

$$L_{ss} = (1 - \alpha) MC_{ss} \frac{Y_{ss}}{W_{ss}} \tag{4.23}$$

$$K_{ss} = \alpha MC_{ss} \frac{Y_{ss}}{R_{ss}} \tag{4.24}$$

$$Y_{ss} = K_{ss}^{\alpha} L_{ss}^{1-\alpha} \tag{4.25}$$

$$MC_{ss} = \left(\frac{W_{ss}}{1 - \alpha} \right)^{1-\alpha} \left(\frac{R_{ss}}{\alpha} \right)^{\alpha} \tag{4.26}$$

$$P_{ss} = \left(\frac{\psi}{\psi - 1} \right) \left(\frac{1}{1 - \beta\theta} \right) CM_{ss} \tag{4.27}$$

Equilibrium condition

$$Y_{ss} = C_{ss} + I_{ss} \tag{4.28}$$

Initially, the values of prices (P_{ss}, R_{ss}, W_{ss} and MC_{ss}) must be determined. As "standard" procedure, the general price level is normalized ($P_{ss} = 1$). The values of R_{ss} and CM_{ss} are thus also known.

so, from equation (4.21),

$$R_{ss} = P_{ss} \left[\frac{1}{\beta} - (1 - \delta) \right] \tag{4.29}$$

and equation (4.27),

$$MC_{ss} = \left(\frac{\psi - 1}{\psi} \right) (1 - \beta\theta) P_{ss} \tag{4.30}$$

With R_{ss} and MC_{ss} known, the value of W_{ss} is also known, and from equation (4.26),

$$W_{ss}^{1-\alpha} = MC_{ss}(1 - \alpha)^{1-\alpha} \left(\frac{\alpha}{R_{ss}} \right)^{\alpha}$$

$$W_{ss} = (1 - \alpha) MC_{ss}^{\frac{1}{1-\alpha}} \left(\frac{\alpha}{R_{ss}} \right)^{\frac{\alpha}{1-\alpha}} \tag{4.31}$$

$$I_{ss} = \left(\frac{\delta \alpha MC_{ss}}{R_{ss}}\right) Y_{ss} \tag{4.32}$$

and substituting equation (4.23) in equation (4.20),

$$C_{ss}^{\sigma}\left[(1-\alpha)MC_{ss}\frac{Y_{ss}}{W_{ss}}\right]^{\varphi}\left(\frac{\psi_W}{\psi_W - 1}\right)\left(\frac{P_{ss}}{1-\beta\theta_W}\right) = W_{ss}$$

$$C_{ss}^{\sigma}Y_{ss}^{\varphi} = \frac{W_{ss}}{P_{ss}}\left(\frac{\psi_W - 1}{\psi_W}\right)(1-\beta\theta_W)\left[\frac{W_{ss}}{(1-\alpha)MC_{ss}}\right]^{\varphi}$$

$$C_{ss} = \frac{1}{Y_{ss}^{\frac{\varphi}{\sigma}}}\left\{(1-\beta\theta_W)\left(\frac{\psi_W - 1}{\psi_W}\right)\frac{W_{ss}}{P_{ss}}\left[\frac{W_{ss}}{(1-\alpha)MC_{ss}}\right]^{\varphi}\right\}^{\frac{1}{\sigma}} \tag{4.33}$$

the expressions for investment and consumption are obtained. Lastly, in order to determine the steady state output (Y_{ss}), it is necessary to meet the equilibrium condition with equations (4.32) and (4.33) in equation (4.28),

$$Y_{ss} = \left(\frac{\delta \alpha MC_{ss}}{R_{ss}}\right) Y_{ss} + \frac{1}{Y_{ss}^{\frac{\varphi}{\sigma}}}\left\{(1-\beta\theta_W)\left(\frac{\psi_W - 1}{\psi_W}\right)\frac{W_{ss}}{P_{ss}}\left[\frac{W_{ss}}{(1-\alpha)MC_{ss}}\right]^{\varphi}\right\}^{\frac{1}{\sigma}}$$

$$\left(1 - \frac{\delta \alpha MC_{ss}}{R_{ss}}\right) Y_{ss} = \frac{1}{Y_{ss}^{\frac{\varphi}{\sigma}}}\left\{(1-\beta\theta_W)\left(\frac{\psi_W - 1}{\psi_W}\right)\frac{W_{ss}}{P_{ss}}\left[\frac{W_{ss}}{(1-\alpha)MC_{ss}}\right]^{\varphi}\right\}^{\frac{1}{\sigma}}$$

$$Y_{ss}^{1+\frac{\varphi}{\sigma}} = \left(\frac{R_{ss}}{R_{ss} - \delta \alpha MC_{ss}}\right)\left\{(1-\beta\theta_W)\left(\frac{\psi_W - 1}{\psi_W}\right)\frac{W_{ss}}{P_{ss}}\left[\frac{W_{ss}}{(1-\alpha)MC_{ss}}\right]^{\varphi}\right\}^{\frac{1}{\sigma}}$$

thus, the steady state output is:

$$Y_{ss} = \left(\frac{R_{ss}}{R_{ss} - \delta \alpha MC_{ss}}\right)^{\frac{\sigma}{\sigma+\varphi}}$$

$$\left\{(1-\beta\theta_W)\left(\frac{\psi_W - 1}{\psi_W}\right)\frac{W_{ss}}{P_{ss}}\left[\frac{W_{ss}}{(1-\alpha)MC_{ss}}\right]^{\varphi}\right\}^{\frac{1}{\sigma+\varphi}} \tag{4.34}$$

The previous procedures are summarized in the presentation of the steady state below:

$$A_{ss} = 1$$

$$P_{ss} = 1$$

$$R_{ss} = P_{ss}\left[\frac{1}{\beta} - (1-\delta)\right]$$

$$MC_{ss} = \left(\frac{\psi - 1}{\psi}\right)(1 - \beta\theta)P_{ss}$$

$$W_{ss} = (1-\alpha)MC_{ss}^{\frac{1}{1-\alpha}}\left(\frac{\alpha}{R_{ss}}\right)^{\frac{\alpha}{1-\alpha}}$$

$$Y_{ss} = \left(\frac{R_{ss}}{R_{ss} - \delta\alpha MC_{ss}}\right)^{\frac{\sigma}{\sigma+\varphi}}$$

$$\left\{(1-\beta\theta_W)\left(\frac{\psi_W - 1}{\psi_W}\right)\frac{W_{ss}}{P_{ss}}\left[\frac{W_{ss}}{(1-\alpha)MC_{ss}}\right]^{\varphi}\right\}^{\frac{1}{\sigma+\varphi}}$$

$$L_{ss} = (1-\alpha)MC_{ss}\frac{Y_{ss}}{W_{ss}}$$

$$K_{ss} = \alpha MC_{ss}\frac{Y_{ss}}{R_{ss}}$$

$$I_{ss} = \delta K_{ss}$$

$$C_{ss} = \frac{1}{Y_{ss}^{\frac{\varphi}{\sigma}}}\left\{(1-\beta\theta_W)\left(\frac{\psi_W - 1}{\psi_W}\right)\frac{W_{ss}}{P_{ss}}\left[\frac{W_{ss}}{(1-\alpha)MC_{ss}}\right]^{\varphi}\right\}^{\frac{1}{\sigma}}$$

Tables 4.2 and 4.3 show the calibrated values that will be used in the simulation and the steady state values, respectively.

Table 4.2: Values of the structural model's parameters.

Parameter	Meaning of the parameter	Calibrated value
σ	Relative risk aversion coefficient	2
φ	Marginal disutility with regard to labor supply	1.5
α	Elasticity of output with regard to capital	0.35
β	Discount factor	0.985
δ	Depreciation rate	0,025
ρ_A	Autoregressive parameter of productivity	0.95
σ_A	Standard deviation of productivity	0.01
θ	Price stickiness parameter	0.75
ψ	Elasticity of substitution between intermediate goods	8
θ_W	Wage stickiness parameter	0.75
ψ_W	Elasticity of substitution between differentiated labors	21

Table 4.3: Values of variables at the steady state.

Variable	Steady state
A	1
R	0.040
MC	0.2286
W	0.2152
Y	0.523
I	0.026
C	0.4968
L	0.361
K	1.040

Log-linearization (Uhlig's method)

The tool developed by Uhlig continues to be used for the model's log-linearization. Results from previous chapters that coincide with those of the present model will be used. The new fact here is the log-linearization of the optimal wage and the aggregate wage level rules: Thus, using equations:

$$\frac{\sigma}{\beta}(E_t\tilde{C}_{t+1} - \tilde{C}_t) = \frac{R_{ss}}{P_{ss}}E_t(\tilde{R}_{t+1} - \tilde{P}_{t+1}) \tag{4.35}$$

$$\tilde{K}_{t+1} = (1-\delta)\tilde{K}_t + \delta\tilde{I}_t \tag{4.36}$$

$$\tilde{Y}_t = \tilde{A}_t + \alpha\tilde{K}_t + (1-\alpha)\tilde{L}_t \tag{4.37}$$

$$\tilde{K}_t = \widetilde{MC}_t + \tilde{Y}_t - \tilde{R}_t \tag{4.38}$$

$$\tilde{L}_t = \widetilde{MC}_t + \tilde{Y}_t - \tilde{W}_t \tag{4.39}$$

$$\widetilde{MC}_t = [(1-\alpha)\tilde{W}_t + \alpha\tilde{R}_t - \tilde{A}_t] \tag{4.40}$$

$$\tilde{\pi}_t = \beta E_t\tilde{\pi}_{t+1} + \left[\frac{(1-\theta)(1-\beta\theta)}{\theta}\right](\widetilde{MC}_t - \tilde{P}_t) \tag{4.41}$$

$$\tilde{\pi}_t = \tilde{P}_t - \tilde{P}_{t-1} \tag{4.42}$$

$$Y_{ss}\tilde{Y}_t = C_{ss}\tilde{C}_t + I_{ss}\tilde{I}_t \tag{4.43}$$

$$\tilde{A}_t = \rho_A\tilde{A}_{t-1} + \epsilon_t \tag{4.44}$$

Log-linearization of the wage rule

First, equation (4.10) must be log-linearized,

$$W_{ss}(1 + \tilde{W}_t^*) = \left(\frac{\psi_W}{\psi_W - 1}\right)\left(\frac{1-\beta\theta_W}{1-\beta\theta_W}\right)C_{ss}^\sigma L_{ss}^\varphi P_{ss}E_t$$

$$\sum_{i=0}^{\infty} (\beta \theta_W)^i [1 + \sigma \widetilde{C}_{t+i} + \varphi \widetilde{L}_{t+i} + \widetilde{P}_{t+i}]$$

Recalling that $W_{ss} = \left(\frac{\psi_W}{\psi_W - 1} \right) \left(\frac{C_{ss}^{\sigma} L_{ss}^{\varphi} P_{ss}}{1 - \beta \theta_W} \right)$,

$$\widetilde{W}_t^* = (1 - \beta \theta_W) E_t \sum_{i=0}^{\infty} (\beta \theta_W)^i (\sigma \widetilde{C}_{t+i} + \varphi \widetilde{L}_{t+i} + \widetilde{P}_{t+i}) \qquad (4.45)$$

Next, equation (4.11),

$$W_{ss}^{1-\psi_W}[1 + (1 - \psi_W)\widetilde{W}_t] = \theta_W W_{ss}^{1-\psi_W}[1 + (1 - \psi_W)\widetilde{W}_{t-1}]$$
$$+ (1 - \theta_W) W_{ss}^{1-\psi_W}[1 + (1 - \psi_W)\widetilde{W}_t^*]$$

$$1 + (1 - \psi_W)\widetilde{W}_t] = \theta_W + \theta_W(1 - \psi_W)\widetilde{W}_{t-1} + 1 - \theta_W + (1 - \theta_W)(1 - \psi_W)\widetilde{W}_t^*$$

$$\widetilde{W}_t = \theta_W \widetilde{W}_{t-1} + (1 - \theta_W)\widetilde{W}_t^* \qquad (4.46)$$

Substituting (4.45) in (4.46),

$$\widetilde{W}_t = \theta_W \widetilde{W}_{t-1} + (1 - \theta_W)(1 - \beta \theta_W) E_t \sum_{i=0}^{\infty} (\beta \theta_W)^i (\sigma \widetilde{C}_{t+i} + \varphi \widetilde{L}_{t+i} + \widetilde{P}_{t+i})$$

To use the quasi-differencing technique[5] it is necessary to multiply both sides of the previous equation by $(1 - L^{-1}\beta \theta_W)$,

$$\widetilde{W}_t - \beta \theta_W E_t \widetilde{W}_{t+1} = \theta_W \widetilde{W}_{t-1} + (1 - \theta_W)(1 - \beta \theta_W)$$
$$E_t \sum_{i=0}^{\infty} (\beta \theta_W)^i (\sigma \widetilde{C}_{t+i} + \varphi \widetilde{L}_{t+i} + \widetilde{P}_{t+i})$$

or,

$$-\beta \theta_W \theta_W \widetilde{W}_t - (1 - \theta_W)(1 - \beta \theta_W)\beta \theta_W$$
$$E_t \sum_{i=0}^{\infty} (\beta \theta_W)^i (\sigma \widetilde{C}_{t+1+i} + \varphi \widetilde{L}_{t+1+i} + \widetilde{P}_{t+1+i})$$

Then,

$$\widetilde{W}_t - \beta \theta_W E_t \widetilde{W}_{t+1} = \theta_W \widetilde{W}_{t-1} + (1 - \theta_W)(1 - \beta \theta_W)(\sigma \widetilde{C}_t + \varphi \widetilde{L}_t + \widetilde{P}_t)$$

---

[5] Presented in the previous chapter when log-linearizing price levels.

$$-\beta\theta_W\theta_W\widetilde{W}_t$$

Adding and subtracting $\widetilde{W}_t = (1-\theta_W)(1-\beta\theta_W)$ on the right-hand side of the previous equation,

$$\widetilde{W}_t - \beta\theta_W E_t\widetilde{W}_{t+1} = \theta_W\widetilde{W}_{t-1} + (1-\theta_W)(1-\beta\theta_W)(\sigma\widetilde{C}_t + \varphi\widetilde{L}_t + \widetilde{P}_t - \widetilde{W}_t)$$

$$-\beta\theta_W\theta_W\widetilde{W}_t + \widetilde{W}_t - \beta\theta_W\widetilde{W}_t - \theta_W\widetilde{W}_t + \beta\theta_W\theta_W\widetilde{W}_t$$

Dividing the previous equation by θ_W, and assuming the gross wage inflation rate in the log-linear form, $\widetilde{\pi_W}_t = \widetilde{W}_t - \widetilde{W}_{t-1}$ e $\widetilde{\pi_W}_{t+1} = \widetilde{W}_{t+1} - \widetilde{W}_t$, the Phillips equation for wages is:

$$\widetilde{\pi_W}_t = \beta\widetilde{\pi_W}_{t+1} + \left[\frac{(1-\theta_W)(1-\beta\theta_W)}{\theta_W}\right][\sigma\widetilde{C}_t + \varphi\widetilde{L}_t - (\widetilde{W}_t - \widetilde{P}_t)] \quad (4.47)$$

As a consequence, note that the gross wage inflation rate is determined by agents' expectations ($\beta\widetilde{\pi_W}_{t+1}$), by the preferences of households ($MRS_{t,leisure-C} = \sigma\widetilde{C}_t + \varphi\widetilde{L}_t$) and by labor supply and demand conditions (that define real wages: $\widetilde{W}_t - \widetilde{P}_t$).

Table 4.4 summarizes the log-linear model.

Productivity shock

In this section, the results of a productivity shock on the NKWR model will be presented. First, the effects of the shock on the model in isolation will be discussed (figure 4.2), following which the differences in relation to the other two models (RBC and NK) will be analyzed (figures 4.3 and 4.4).

Qualitatively, the results of the productivity shock on this model are not very different from the previous chapters. With the shock, the marginal productivities of capital and labor rise, allowing firms to increase demand for these inputs. Differently from the other models, the wage level is slower to adjust to this higher demand for labor, which limits the increase in household income and increases the supply of labor (initially, the income effect is less sensitive). The aggregate demand variables respond positively to the shock, with a significant rise in investments.

Comparing the three models (figure 4.3), one can generally see that, as frictions are incorporated, the variables become more persistent, especially output, capital stock and consumption. Differ-

Table 4.4: Structure of the log-linear model.

Equation	(Definition)
$\widetilde{\pi_W}_t = \beta\widetilde{\pi_W}_{t+1} +$ $\left[\frac{(1-\theta_W)(1-\beta\theta_W)}{\theta_W}\right][\sigma\tilde{C}_t + \varphi\tilde{L}_t -$ $(\widetilde{W}_t - \tilde{P}_t)]$	(Phillips equation for wages)
$\widetilde{\pi_W}_t = \widetilde{W}_t - \widetilde{W}_{t-1}$	(Gross wage inflation rate)
$\frac{\sigma}{\beta}(E_t\tilde{C}_{t+1} - \tilde{C}_t) = \frac{R_{ss}}{P_{ss}}E_t(\tilde{R}_{t+1} - \tilde{P}_{t+1})$	(Euler Equation)
$\tilde{K}_{t+1} = (1-\delta)\tilde{K}_t + \delta\tilde{I}_t$	(Law of motion of capital)
$\tilde{Y}_t = \tilde{A}_t + \alpha\tilde{K}_t + (1-\alpha)\tilde{L}_t$	(Production function)
$\tilde{K}_t = \widetilde{CM}_t + \tilde{Y}_t - \tilde{R}_t$	(Demand for capital)
$\tilde{L}_t = \widetilde{CM}_t + \tilde{Y}_t - \widetilde{W}_t$	(Demand for labor)
$\widetilde{CM}_t = [(1-\alpha)\widetilde{W}_t + \alpha\tilde{R}_t - \tilde{A}_t]$	(Marginal cost)
$\tilde{\pi}_t = \beta E_t\tilde{\pi}_{t+1} +$ $\left[\frac{(1-\theta)(1-\beta\theta)}{\theta}\right](\widetilde{CM}_t - \tilde{P}_t)$	(Phillips equation)
$\tilde{\pi}_t = \tilde{P}_t - \tilde{P}_{t-1}$	(Gross inflation rate)
$Y_{ss}\tilde{Y}_t = C_{ss}\tilde{C}_t + I_{ss}\tilde{I}_t$	(Equilibrium condition)
$\tilde{A}_t = \rho_A\tilde{A}_{t-1} + \epsilon_t$	(Productivity shock)

ently from the other models, wages show "adjustment stickiness", causing labor supply to initially increase more than in the other models.

Figure 4.4 shows the leisure-wage locus for the three models. Note that with wage stickiness, the inflection point between the periods in which the income and substitution effects are predominant, increases from 57% and 98% respectively, for the RBC and NK models, to 127% in the NKWR model.

It can be seen that the pattern of income and substitution effects changes when frictions are included. In the RBC model, when the inflection point was reached, the substitution effect began to dominate. In the other two models (mainly the NKWR model), it is

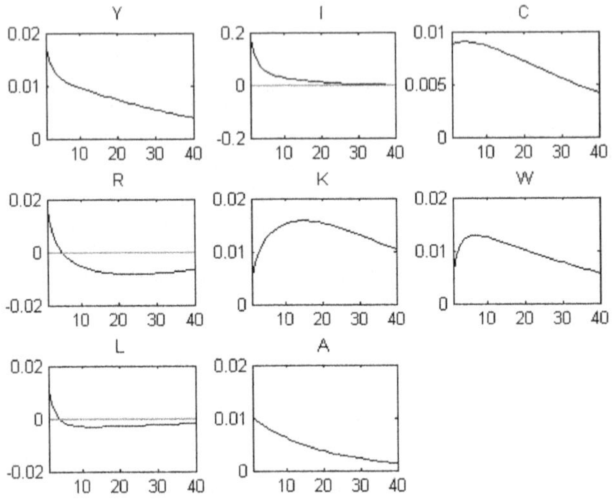

Figure 4.2: Effects of a productivity shock.   Dynare simulation results (Impulse-response functions).

more important to analyze whether leisure increased or decreased in relation to its steady state after a productivity shock. If real wages increase, then leisure increases (income effect), this behavior persisting until the curve's inflection point is reached. Thus, the shape of the leisure-wage locus is no longer an inverted C (RBC model) but an inverted V (NK and NKWR models).

Is there an interpretation problem related to the assumption of the presence or absence of frictions in the model's prices and wages?

Putting another question to further clarify the intention of this subsection: "What would be the outcome if an analyst, studying the possibility of a fall in productivity in a certain economy, uses an RBC model, when the more appropriate model would really be an NKWR model"?

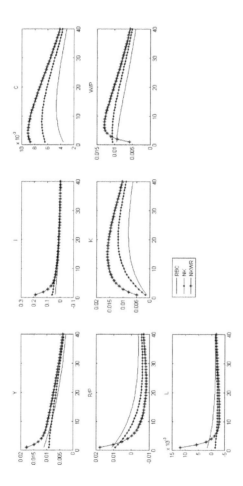

Figure 4.3: Comparison between the RBC, NK and NKWR's impulse-response functions.

To answer this question, it is necessary to analyze figure 4.5, which represents a negative productivity shock. The tendency would be for the analyst in question to underestimate the effects of a fall in productivity and thus indicate a countercyclical policy that is weaker than is needed for economic stability[6]. This can be seen in the graphs in figure 4.5: the expected fall in output in relation to the steady state for the RBC model is 0.012, while in the NKWR it is 0.016[7]. The opposite situation (choosing an NKWR model when an RBC model would be more appropriate) would also be problematic, as it would call for an economic policy stronger than needed, to stabilize the economy.

In short, choosing the appropriate DSGE model is relevant to the analysis of any economic phenomenon. This has been shown by the joint analysis of the three models studied in the first part of this book (figures 4.3-4.5). The next two chapters develop other frictions for households and firms, always seeking to better adjust projected data to real data.

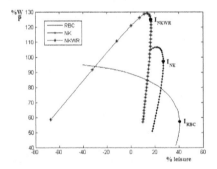

Figure 4.4: Leisure-wage locus. The x and y axes measure the variable's deviation in relation to the steady state in percentage terms. Point I is the inflection point between the periods in which the substitution effect and income effect are predominant.

---

[6] For the purposes of this exercise, the fact that this analyst, having chosen an RBC model, may not believe in countercyclical policy, is not being considered.

[7] Given that the steady states are 2.338 and 0.523 for the RBC and NKWR models, respectively. The falls, in percentage terms, would be:

- for the RBC model: $\frac{0.012}{2.338} = -0.51\%$
- for the NKWR model: $\frac{0.016}{0.523} = -3.06\%$

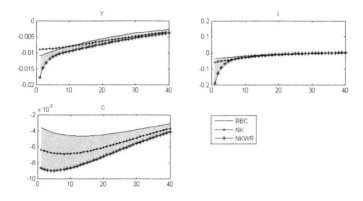

Figure 4.5: Negative productivity shock. The gray area represents the difference between the NKWR and RBC models' results.

BOX 4.1 - Log-linear NK model with wage stickiness on Dynare.

```
//NK model with wage stickiness -
//Chapter 4 (UNDERSTANDING DSGE MODELS)
var Y I C R K W L PIW P PI A CM;
varexo e;
parameters sigma phi alpha beta delta rhoa psi theta thetaW psiW;

sigma = 2;
phi = 1.5;
alpha = 0.35;
beta = 0.985;
delta = 0.025;
rhoa = 0.95;
psi = 8;
theta = 0.75;
thetaW = 0.75;
psiW = 21;

model(linear);
#Pss = 1;
#Rss = Pss*((1/beta)-(1-delta));
#CMss = ((psi-1)/psi)*(1-beta*theta)*Pss;
#Wss = (1-alpha)*(CMss^(1/(1-alpha)))*((alpha/Rss)^(alpha/(1-alpha)));
#Yss = ((Rss/(Rss-delta*alpha*CMss))^(sigma/(sigma+phi)))*((1-beta*thetaW)
*((psiW-1)/psiW)*(Wss/Pss)*(Wss/((1-alpha)*CMss))^phi)^(1/(sigma+phi));
#Kss = alpha*CMss*(Yss/Rss);
#Iss = delta*Kss;
#Css = Yss - Iss;
#Lss = (1-alpha)*CMss*(Yss/Wss);
//1-Phillips equation for wages
PIW = beta*PIW(+1)+((1-thetaW)*(1-beta*thetaW)/thetaW)*(sigma*C+phi*L-(W-P));
//2-Gross wage inflation rate
PIW = W - W(-1);
//3-Euler equation
(sigma/beta)*(C(+1)-C)=(Rss/Pss)*(R(+1)-P(+1));
//4-Law of motion of capital
K = (1-delta)*K(-1) + delta*I;
//5-Production function
Y = A + alpha*K(-1) + (1-alpha)*L;
//6-Demand for capital
K(-1) = Y - R;
//7-Demand for labor
L = Y - W;
//8-Marginal cost
CM = ((1-alpha)*W + alpha*R - A);
//9-Phillips equation
PI = beta*PI(+1)+((1-theta)*(1-beta*theta)/theta)*(CM-P);
//10-Gross inflation rate
PI = P - P(-1);
//11-Equilibrium condition
Yss*Y = Css*C + Iss*I;
//12-Productivity shock
A = rhoa*A(-1) + e;
end;
```

```
model_diagnostics;
steady;
check (qz_zero_threshold=1e-20);


shocks;
var e;
stderr 0.01;
end;

stoch_simul(qz_zero_threshold=1e-20) Y I C R K W L PI A;
```

Part II

Extensions

Chapter 5

New-Keynesian model with habit formation and non-Ricardian agents

Up to this point, the only frictions included have involved transforming an RBC model into an NK model (price and wage frictions). The utility of households in t depended only on current consumption and not on previous consumption. Moreover, it was assumed that households were made up of Ricardian agents only. In other words, the models were simple and their results were not completely in tune with real data.

To address this, we begin conferring flexibility to the assumption that the utility function is intertemporally separable, an assumption useful for the mathematical treatability of the problem of the consumer. However, empirical evidence shows that it would be most appropriate to consider the utility function as intertemporally non-separable. This assumption is related to the idea that the behavior of households follows a regular pattern. Thus, if a household is used to a certain level of consumption and suddenly a shock alters its income, it does not immediately change its pattern of consumption, but uses its savings to mitigate this alteration. This friction, in the literature, is known as habit formation or consumption habits.

Another simplification is that households are rational optimizers and choose their "optimal" path of intertemporal consumption to maximize their utility. This is the idea behind the life-cycle hypothesis, in which consumption in a given period does not depend on total income, but on what is called permanent income. This description involves the assumption that these agents have access to the financial market, and can "transport" income between periods. Empirical evidence shows that there are deviations to the permanent income hypothesis. In this sense, there are many explanations that demonstrate these deviations, one of the being an imperfect capital market and liquidity restrictions. This means that some households do not have access to credit, which would be a barrier for intertemporal optimization. This idea is applied to DSGE models, considering that some households possess liquidity restrictions and do not have access to credit. This type of household in the literature is called a non-Ricardian agent. Considering this type of agent has important consequences when studying shocks, mainly fiscal policy issues.

Brief theoretical review: household rigidity

This section presents the two frictions that involve households: habit-formation and non-Ricardian agents. The former is presented demonstrating why it needs to be applied and the way the literature uses it in modelling. Next, the idea of non-Ricardian agents is presented. In both cases, the aim is to meet the adjustment principle (Definition 1.0.1) and how consumption distances itself from the ideas of permanent income and life-cycles.

Habit formation

The basic models in this book assumed that a period's utility depends only on the consumption in that period, not being affected by the consumption in other periods. This means that the utility function would be intertemporally additively separable. However, an empirical characteristic found in household consumption patterns is what the literature calls habit formation (or consumption habits).

> **Definition 5.1.1** (Habit formation). *This is the consumption adjustment cost when a shock occurs that alters a household's income. These adjustment costs are measured in terms of utility. Thus, if habit formation is particularly significant in relation to a certain shock, consumption will adjust very slowly over time.*

The existence of habit formation is a factor that can explain consumption's overly mild response in relation to changes in output levels, as in this case preferences are not separable in time. Moreover, as shown by Boldrin, Christiano and Fischer (2001), it can also explain the deviation from the permanent income hypothesis, which is the excess of sensitivity in consumption in relation to changes in income levels.

Definition 5.1.2 (Permanent income hypothesis). *Friedman (1957) suggested that income Y is made up of two components: permanent income Y^P and transitory income Y^T. In other words, $Y = Y^P + Y^T$. Permanent income is the fraction of income that households expect will persist in the future, while transitory income is the fraction of income that households expect will not persist. The former can be thought of as an average and the latter as transient deviations.*
Friedman maintains that consumption should depend mainly on permanent income, because households use savings and loans to stabilize consumption in relation to transitory changes in income, that is, $C = \alpha Y^P$, where α is a constant that measures the fraction of permanent income consumed.

Habit formation was introduced into DSGE models with the aim of explaining the main dynamics observed in economics and of addressing the adjustment principle. With that said, data indicate that the response of consumption to a positive shock in income has a bell shaped curve. In particular, habit formation implies the intertemporal non-separability of consumption. Considering this assumption, a rise/fall in current consumption decreases/increases the marginal utility of current consumption, but increases/decreases marginal utility in subsequent periods. Thus, the problem of the household to be solved is technically more complex, because of to the fact that consumption decisions in the current period are not only determined directly by the period's utility, but also by future utility.

The literature works with two possibilities of habit formation: one external and the other internal. Assuming that consumption habits are external to the household means that habits do not depend on these agents' past decisions with regard to individual consumption, but on the economy's aggregate consumption, an assumption known in the literature as "catching up with the Joneses". This is the specification used by Duesenberry (1949), Pollak (1970) and Abel (1990). Another possibility is considering internal habit formation, which refers to a specification in which individuals' habits are determined in terms of their past consumption. This is the specification used by Constantinides (1990). Fortunately, as pointed out by Schmitt-Grohé and Uribe (2012), the dynamics of both the assumptions' models are similar, especially if it is considered that the representative agent's preference coincides with the aggregate per capita preference[1].

In the literature, we find a large variety of specifications when introducing habit formation. The most common functional form is introducing a quasi-difference in consumption into the utility function, that is, a current consumption function minus a proportion of the previous period's consumption, $U\left(C_t - \phi_c C_{t-1}\right)$, where $\phi_c > 0$ is the persistence coefficient of habit formation, which represents the degree to which preferences are non-separable over time. Thus, a household's utility in a certain period does not depend on the period's level of consumption, but on the quasi-difference.

Another common way of introducing this kind of friction is to consider the utility function as a quasi-ratio of consumption. This kind of utility function is a function of all past levels of consumption, $U\left(C_t - \phi_c X_{t-1}\right)$, where $X_{t-1} = X\left(C_{t-1}, C_{t-2}, \ldots\right)$, with X_{t-1} representing the stock of consumption habits in period t. In general terms, it is assumed that the stock of consumption habits follows a process, $X_t = (1 - \delta_x)X_{t-1} + \theta_c C_t$, where δ_x is the depreciation rate of the stock of habits and θ_c measures the sensitivity of this stock in relation to current consumption.

In the literature, habit formation has special relevance when explaining the so-called "equity premium puzzle", fundamentally because of to the rising discrepancy between the representative agent's relative risk aversion and consumption's intertemporal elasticity of substitution (Constantinides, 1990). Carroll, Overland and Weil (2000) use habit formation to explain the existence of a positive relation between savings and growth. In this sense, the study shows that high growth causes high savings, which contradicts standard models of economic growth, in which "forward-looking agents" would save less in an economy with high growth owing to knowing that they will be richer in the future. Thus, the authors show that, with

---

[1]External habit formation is $U\left(C_{j,t} - \phi_c C_{t-1}\right)$, whereas internal habit formation is $U\left(C_{j,t} - \phi_c C_{j,t-1}\right)$. If the idea of a representative household is being used, preferences will be equal among households. Therefore, both habit formation assumptions will be similar.

habit formation, results are consistent with empirical evidence. Moreover, Boldrin, Christiano and Fischer (2001) show that, when habit formation is considered, a large variety of empirical characteristics are explained, such as the excess of sensitivity of consumption in relation to income alterations, output persistence and negative correlation between interest rates and future consumption.

Non-Ricardian agents

Basic models use agents that the literature calls Ricardian, because of to a behavior that seeks to satisfy the principle of Ricardian equivalence. These basic assumptions imply that agents are optimizers and use savings to maximize their levels of utility throughout their lives. Thus, savings is considered a variable that agents use to separate the temporal profile of their consumption from the temporal profile of their income, with the aim of maximizing utility. This causes consumption, at a certain moment, not to depend on the current period's income, but on the level of income throughout agents' life-cycles.

The main assumption regarding the basis of the aforementioned behavior stems from the fact that savings is merely an instrument used for choosing optimal consumption at each moment in time and that agents can move income between periods. Thus, agents have free access to the financial market, for carrying forward present income to the future and for bringing future income to the present. While the first case is always true (any individual can save), the second may not be. Thus, it is possible to find an individual who wishes to have a higher level of consumption today, but this can only occur if the individual has access to credit, otherwise consumption is restricted to current income. When this occurs, it is said that the financial market is imperfect, and that liquidity constraints exist.

In practice, many agents face liquidity constraints, that is, they would be willing to go into debt to increase their present consumption levels, but do not have access to credit. This implies that these agents cannot maximize their intertemporal utility. Such agents are called non-Ricardian or rule-of-thumb agents. Many empirical studies, in both macro- and microeconomics, show that a significant proportion of the population is subject to liquidity constraints[2].

---

[2] For further information, see: Campbell and Mankiw, 1989; Deaton, 1992; Wolff, 1998; Souleles, 1999; and Johnson, Paarker and Souleles, 2006.

Definition 5.1.3 (Principle of Ricardian equivalence). *House-holds are forward looking and therefore base their spending not only on current income, but also on expected future income. Thus, if the fiscal authority implements a tax cut without plans to reduce spending, it will have to finance this cut with a bud-get deficit (an increase in public debt). At some moment in the future, the government will have to increase taxes to pay off the debt and the accumulated interest. Thus, this fiscal policy actu-ally represents a tax cut today that will be followed by a rise in taxes in the future. Tax relaxation therefore provides only tran-sitory income to households that will eventually be taken back. Thus, households would not be in a better situation and con-sumption would remain unchanged.*

Definition 5.1.4 (Life-cycle hypothesis). *According to this hy-pothesis, income varies systematically throughout peoples' lives, and savings (or credit) allows households to transfer income from periods of highs to periods of lows. Thus, if an individ-ual expects to live T years, has wealth W (or access to credit) and expects to receive income Y until retirement, which will happen in X years, the individual's resources throughout his/her life correspond to the initial wealth W and the income XY ob-tained throughout productive life (to simplify matters, income obtained from interest is not being considered). Thus, the in-dividual can divide his/her resources throughout life to main-tain a stable level of consumption, $C = \frac{W+XY}{T}$, or $C = \alpha W + \beta Y$, where $\alpha = \frac{1}{T}$ and $\beta = \frac{X}{T}$. Therefore, it can be seen that consump-tion depends on income and wealth.*

In the basic model, a positive shock in government spending has a negative effect on wealth, causing agents to decrease their levels of consumption and increase labor supply. This result is, in prin-ciple, at odds with empirical literature, which establishes the effect on consumption as positive, or at least not significant. If the exis-tence of non-Ricardian agents is not considered, the negative effect on agents' wealth is forward looking, so their levels of consumption depend on permanent income as it satisfies the principle of Ricardian equivalence. The inclusion of non-Ricardian agents causes the level of aggregate consumption to rise in response to a shock in public spending, as shown by Mankiw (2000).

Galí *et al.* (2007) developed a model with Ricardian and non-Ricardian agents. In this context, the effect of a public spending shock on private consumption will be positive if the proportion of non-Ricardian agents in the economy is greater than 60% in the case of a competitive market structure. This proportion drops to 25% in the case of a competitive labor market only.

The model

In this section, the structural model of the economy proposed in this chapter is presented and solved, step by step. The alterations in this chapter are related to the structure of the household agent, which now considers habit formation and is divided into two groups: Ricardian and non-Ricardian agents. With regard to firms, there are no alterations in relation to the previous chapter. Of the general assumptions, 2.2.1 and 2.2.2 remain valid, while assumption 2.2.3 does not, as adjustment costs on consumption (habit formation) are now being considered.

Households

In this model, households will be altered, with the inclusion of habit formation and non-Ricardian agents. There is a continuum of households indexed by $j \in [0,1]$. A fraction ω_R of this continuum of households, indexed by $R \in [0, \omega_R)$ has access to the financial market and acts as Ricardian-agents, that is, this type of household maximizes its utility intertemporally. The remaining households, indexed by $NR \in [\omega_R, 1]$ do not have access to the financial market and simply consume current available income, thus acting as non-Ricardian agents. For households, assumptions 2.2.4 and 2.2.6 remain valid, while assumption 2.2.5 ceases to be so owing to the aforementioned alterations. Assumptions 4.2.1 and 4.2.2 also remain valid.

Assumption 5.2.1. *The utility function is intertemporally non-separable and depends on the quasi-difference of consumption, $C_{j,t} - \phi_c C_{j,t-1}$ (internal habit formation), where $\phi_c > 0$ is the parameter for the persistence of consumption habits.*

Determining consumption and savings in Ricardian households

It is assumed that each Ricardian household maximizes its intertemporal utility function in terms of consumption ($C_{R,t}$) and leisure (with labor, $L_{R,t}$). The problem of this agent is defined as:

$$\max_{C_{R,t}, K_{t+1}} E_t \sum_{t=0}^{\infty} \beta^t \left[\frac{\left(C_{R,t} - \phi_c C_{R,t-1}\right)^{1-\sigma}}{1-\sigma} - \frac{L_{R,t}^{1+\varphi}}{1+\varphi} \right] \qquad (5.1)$$

subject to,

$$P_t(C_{R,t} + I_t) = W_t L_{R,t} + R_t K_t \qquad (5.2)$$

with the law of motion of capital,

$$K_{R,t+1} = (1 - \delta)K_t + I_t \qquad (5.3)$$

Using the Lagrangian to solve the problem of the Ricardian household,

$$\mathcal{L} = E_t \sum_{t=0}^{\infty} \beta^t \left\{ \left[\frac{\left(C_{R,t} - \phi_c C_{R,t-1}\right)^{1-\sigma}}{1-\sigma} - \frac{L_{R,t}^{1+\varphi}}{1+\varphi} \right] \right.$$

$$\left. - \lambda_{R,t} \left[P_t C_{R,t} + P_t K_{t+1} - P_t(1-\delta)K_t t - W_t L_{R,t} - R_t K_{R,t} \right] \right. \qquad (5.4)$$

This agent's first-order conditions are:

$$\frac{\partial \mathcal{L}}{\partial C_{R,t}} = \left(\frac{1}{1-\sigma}\right) \frac{\partial \left[\left(C_{R,t} - \phi_c C_{R,t-1}\right)^{1-\sigma} \right]}{\partial C_{R,t}}$$

$$-\lambda_{R,t} P_t + \left(\frac{1}{1-\sigma}\right) \beta \frac{\partial \left[\left(E_t C_{R,t+1} - \phi_c C_{R,t}\right)^{1-\sigma} \right]}{\partial C_{R,t}} = 0$$

With,

$$\frac{\partial\left[\left(C_{R,t} - \phi_c C_{R,t-1}\right)^{1-\sigma}\right]}{\partial C_{R,t}} = (1-\sigma)\left(C_{R,t} - \phi_c C_{R,t-1}\right)^{-\sigma}$$

and,

$$\frac{\partial\left[\left(E_t C_{R,t+1} - \phi_c C_{R,t}\right)^{1-\sigma}\right]}{\partial C_{R,t}} = -\phi_c(1-\sigma)\left(E_t C_{R,t+1} - \phi_c C_{R,t}\right)^{-\sigma}$$

Thus, the previous result is:

$$\left(C_{R,t} - \phi_c C_{R,t-1}\right)^{-\sigma} - \lambda_{R,t} P_t - \phi_c \beta \left(E_t C_{R,t+1} - \phi_c C_{R,t}\right)^{-\sigma} = 0 \quad (5.5)$$

$$\frac{\partial \mathscr{L}}{\partial K_{t+1}} = -\lambda_{R,t} P_t + \beta E_t \lambda_{R,t+1}\left[(1-\delta)E_t P_{t+1} + E_t R_{t+1}\right] = 0 \quad (5.6)$$

From equation (5.5),

$$\lambda_{R,t} = \frac{\left(C_{R,t} - \phi_c C_{R,t-1}\right)^{-\sigma}}{P_t} - \phi_c \beta \frac{\left(E_t C_{R,t+1} - \phi_c C_{R,t}\right)^{-\sigma}}{P_t} \quad (5.7)$$

The relevance of the assumption of habit formation can be seen by looking at the periods involved in household consumption decision-making. If, in the basic model, households look at t and t+1 to make decisions, with habit formation, the periods involved in intertemporal choice are t-1, t, t+1 and t+2, which attenuates consumption alterations between periods.

From equation (5.6), the Euler equation is derived,

$$\lambda_{R,t} P_t = \beta E_t \lambda_{R,t+1}\left[(1-\delta)E_t P_{t+1} + E_t R_{t+1}\right] \quad (5.8)$$

Determining the consumption of non-Ricardian households

The behavior of non-Ricardian households is simpler owing to liquidity restrictions that do not allow intertemporal maximization. Thus, the consumption of non-Ricardian agents must equal income in each in period. Actually, even without access to credit, these agents can take present income to the future (via savings). To make the model more treatable, it is also assumed that these agents do not save. The problem faced by these agents is:

$$\max_{C_{NR,t}} E_t \sum_{t=0}^{\infty} \beta^t \left[\frac{\left(C_{NR,t} - \phi_c C_{NR,t-1}\right)^{1-\sigma}}{1-\sigma} - \frac{L_{NR,t}^{1+\varphi}}{1+\varphi} \right] \qquad (5.9)$$

subject to the following budget constraint:

$$P_t C_{NR,t} = W_t L_{NR,t} \qquad (5.10)$$

Using the Lagrangian to solve this problem,

$$\mathscr{L} = E_t \sum_{t=0}^{\infty} \beta^t \left\{ \left[\frac{\left(C_{NR,t} - \phi_c C_{NR,t-1}\right)^{1-\sigma}}{1-\sigma} - \frac{L_{NR,t}^{1+\varphi}}{1+\varphi} \right] \right.$$

$$\left. - \lambda_{NR,t} \left[P_t C_{NR,t} - W_t L_{NR,t} \right] \right\} \qquad (5.11)$$

The first-order conditions for the previous problem are:

$$\frac{\partial \mathscr{L}}{\partial C_{NR,t}} = \left(C_{NR,t} - \phi_c C_{NR,t-1}\right)^{-\sigma}$$

$$- \lambda_{NR,t} P_t - \phi_c \beta \left(E_t C_{NR,t+1} - \phi_c C_{NR,t}\right)^{-\sigma} = 0 \qquad (5.12)$$

So, from equation (5.12),

$$\lambda_{NR,t} = \frac{\left(C_{NR,t} - \phi_c C_{NR,t-1}\right)^{-\sigma}}{P_t} - \phi_c \beta \frac{\left(E_t C_{NR,t+1} - \phi_c C_{NR,t}\right)^{-\sigma}}{P_t}$$

$$\qquad (5.13)$$

Determining wages for Ricardian and non-Ricardian agents

As far as the problem of determining wages is concerned, there is no difference between the types of household involved. Thus, $x = \{R, NR\}$, and the problem is the same as in the previous chapter:

$$\max_{W_{j,t}^*} E_t \sum_{i=0}^{\infty} (\beta \theta_W)^i \left\{ -\frac{L_{x,j,t+i}^{1+\varphi}}{1+\varphi} + \lambda_{x,t+i} \left[W_{j,t}^* L_{x,j,t+i} \right] \right\} \qquad (5.14)$$

subject to,

$$L_{x,j,t} = L_{x,t}\left(\frac{W_t}{W_{j,t}{}^*}\right)^{\psi_W} \tag{5.15}$$

Thus, the maximization problem is:

$$\max_{W_{j,t}^*} E_t \sum_{i=0}^{\infty} (\beta\theta_W)^i \left\{ -\frac{1}{1+\varphi}\left[L_{x,t+i}\left(\frac{W_{t+i}}{W_{j,t}{}^*}\right)^{\psi_W}\right]^{1+\varphi}\right.$$

$$\left. + \lambda_{x,t+i}\left[W_{j,t}^* L_{x,t+i}\left(\frac{W_{t+i}}{W_{j,t}{}^*}\right)^{\psi_W}\right]\right\} \tag{5.16}$$

The first-order condition for the problem of determining wages is:

$$0 = E_t \sum_{i=0}^{\infty} (\beta\theta_W)^i \left\{ \psi_W\left[L_{x,t+i}\left(\frac{W_{t+i}}{W_{j,t}{}^*}\right)^{\psi_W}\right]^{\varphi} L_{x,t+i}\left(\frac{W_{t+i}}{W_{j,t}{}^*}\right)^{\psi_W}\frac{1}{W_{j,t}{}^*}\right.$$

$$\left. +(1-\psi_W)\lambda_{x,t+i}L_{x,t+i}\left(\frac{W_{t+i}}{W_{j,t}{}^*}\right)^{\psi_W}\right\}$$

or,

$$0 = E_t \sum_{i=0}^{\infty} (\beta\theta_W)^i \left\{ \psi_W\left[L_{x,t+i}\left(\frac{W_{t+i}}{W_{j,t}{}^*}\right)^{\psi_W}\right]^{\varphi}\frac{1}{W_{j,t}{}^*}\right.$$

$$\left. +(1-\psi_W)\lambda_{x,t+i}\right\}$$

Therefore, the optimal wage is obtained thus:

$$W_{j,t}{}^* = \left(\frac{\psi_W}{\psi_W-1}\right)E_t\sum_{i=0}^{\infty}(\beta\theta_W)^i\left(\frac{L_{x,j,t+i}^{\varphi}}{\lambda_{x,t+i}}\right) \tag{5.17}$$

or,

$$W_{j,t}{}^* = \left(\frac{\psi_W}{\psi_W-1}\right)E_t\sum_{i=0}^{\infty}(\beta\theta_W)^i\left(\frac{L_{R,j,t+i}^{\varphi}}{\lambda_{R,t+i}}\right) \tag{5.18}$$

$$W_{j,t}{}^* = \left(\frac{\psi_W}{\psi_W-1}\right)E_t\sum_{i=0}^{\infty}(\beta\theta_W)^i\left(\frac{L_{NR,j,t+i}^{\varphi}}{\lambda_{NR,t+i}}\right) \tag{5.19}$$

and the wage level,

$$W_t = \left[\theta_W W_{t-1}^{1-\psi_W} + (1-\theta_W)W_t^{*1-\psi_W}\right]^{\frac{1}{1-\psi_W}} \qquad (5.20)$$

Aggregating Consumption and Labor

The aggregate value for consumption and labor is given by the following aggregation form:

$$X_t = \int_0^{\omega_R} X_{R,j,t}\,dj + \int_{\omega_R}^1 X_{NR,j,t}\,dj = \omega_R X_{R,t} + (1-\omega_R)X_{NR,t}$$

Therefore, aggregate consumption and labor is:

$$C_t = \omega_R C_{R,t} + (1-\omega_R)C_{NR,t} \qquad (5.21)$$

$$L_t = \omega_R L_{R,t} + (1-\omega_R)L_{NR,t} \qquad (5.22)$$

Firms

The assumptions of the firms groups 3.2.1-3.2.6 remain valid. Consequently, the results from chapter 3 will be used:

Equation (3.10),

$$Y_{j,t} = A_t K_{j,t}^{\alpha} L_{j,t}^{1-\alpha} \qquad (5.23)$$

Equation (3.11),

$$\log A_t = (1-\rho_A)\log A_{ss} + \rho_A \log A_{t-1} + \varepsilon_t \qquad (5.24)$$

Equation (3.15),

$$L_{j,t} = (1-\alpha)MC_{j,t}\frac{Y_{j,t}}{W_t} \qquad (5.25)$$

Equation (3.16),

$$K_{j,t} = \alpha MC_{j,t}\frac{Y_{j,t}}{R_t} \qquad (5.26)$$

Equation (3.22),

$$MC_{j,t} = \frac{1}{A_t}\left(\frac{W_t}{1-\alpha}\right)^{1-\alpha}\left(\frac{R_t}{\alpha}\right)^{\alpha}$$

(5.27)

Equation (3.25),

$$P_{j,t}^* = \left(\frac{\psi}{\psi-1}\right)E_t\sum_{i=0}^{\infty}(\beta\theta)^i\,MC_{j,t+i}$$

(5.28)

Equation (3.26),

$$P_t = \left[\theta P_{t-1}^{1-\psi} + (1-\theta)P_t^{*\,1-\psi}\right]^{\frac{1}{1-\psi}}$$

(5.29)

The model's equilibrium conditions

The model reaches its conclusion with the following equilibrium condition for the goods market:

$$Y_t = C_t + I_t$$

(5.30)

This economy's model is composed of the equations from Table 5.1.

Table 5.1: Structure of the model.

Equation	(Definition)
$\lambda_{R,t} =$ $\frac{(C_{R,t}-\phi_c C_{R,t-1})^{-\sigma}}{P_t} - \phi_c\beta\frac{(E_t C_{R,t+1}-\phi_c C_{R,t})^{-\sigma}}{P_t}$	(Ricardian household Lagrangian)
$W_{j,t}^* = \left(\frac{\psi_W}{\psi_W-1}\right)E_t\sum_{i=0}^{\infty}(\beta\theta_W)^i\left(\frac{L_{R,j,t+i}^{\varphi}}{\lambda_{R,t+i}}\right)$	(Definition of optimal wages of Ricardian household)
$W_t =$ $\left[\theta_W W_{t-1}^{1-\varphi_W} + (1-\theta_W)W_t^{*\,1-\varphi_W}\right]^{\frac{1}{1-\varphi_W}}$	(Level of aggregate wages)
$\pi_{W,t} = W_t/W_{t-1}$	(Gross wage inflation rate)
$\lambda_{R,t}P_t = \beta E_t\{\lambda_{R,t+1}[(1-\delta)P_{t+1} + R_{t+1}]\}$	(Euler equation)
$K_{t+1} = (1-\delta)K_t + I_t$	(Law of motion of capital)

$$\lambda_{NR,t} = \frac{(C_{NR,t} - \phi_c C_{NR,t-1})^{-\sigma}}{P_t} -$$
$$\phi_c \beta \frac{(E_t C_{NR,t+1} - \phi_c C_{NR,t})^{-\sigma}}{P_t}$$

(Non-Ricardian household Lagrangian)

$$W_{j,t}^* = \left(\frac{\psi_W}{\psi_W - 1}\right) E_t \sum_{i=0}^{\infty} (\beta \theta_W)^i \left(\frac{L_{NR,j,t+i}^{\varphi}}{\lambda_{NR,t+i}}\right)$$

(Budget constraint of non-Ricardian agent)

$$P_t C_{NR,t} = W_t L_{NR,t}$$

(Restrição orçamentária para o agente não ricardiano)

$$C_t = \omega_R C_{R,t} + (1 - \omega_R) C_{NR,t}$$

(Aggregate consumption)

$$L_t = \omega_R L_{R,t} + (1 - \omega_R) L_{NR,t}$$

(Aggregate Labor)

$$Y_t = A_t K_t^{\alpha} L_t^{1-\alpha}$$

(Production function)

$$K_t = \alpha MC_t \frac{Y_t}{R_t}$$

(Demand for capital)

$$L_t = (1 - \alpha) MC_t \frac{Y_t}{W_t}$$

(Demand for labor)

$$MC_t = \frac{1}{A_t} \left(\frac{W_t}{1-\alpha}\right)^{1-\alpha} \left(\frac{R_t}{\alpha}\right)^{\alpha}$$

(Marginal Cost)

$$P_t^* = \left(\frac{\psi}{\psi - 1}\right) E_t \sum_{i=0}^{\infty} (\beta \theta)^i MC_{t+i}$$

(Optimal price level)

$$P_t = \left[\theta P_{t-1}^{1-\psi} + (1 - \theta) P_t^{*\,1-\psi}\right]^{\frac{1}{1-\psi}}$$

(General price level)

$$\pi_t = P_t / P_{t-1}$$

(Gross inflation rate)

$$Y_t = C_t + I_t$$

(Equilibrium condition)

$$\log A_t = (1 - \rho_A) \log A_{ss} + \rho_A \log A_{t-1} + \epsilon_t$$

(Productivity shock)

Steady state

This section keeps to the same procedure adopted in other chapters for solving the steady state.

Households

$$1 = \beta \left(1 - \delta + \frac{R_{ss}}{P_{ss}}\right) \tag{5.31}$$

$$\delta K_{ss} = I_{ss} \tag{5.32}$$

$$W_{ss} = \left(\frac{\psi_W}{\psi_W - 1}\right)\left[\frac{C_{R,ss}^{\sigma} L_{R,ss}^{\varphi} P_{ss}}{(1 - \beta\theta_W)(1 - \phi_c)^{-\sigma}(1 - \phi_c\beta)}\right] \tag{5.33}$$

$$W_{ss} = \left(\frac{\psi_W}{\psi_W - 1}\right)\left[\frac{C_{NR,ss}^{\sigma} L_{NR,ss}^{\varphi} P_{ss}}{(1 - \beta\theta_W)(1 - \phi_c)^{-\sigma}(1 - \phi_c\beta)}\right] \tag{5.34}$$

where: $\sum_{i=0}^{\infty}(\beta\theta_W)^i = \frac{1}{1-\beta\theta_W}$

$$C_{ss} = \omega_R C_{R,ss} + (1 - \omega_R)C_{NR,ss} \tag{5.35}$$

$$L_{ss} = \omega_R L_{R,ss} + (1 - \omega_R)L_{NR,ss} \tag{5.36}$$

Firms

$$L_{ss} = (1 - \alpha)MC_{ss}\frac{Y_{ss}}{W_{ss}} \tag{5.37}$$

$$K_{ss} = \alpha MC_{ss}\frac{Y_{ss}}{R_{ss}} \tag{5.38}$$

$$Y_{ss} = K_{ss}^{\alpha} L_{ss}^{1-\alpha} \tag{5.39}$$

$$MC_{ss} = \left(\frac{W_{ss}}{1 - \alpha}\right)^{1-\alpha}\left(\frac{R_{ss}}{\alpha}\right)^{\alpha} \tag{5.40}$$

$$P_{ss} = \left(\frac{\psi}{\psi - 1}\right)\left(\frac{1}{1 - \beta\theta}\right)MC_{ss} \tag{5.41}$$

where: $\sum_{i=0}^{\infty}(\beta\theta)^i = \frac{1}{1-\beta\theta}$.

Equilibrium condition

$$Y_{ss} = C_{ss} + I_{ss} \tag{5.42}$$

Next, the values of the prices (P_{ss}, R_{ss}, W_{ss} and MC_{ss}) must be determined. The general price level is normalized ($P_{ss} = 1$), thus, from equation (5.31),

$$R_{ss} = P_{ss}\left[\frac{1}{\beta} - (1-\delta)\right] \tag{5.43}$$

the value of R_{ss} is found, while the value of MC_{ss} is derived from equation (5.41):

$$MC_{ss} = \left(\frac{\psi - 1}{\psi}\right)(1 - \beta\theta)P_{ss} \tag{5.44}$$

With the values of R_{ss} and MC_{ss} known, the value of W_{ss} is also known, and from equation (5.40),

$$W_{ss}^{1-\alpha} = MC_{ss}(1-\alpha)^{1-\alpha}\left(\frac{\alpha}{R_{ss}}\right)^{\alpha}$$

$$W_{ss} = (1-\alpha)MC_{ss}^{\frac{1}{1-\alpha}}\left(\frac{\alpha}{R_{ss}}\right)^{\frac{\alpha}{1-\alpha}} \tag{5.45}$$

Having determined the prices, the next step is to obtain the variables that compose aggregate demand (C_{ss} e I_{ss}). Substituting equation (5.38) in equation (5.32),

$$I_{ss} = \left(\frac{\delta\alpha CM_{ss}}{R_{ss}}\right)Y_{ss} \tag{5.46}$$

At the steady state, $C_{ss} = C_{R,ss} = C_{NR,ss}$ e $L_{ss} = L_{R,ss} = L_{NR,ss}$, substituting equation (5.37) in equation (5.33),

$$W_{ss} = \left(\frac{\psi_W}{\psi_W - 1}\right)\left\{\frac{C_{ss}^{\sigma}\left[(1-\alpha)MC_{ss}\frac{Y_{ss}}{W_{ss}}\right]^{\varphi}P_{ss}}{(1-\beta\theta_W)(1-\phi_c)^{-\sigma}(1-\phi_c\beta)}\right\}$$

$$C_{ss}^{\sigma}Y_{ss}^{\varphi} = (1-\phi_c)^{-\sigma}(1-\phi_c\beta)(1-\beta\theta_W)\left(\frac{\psi_W - 1}{\psi_W}\right)\frac{W_{ss}}{P_{ss}}\left[\frac{W_{ss}}{(1-\alpha)MC_{ss}}\right]^{\varphi}$$

$$C_{ss} = \frac{1}{Y_{ss}^{\frac{\varphi}{\sigma}}}\left\{(1-\phi_c)^{-\sigma}(1-\phi_c\beta)(1-\beta\theta_W)\right.$$

$$\left.\left\{\left(\frac{\psi_W - 1}{\psi_W}\right)\frac{W_{ss}}{P_{ss}}\left[\frac{W_{ss}}{(1-\alpha)MC_{ss}}\right]^{\varphi}\right\}^{\frac{1}{\sigma}} \tag{5.47}$$

Substituting (5.46) and (5.47) in (5.42),

$$Y_{ss} = \frac{1}{Y_{ss}^{\frac{\varphi}{\sigma}}} \left\{ (1 - \phi_c)^{-\sigma} (1 - \phi_c\beta)(1 - \beta\theta_W) \right\}$$

$$\left\{ \left(\frac{\psi_W - 1}{\psi_W} \right) \frac{W_{ss}}{P_{ss}} \left[\frac{W_{ss}}{(1-\alpha)MC_{ss}} \right]^{\varphi} \right\}^{\frac{1}{\sigma}}$$

$$+ \left(\frac{\delta\alpha MC_{ss}}{R_{ss}} \right) Y_{ss}$$

$$\left[1 - \left(\frac{\delta\alpha MC_{ss}}{R_{ss}} \right) \right] Y_{ss} = \frac{1}{Y_{ss}^{\frac{\varphi}{\sigma}}}$$

$$\left\{ (1 - \phi_c)^{1-\sigma} (1 - \beta\theta_W) \left(\frac{\psi_W - 1}{\psi_W} \right) \frac{W_{ss}}{P_{ss}} \right\}$$

the product at the steady state is:

$$Y_{ss} = \left(\frac{R_{ss}}{R_{ss} - \delta\alpha MC_{ss}} \right)^{\frac{\sigma}{\sigma+\varphi}}$$

$$\left\{ (1 - \phi_c)^{-\sigma} (1 - \phi_c\beta)(1 - \beta\theta_W) \left(\frac{\psi_W - 1}{\psi_W} \right) \frac{W_{ss}}{P_{ss}} \right.$$

$$\left. \left\{ \left[\frac{W_{ss}}{(1-\alpha)MC_{ss}} \right]^{\varphi} \right\} \right\}^{\frac{1}{\sigma+\varphi}} \tag{5.48}$$

The previous procedures are summed up in the presentation of the steady state below:

$$A_{ss} = 1$$

$$P_{ss} = 1$$

$$R_{ss} = P_{ss} \left[\frac{1}{\beta} - (1 - \delta) \right]$$

$$MC_{ss} = \left(\frac{\psi - 1}{\psi} \right) (1 - \beta\theta) P_{ss}$$

$$W_{ss} = (1-\alpha)MC_{ss}^{\frac{1}{1-\alpha}}\left(\frac{\alpha}{R_{ss}}\right)^{\frac{\alpha}{1-\alpha}}$$

$$Y_{ss} = \left(\frac{R_{ss}}{R_{ss}-\delta\alpha MC_{ss}}\right)^{\frac{\sigma}{\sigma+\varphi}}$$

$$\left\{(1-\phi_c)^{-\sigma}(1-\phi_c\beta)(1-\beta\theta_W)\left(\frac{\psi_W-1}{\psi_W}\right)\frac{W_{ss}}{P_{ss}}\right\}$$

$$\left\{\left[\frac{W_{ss}}{(1-\alpha)MC_{ss}}\right]^{\varphi}\right\}^{\frac{1}{\sigma+\varphi}}$$

$$L_{ss} = (1-\alpha)MC_{ss}\frac{Y_{ss}}{W_{ss}}$$

Remembering that,

$$L_{ss} = L_{R,ss} = L_{NR,ss}$$

$$K_{ss} = \alpha MC_{ss}\frac{Y_{ss}}{R_{ss}}$$

$$I_{ss} = \delta K_{ss}$$

$$C_{ss} = \frac{1}{Y_{ss}^{\frac{\varphi}{\sigma}}}\left\{(1-\phi_c)^{1-\sigma}(1-\beta\theta_W)\right\}$$

$$\left\{\left(\frac{\psi_W-1}{\psi_W}\right)\frac{W_{ss}}{P_{ss}}\left[\frac{W_{ss}}{(1-\alpha)MC_{ss}}\right]^{\varphi}\right\}^{\frac{1}{\sigma}}$$

Also remembering that,

$$C_{ss} = C_{R,ss} = C_{NR,ss}$$

Table 5.2 shows the calibrated values that will be used in the simulation, while table 5.3 shows the model's steady state values.

Table 5.2: Values of the structural model's parameters.

Parameter	Meaning of the parameter	Calibrated value
σ	Relative risk aversion coefficient	2
φ	Marginal disutility with respect to labor supply	1.5
α	Elasticity of output with respect to capital	0.35
β	Discount factor	0.985
δ	Depreciation rate	0.025
ρ_A	Autoregressive parameter of productivity	0.95
σ_A	Standard deviation of productivity	0.01
θ	Price stickiness parameter	0.75
ψ	Elasticity of substitution between intermediate goods	8
θ_W	Wage stickiness parameter	0.75
ψ_W	Elasticity of substitution between differentiated labor	21
ϕ_c	Habit persistence	0.8
ω_R	Participation of Ricardian agents in consumption and labor	0.5

Table 5.3: Values of variables at the steady state.

Variable	Steady state
A	1
R	0.040
MC	0.229
W	0.215
Y	0.842
I	0.042
C	0.800
L	0.581
K	1.674

Log-linearization (Uhlig's method)

Uhlig's method continues to be used as a tool for log-linearizing the model. The law of motion of capital is the same as in the other chapters,

$$\tilde{K}_{t+1} = (1-\delta)\tilde{K}_t + \delta\tilde{I}_t \tag{5.49}$$

The Lagrangian of Ricardian and non-Ricardian households

Habit formation and the introduction of non-Ricardian agents are new elements in this chapter. Thus, more attention is necessary when log-linearizing the equations that involve them.

From equation (5.7),

$$\lambda_{R,t}P_t = \left(C_{R,t} - \phi_c C_{R,t-1}\right)^{-\sigma} - \phi_c\left(C_{R,t+1} - \phi_c C_{R,t}\right)^{-\sigma}$$

whose steady state is:

$$\lambda_{R,ss}P_{ss} = C_{R,ss}^{-\sigma}(1-\phi_C)^{-\sigma}(1-\phi_c\beta)$$

To log-linearize the Lagrangian equation of the non-Ricardian agents, two auxiliary variables will be used,

$$CC_{R,t} = C_{R,t} - \phi_c C_{R,t-1}$$

and,

$$CC_{R,t+1} = C_{R,t+1} - \phi_c C_{R,t}$$

with the following steady state,

$$CC_{R,ss} = C_{R,ss}(1-\phi_c)$$

and log-linearization:

$$CC_{R,ss}(1+\widetilde{CC}_{R,t}) = C_{R,ss}(1+\tilde{C}_{R,t}) - \phi_c C_{R,ss}(1+\tilde{C}_{R,t-1})$$

with $CC_{R,ss} = C_{R,ss}(1-\phi_c)$, the log-linearization of $CC_{R,ss}$ is:

$$\widetilde{CC}_{R,t} = \left(\frac{1}{1-\phi_c}\right)(\tilde{C}_{R,t} - \phi_c\tilde{C}_{R,t-1}) \tag{5.50}$$

Similarly,

$$\widetilde{CC}_{R,t+1} = \left(\frac{1}{1-\phi_c}\right)(\widetilde{C}_{R,t+1} - \phi_c \widetilde{C}_{R,t}) \tag{5.51}$$

Rewriting the Lagrangian equation of the Ricardian agents using the auxiliary variables,

$$\lambda_{R,t} P_t = CC_{R,t}^{-\sigma} - \phi_c \beta E_t CC_{R,t+1}^{-\sigma}$$

$$\lambda_{R,ss} P_{ss}(1+\tilde{\lambda}_{R,t}+\tilde{P}_t) = CC_{R,ss}^{-\sigma}(1-\sigma\widetilde{CC}_{R,t}) - \phi_c \beta CC_{R,ss}^{-\sigma}(1-\sigma E_t \widetilde{CC}_{R,t+1})$$

$$C_{R,ss}^{-\sigma}(1-\phi_c)^{-\sigma}(1-\phi_c\beta)(\tilde{\lambda}_{R,t} + \tilde{P}_t)$$
$$= C_{R,ss}^{-\sigma}(1-\phi_c)^{-\sigma}\sigma(\phi_c \beta E_t \widetilde{CC}_{R,t+1} - \widetilde{CC}_{R,t})$$

$$\tilde{\lambda}_{R,t} + \tilde{P}_t = \left[\frac{\sigma}{(1-\phi_c\beta)}\right](\phi_c \beta E_t \widetilde{CC}_{R,t+1} - \widetilde{CC}_{R,t})$$

Substituting the auxiliary variables in the previous expression,

$$\tilde{\lambda}_{R,t} + \tilde{P}_t = \left[\frac{\sigma}{(1-\phi_c\beta)}\right]\left[\phi_c\beta\left(\frac{1}{1-\phi_c}\right)(E_t\tilde{C}_{R,t+1} - \phi_c\tilde{C}_{R,t})\right.$$
$$\left. -\left(\frac{1}{1-\phi_c}\right)(\tilde{C}_{R,t} - \phi_c\tilde{C}_{R,t-1})\right]$$

$$\tilde{\lambda}_{R,t} = \left[\frac{\sigma}{(1-\phi_c)(1-\phi_c\beta)}\right]$$
$$[\phi_c\beta(E_t\tilde{C}_{R,t+1} - \phi_c\tilde{C}_{R,t}) - (\tilde{C}_{R,t} - \phi_c\tilde{C}_{R,t-1})] - \tilde{P}_t \tag{5.52}$$

Similarly for non-Ricardian households,

$$\tilde{\lambda}_{NR,t} = \left[\frac{\sigma}{(1-\phi_c)(1-\phi_c\beta)}\right]$$
$$[\phi_c\beta(E_t\tilde{C}_{NR,t+1} - \phi_c\tilde{C}_{NR,t}) - (\tilde{C}_{NR,t} - \phi_c\tilde{C}_{NR,t-1})] - \tilde{P}_t \tag{5.53}$$

As for the Phillips equation for wages, from equation (5.18),

$$W_{ss}(1 + \widetilde{W}_t^*) = \left(\frac{\psi_W}{\psi_W - 1}\right)\left(\frac{1 - \beta\theta_W}{1 - \beta\theta_W}\right)\left(\frac{L_{R,ss}}{\lambda_{R,ss}}\right)$$

$$E_t \sum_{i=0}^{\infty} (\beta\theta_W)^i (1 + \widetilde{L}_{R,t+i} - \widetilde{\lambda}_{R,t+i})$$

Remembering that at the steady state, $W_{ss} = \left(\frac{\psi_W}{\psi_W - 1}\right)\left(\frac{1}{1 - \beta\theta_W}\right)$ $\left(\frac{L_{R,ss}}{\lambda_{R,ss}}\right)$,

$$\widetilde{W}_t^* = (1 - \beta\theta_W)E_t \sum_{i=0}^{\infty} (\beta\theta_W)^i (\widetilde{L}_{R,t+i} - \widetilde{\lambda}_{R,t+i}) \qquad (5.54)$$

Using equation (4.46),

$$\widetilde{W}_t = \theta_W \widetilde{W}_{t-1} + (1 - \theta_W)\widetilde{W}_t^* \qquad (5.55)$$

Substituting (5.54) in (5.55),

$$\widetilde{W}_t = \theta_W \widetilde{W}_{t-1} + (1 - \theta_W)(1 - \beta\theta_W)E_t \sum_{i=0}^{\infty} (\beta\theta_W)^i (\widetilde{L}_{R,t+i} - \widetilde{\lambda}_{R,t+i})$$

Using the quasi-differencing procedure. Thus, multiplying the previous expression by $(1 - L^{-1}\beta\theta_W)$:

$$\widetilde{W}_t - \beta\theta_W E_t \widetilde{W}_{t+1} = \theta_W \widetilde{W}_{t-1} + (1-\theta_W)(1-\beta\theta_W)E_t \sum_{i=0}^{\infty} (\beta\theta_W)^i (\widetilde{L}_{R,t+i} - \widetilde{\lambda}_{R,t+i})$$

$$- \beta\theta_W \theta_W \widetilde{W}_t - (1 - \theta_W)(1 - \beta\theta_W)E_t \sum_{i=0}^{\infty} (\beta\theta_W)^i (\widetilde{L}_{R,t+1+i} - \widetilde{\lambda}_{R,t+1+i})$$

$$\widetilde{W}_t - \beta\theta_W E_t \widetilde{W}_{t+1} = \theta_W \widetilde{W}_{t-1} - \beta\theta_W \theta_W \widetilde{W}_t + (1-\theta_W)(1-\beta\theta_W)(\widetilde{L}_{R,t} - \widetilde{\lambda}_{R,t})$$

Adding and subtracting $\widetilde{W}_t(1-\theta_W)(1-\beta\theta_W) = \widetilde{W}_t(1-\beta\theta_W-\theta_W+\beta\theta_W\theta_W)$ in the previous expression,

$$\widetilde{W}_t - \beta\theta_W E_t \widetilde{W}_{t+1} = \theta_W \widetilde{W}_{t-1} - \beta\theta_W \theta_W \widetilde{W}_t + (1-\theta_W)(1-\beta\theta_W)(\widetilde{L}_{R,t} - \widetilde{\lambda}_{R,t})$$
$$+ \widetilde{W}_t - \beta\theta_W \widetilde{W}_t - \theta_W \widetilde{W}_t + \beta\theta_W \theta_W \widetilde{W}_t$$

$$\theta_W(\widetilde{W}_t - \widetilde{W}_{t-1}) = \theta_W \beta(E_t \widetilde{W}_{t+1} - \widetilde{W}_t) + (1-\theta_W)(1-\beta\theta_W)(\widetilde{L}_{R,t} - \widetilde{\lambda}_{R,t} - \widetilde{W}_t)$$

Dividing both sides of the previous expression by θ_W, assuming $\widetilde{\pi_W}_t = \widetilde{P}_t - \widetilde{P}_{t-1}$ and $\widetilde{\pi_W}_{t+1} = \widetilde{P}_{t+1} - \widetilde{P}_t$, we arrive at the Phillips equation for Ricardian households' wages:

$$\widetilde{\pi_W}_t = \beta E_t \widetilde{\pi_W}_{t+1} + \left[\frac{(1-\theta_W)(1-\beta\theta_W)}{\theta_W} \right] (\widetilde{L}_{R,t} - \widetilde{\lambda}_{R,t} - \widetilde{W}_t) \quad (5.56)$$

Similarly, for non-Ricardian households,

$$\widetilde{\pi_W}_t = \beta E_t \widetilde{\pi_W}_{t+1} + \left[\frac{(1-\theta_W)(1-\beta\theta_W)}{\theta_W} \right] (\widetilde{L}_{NR,t} - \widetilde{\lambda}_{NR,t} - \widetilde{W}_t) \quad (5.57)$$

Euler equation

From equation (5.6),

$$\lambda_{R,t} P_t = \beta E_t \{ \lambda_{R,t+1} [(1-\delta)P_{t+1} + R_{t+1}] \}$$

$$\frac{1}{\beta} \frac{\lambda_{R,t} P_t}{E_t \lambda_{R,t+1}} = E_t [(1-\delta)P_{t+1} + R_{t+1}]$$

$$\left(\frac{P_{ss}}{\beta} \right)(1 + \widetilde{\lambda}_{R,t} + \widetilde{P}_t - E_t \widetilde{\lambda}_{R,t+1}) = E_t \left[(1-\delta)P_{ss}(1 + \widetilde{P}_{t+1}) + R_{ss}(1 + \widetilde{R}_{t+1}) \right]$$

$$\left(\frac{P_{ss}}{\beta} \right)(\widetilde{\lambda}_{R,t} + \widetilde{P}_t - E_t \widetilde{\lambda}_{R,t+1}) = E_t \left[(1-\delta)P_{ss}\widetilde{P}_{t+1} + R_{ss}\widetilde{R}_{t+1} \right] \quad (5.58)$$

Aggregate consumption and labor

From equation (5.21),

$$C_{ss}\widetilde{C}_t = \omega_R C_{R,ss}\widetilde{C}_{R,ss} + (1-\omega_R)C_{NR,ss}\widetilde{C}_{NR,ss}$$

as $C_{ss} = C_{R,ss} = C_{NR,ss}$,

$$\widetilde{C}_t = \omega_R \widetilde{C}_{R,ss} + (1-\omega_R)\widetilde{C}_{NR,ss} \quad (5.59)$$

From equation(5.22),

$$L_{ss}\tilde{L}_t = \omega_R L_{R,ss}\tilde{L}_{R,ss} + (1 - \omega_R)L_{NR,ss}\tilde{L}_{NR,ss}$$

as $L_{ss} = L_{R,ss} = L_{NR,ss}$,

$$\tilde{L}_t = \omega_R \tilde{L}_{R,ss} + (1 - \omega_R)\tilde{L}_{NR,ss} \qquad (5.60)$$

The firms sector is unchanged, thus, the existing log-lineariza-tions are used:

$$\tilde{Y}_t = \tilde{A}_t + \alpha\tilde{K}_t + (1 - \alpha)\tilde{L}_t \qquad (5.61)$$

$$\tilde{K}_t = \widetilde{MC}_t + \tilde{Y}_t - \tilde{R}_t \qquad (5.62)$$

$$\tilde{L}_t = \widetilde{MC}_t + \tilde{Y}_t - \widetilde{W}_t \qquad (5.63)$$

$$\widetilde{MC}_t = [(1 - \alpha)\widetilde{W}_t + \alpha\tilde{R}_t - \tilde{A}_t] \qquad (5.64)$$

$$\tilde{\pi}_t = \beta E_t\tilde{\pi}_{t+1} + \left[\frac{(1-\theta)(1-\beta\theta)}{\theta}\right](\widetilde{MC}_t - \tilde{P}_t) \qquad (5.65)$$

$$\tilde{\pi}_t = \tilde{P}_t - \tilde{P}_{t-1} \qquad (5.66)$$

$$Y_{ss}\tilde{Y}_t = C_{ss}\tilde{C}_t + I_{ss}\tilde{I}_t \qquad (5.67)$$

$$\tilde{A}_t = \rho_A\tilde{A}_{t-1} + \epsilon_t \qquad (5.68)$$

Table 5.4 summarizes the log-linear model.

Table 5.4: Structure of the model.

Equation	(Definition)
$\tilde{\lambda}_{R,t} = \left[\dfrac{\sigma}{(1 - \phi_c)(1 - \phi_c\beta)}\right]$ $[\phi_c\beta(E_t\tilde{C}_{R,t+1} - \phi_c\tilde{C}_{R,t}) - (\tilde{C}_{R,t} - \phi_c\tilde{C}_{R,t-1})] - \tilde{P}_t$	(Ricardian household Lagrangian)
$\widetilde{\pi_W}_t =$ $\beta E_t\widetilde{\pi_W}_{t+1} + \left[\frac{(1-\theta_W)(1-\beta\theta_W)}{\theta_W}\right](\tilde{L}_{R,t} - \tilde{\lambda}_{R,t} - \widetilde{W}_t)$	(Phillips equation for Ricardian household wages)

$$\widetilde{\pi_W}_t = \widehat{W}_t - \widehat{W}_{t-1}$$ (Gross wage inflation rate)

$$\left(\frac{P_{ss}}{\beta}\right)(\widetilde{\lambda}_{R,t} + \widetilde{P}_t - E_t\widetilde{\lambda}_{R,t+1}) =$$ (Euler equation)
$$(1-\delta)E_t\left(P_{ss}\widetilde{P}_{t+1} + R_{ss}\widetilde{R}_{t+1}\right)$$

$$\widetilde{K}_{t+1} = (1-\delta)\widetilde{K}_t + \delta\widetilde{I}_t$$ (Law of motion of capital)

$$\widetilde{\lambda}_{NR,t} = \left[\frac{\sigma}{(1-\phi_c)(1-\phi_c\beta)}\right]$$

$$\left[\phi_c\beta(E_t\widetilde{C}_{NR,t+1} - \phi_c\widetilde{C}_{NR,t}) - (\widetilde{C}_{NR,t} - \phi_c\widetilde{C}_{NR,t-1})\right]$$ (Non-Ricardian household

$$- \widetilde{P}_t$$ Lagrangian)

$$\widetilde{\pi_W}_t = \beta E_t\widetilde{\pi_W}_{t+1} + \left[\frac{(1-\theta_W)(1-\beta\theta_W)}{\theta_W}\right](\widetilde{L}_{NR,t} -$$ (Phillips equation for non-Ricardian
$$\widetilde{\lambda}_{NR,t} - \widehat{W}_t)$$ household wages)

$$\widetilde{P}_t + \widetilde{C}_{NR,t} = \widehat{W}_t + \widetilde{L}_{NR,t}$$ (Budget constraint of non-Ricardian agent)

$$\widetilde{C}_t = \omega_R\widetilde{C}_{R,ss} + (1-\omega_R)\widetilde{C}_{NR,ss}$$ (Aggregate consumption)

$$\widetilde{L}_t = \omega_R\widetilde{L}_{R,ss} + (1-\omega_R)\widetilde{L}_{NR,ss}$$ (Aggregate Labor)

$$\widetilde{Y}_t = \widetilde{A}_t + \alpha\widetilde{K}_t + (1-\alpha)\widetilde{L}_t$$ (Production function)

$$\widetilde{K}_t = \widetilde{MC}_t + \widetilde{Y}_t - \widetilde{R}_t$$ (Demand for capital)

$$\widetilde{L}_t = \widetilde{MC}_t + \widetilde{Y}_t - \widehat{W}_t$$ (Demand for labor)

$$\widetilde{MC}_t = [(1-\alpha)\widehat{W}_t + \alpha\widetilde{R}_t - \widetilde{A}_t]$$ (Marginal Cost)

$$\widetilde{\pi}_t = \beta E_t\widetilde{\pi}_{t+1} + \left[\frac{(1-\theta)(1-\beta\theta)}{\theta}\right](\widetilde{MC}_t - \widetilde{P}_t)$$ (Phillips equation)

$$\widetilde{\pi}_t = \widetilde{P}_t - \widetilde{P}_{t-1}$$ (Gross inflation rate)

$$Y_{ss}\widetilde{Y}_t = C_{ss}\widetilde{C}_t + I_{ss}\widetilde{I}_t$$ (Equilibrium condition)

$$\widetilde{A}_t = \rho_A\widetilde{A}_{t-1} + \epsilon_t$$ (Productivity shock)

Productivity shock

Figure 5.1 shows the results of a positive productivity shock. The shock causes the marginal productivities of labor and capital to rise, and firms respond to this by increasing their demand for factors of production (L, K). In this model, the participation of non-Ricardian agents has a decisive result on labor supply. With the rise in income due to the productivity shock, non-Ricardian households increase their acquisition of consumer goods, but not as much as in the models in the other chapter due to the limitation of habit formation. The excess income that should be used for acquiring financial assets that, as assumed in this model, are not available to these agents, causes them to increase their acquisition of another good, leisure.

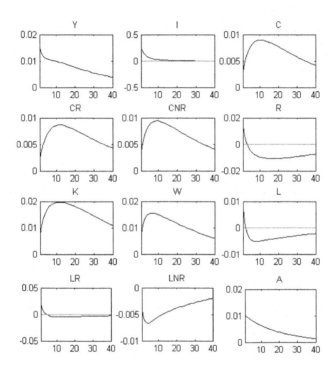

Figure 5.1: Impulse-response functions for the NK model with habit formation and non-Ricardian agents.

In the other models, the income effect was a relevant factor in justifying the labor supply's weak response to a positive shock. With the introduction of agents with liquidity constraints and habit formation, this effect is more robust. In Figure 5.2, it can be seen that the results in terms of real wages are more significant in the model with household frictions (NKFR) and labor supply is less than in other models.

This difference in the income effect between models, which generates a lower labor supply is compensated by a higher supply of capital. Another sign related to frictions included here is consumption's bell-shape. In Figure 5.2, the differences in consumption after a productivity shock between the models is more evident. In the model with habit formation, the response of consumption given a productivity shock is delayed for approximately 10 periods (the point at which the responses of consumption in the NKFR and NKWR models are equal).

Figure 5.3 reinforces the discussion on the income effect. The introduction of this type of agent causes the wage level, at the point of inflection between the regions in which each effect dominates, to increase from 127% in the previous model to 150% in this model, which demonstrates the increased influence of the income effect on this economy's labor supply.

Is there an interpretation problem related to the presence or absence of household frictions (habit formation and non-Ricardian agents)?

The effects of the two types of household friction will be isolated so as to answer the question in this subsection. The first counterfactual exercise (Figure 5.4) concerns habit formation, with three productivity shock simulations having been performed, the ϕ_c parameter assuming the values of 0, 0.4 and 0.8. The first evidence is that, with the increase in ϕ_c, the influence of the income effect becomes stronger, a fall in labor supply, a rise in real wages and increased supply of capital. The participation of non-Ricardian agents is studied in Figure 5.5, in which ω_R (the participation of Ricardian agents) assumes the values of 0.1, 0.5 and 0.9. With an increase in non-Ricardian agents (a decrease in ω_R), the supply of capital is compromised, as this kind of agent does not have access to the financial market. This lower level of savings affects the economy's future performance, with a reduction in household consumption.

In short, when defining a model's assumptions, the economist must carefully consider the inclusion of habit formation and non-Ricardian agents, as the intertemporal allocation of income (via sav-

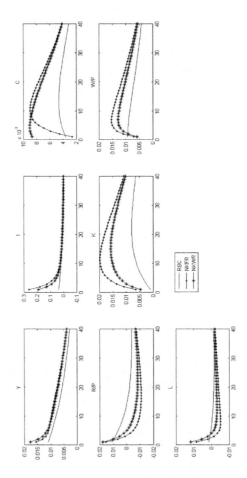

Figure 5.2: Comparison of the RBC, NKWR and NKFR models' impulse-response functions.

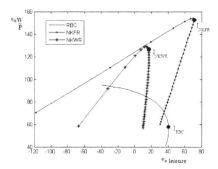

Figure 5.3: Leisure-wage locus. The x and y axes measure the variable's deviation in relation to the steady state in percentage. Point I is the inflection point between which the substitution effect and income effect dominate.

ings) is impaired. This situation has different results on consumption and factors of production, and economic policy may be designed erroneously, expecting results different from those that will actually occur.

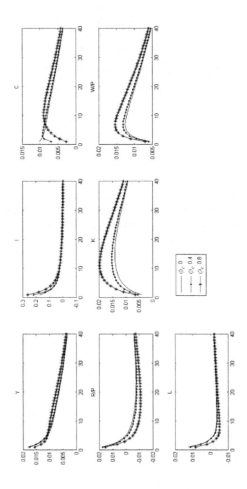

Figure 5.4: Counterfactual analysis of habit formation.

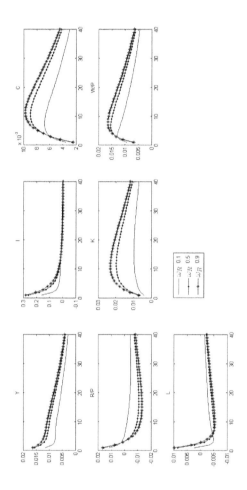

Figure 5.5: Counterfactual analysis of non-Ricardian agents.

BOX 5.1 - Log-linear NK model with household rigidity on Dynare.

```
//NK model with household rigidity
//(Habit formation and non-Ricardian agents)
//Chapter 5 (UNDERSTANDING DSGE MODELS)
var Y I C CR CNR R K W L LR LNR PIW P PI A LAMBDAR LAMBDANR CM;
varexo e;
parameters sigma phi alpha beta delta rhoa psi theta thetaW psiW phic omegaR;

sigma = 2;
phi = 1.5;
alpha = 0.35;
beta = 0.985;
delta = 0.025;
rhoa = 0.95;
psi = 8;
theta = 0.75;
thetaW = 0.75;
psiW = 21;
phic = 0.8;
omegaR = 0.5;

model(linear);
#Pss = 1;
#Rss = Pss*((1/beta)-(1-delta));
#CMss = ((psi-1)/psi)*(1-beta*theta)*Pss;
#Wss = (1-alpha)*(CMss^(1/(1-alpha)))*((alpha/Rss)^(alpha/(1-alpha)));
#Yss = ((Rss/(Rss-delta*alpha*CMss))^(sigma/(sigma+phi)))
*((1-phic*beta)*((1-phic)^(-sigma))*(1-beta*thetaW)*((psiW-1)/psiW)*(Wss/Pss)
*(Wss/((1-alpha)*CMss))^phi)^(1/(sigma+phi)));
#Kss = alpha*CMss*(Yss/Rss);
#Iss = delta*Kss;
#Css = Yss - Iss;
#Lss = (1-alpha)*CMss*(Yss/Wss);
#CRss = Css;
#CNRss = Css;
#LRss = Lss;
#LNRss = Lss;
#LAMBDARss = (1/Pss)*(CRss^(-sigma))*((1-phic)^(-sigma))*(1-phic*beta);
#LAMBDANRss = (1/Pss)*(CNRss^(-sigma))*((1-phic)^(-sigma))*(1-phic*beta);
//1-Ricardian household Lagrangian
LAMBDAR = (sigma/((1-phic)*(1-phic*beta)))*(phic*beta*(CR(+1)-phic*CR)
-(CR-phic*CR(-1)))-P;
//2-Phillips equation for Ricardian households' wages
PIW = beta*PIW(+1)+((1-thetaW)*(1-beta*thetaW)/thetaW)*(LR-LAMBDAR-W);
//3-Gross inflation rate for wages
PIW = W - W(-1);
//4-Euler equation
(Pss/beta)*(LAMBDAR+P-LAMBDAR(+1))=(1-delta)*Pss*P(+1) + Rss*R(+1);
//5-Law of motion of capital
K = (1-delta)*K(-1) + delta*I;
//6-Non-Ricardian household Lagrangian
LAMBDANR = (sigma/((1-phic)*(1-phic*beta)))*(phic*beta*(CNR(+1)-phic*CNR)
-(CNR-phic*CNR(-1)))-P;
```

```
//7-Phillips equation for non-Ricardian households' wages
PIW = beta*PIW(+1)+((1-thetaW)*(1-beta*thetaW)/thetaW)*(LNR-LAMBDANR-W);
//8-Non-Ricardian household budget constraint
P+CNR=W+LNR;
//9-Aggregate consumption
Css*C = omegaR*CRss*CR + (1-omegaR)*CNRss*CNR;
//10-Aggregate labor
Lss*L = omegaR*LRss*LR + (1-omegaR)*LNRss*LNR;
//11-Production function
Y = A + alpha*K(-1) + (1-alpha)*L;
//12-Demand for capital
K(-1) = Y - R;
//13-Demand for labor
L = Y - W;
//14-Marginal cost
CM = ((1-alpha)*W + alpha*R - A);
//15-Phillips equation
PI = beta*PI(+1)+((1-theta)*(1-beta*theta)/theta)*(CM-P);
//16-Gross inflation rate
PI = P - P(-1);
//17-Equilibirum condition
Yss*Y = Css*C + Iss*I;
//18-Productivity shock
A = rhoa*A(-1) + e;
end;

model_diagnostics;
steady;
check (qz_zero_threshold=1e-20);


shocks;
var e;
stderr 0.01;
end;

stoch_simul(qz_zero_threshold=1e-20)Y I C CR CNR R K W L LR LNR PIW PI A;
```

New Keynesian Model with adjustment costs on investment and the under-utilization of maximum installed capacity

The first part of the extension of the basic models involved the development of household consumption-related frictions. In this chapter, two types of friction will be addressed: the first is related to costs a firm faces when deciding upon its level of investment, while the second involves costs that the firm will have to defray when deciding its level of utilization of installed capacity.

In the basic model, it is assumed that capital can change from one period to the next, without any constraint on the investment process. However, in the real world, capital stock signifies warehouses, machinery, etc., which cannot be instantaneously built and installed. Therefore, one important aspect that should be considered involves the inclusion of an adjustment cost in the investment process. This means that the capital stock would not be at its optimal level in the current period, as the agents would not be making their investment decisions immediately, to fully cover this requirement. Rather they would seek to change the capital stock gradually, with smooth movements in investment.

Another assumption made by the more simplistic models is that the use of installed capital would be a constant 100% so that the only decision to be made would concern the stock's adjustment velocity. However, empirical evidence demonstrates situations in which the use of capital is lower than 100%, this level basically being related to business cycles. In other words, a firm might have built a plant, but because of to a weakening economy, it would be functioning below its maximum capacity. At the very least this would present an opportunity cost.

A brief theoretical review: adjustment costs on investment and the under-utilization of maximum installed capacity

This section aims to present a basic review of investment and the frictions associated with the level of capital. It begins with a presentation of the adjustment cost on investment, and then demonstrates the cost of not using maximum installed capacity.

Adjustment Cost on Investment

The basic model presents no form of constraint with regard to investment, so the capital stock can be adjusted instantaneously. However, empirical evidence shows that the capital stock in firms is a variable that possesses a degree of rigidity, meaning that any adjustment to this variable is not so quick. In this section, the idea will be introduced of the existence of adjustment costs in the investment process. The more quickly the firm intends to adjust its capital, the higher the adjustment cost. Two distinct types of adjustment cost may be cited: external and internal.

The external adjustment cost occurs when firms desire a perfectly elastic supply of capital. In reality, however, the availability of capital goods occurs at different velocities. Some types of capital have immediate availability, while others do not. This has the effect of making the price of capital dependent upon the timing of the desire for this availability: the quicker the desire for capital, the higher the price of this input. The internal adjustment cost is measured in terms of production loss. When new capital is introduced, a portion of production resources will be diverted to its installation. These resources would be temporarily unavailable for production, resulting in production shortfalls.

In general, the adjustment cost on capital can be differentiated from the adjustment cost on investment. The existence of the former emanates from the evolution of Tobin's Q theory, while the latter comes from Jorgenson (1963). Tobin (1969) developed a theory in which firms' investment decisions are a function of the value of a ratio known as Q. Any element that affects investment does so by way of an effect on this variable. On the other hand, Jorgenson

(1963) introduced the existence of adjustment cost on investment as a lag structure linked to investment.

Definition 6.1.1 (Tobin's Q). *Relationship between a company's market value and the replacement value of its physical assets. Thus, it represents the ratio between two values assigned to the same group of assets (Reinhart, 1977). Tobin's Q, in its basic form, may be expressed as:*

$$Q = \frac{market\ value\ of\ the\ shares}{replacement\ value\ of\ firm's\ assets}$$

Hayashi (1982) shows that, under certain conditions, Tobin's Q is equivalent to the marginal value of capital. In this context, if Q > 1, at the margin, firms will have an incentive to invest since the value of the new capital invested will exceed its cost (Lindenberg and Ross, 1981).

The existence of adjustment costs on capital is covered in the literature in works such as Hayashi (1982), Abel and Blanchard (1983), Shapiro (1986), among others. Generally speaking, the following function of adjustment cost on capital may be defined: $S(.) = S(\frac{I_t}{K_t})$, in which this cost depends on the volume of investment in relation to the capital stock. This function should fulfill the following characteristics: $S(\delta) = 0$, $S' > 0$ and $S'' > 0$, in other words, if the aim is simply to maintain a constant level of capital, the cost will be zero. On the other hand, its second derivative is positive, indicating that this cost rises more than proportionately – an increasing, convex function.

The existence of adjustment cost on investment means that there is a loss of capital or an additional cost in the investment process. This notion suggests that marginal productivity of capital should be equal to an expression in which the cost of capital appears, as well as the net function of investment of the cost of this adjustment. In other words, in a period of growth, a firm's capital stock will be lower than its optimal level in the current period, causing the firm not to carry out the full, desired investment immediately as the adjustment cost could be significant, leading it to carry out its investments gradually over a longer period of time.

In this way, the adjustment cost associated with investments makes reference to the existence of costs in terms of period-to-period investment variations. The most common way of defining the adjustment cost on investment is by means of the following function: $S(.) = S\left(\frac{I_t}{I_{t-1}}\right)$, where $S(1) = 0$, $S^{'}(1) = 0$ and $S^{''} > 0$, indicating that the cost associated with the change in the level of investment is zero when the objective is simply to maintain a constant level of capital, i.e., a steady state. Consequently, the usual form of considering the existence of adjustment costs on investment is to assume that the law of motion of capital is: $K_{t+1} = (1 - \delta)K_t +$ $I_t\left[1 - \frac{\chi}{2}\left(\frac{I_t}{I_{t-1}} - 1\right)^2\right]$, where I_t is the gross investment and $\left[1 - \frac{\chi}{2}\left(\frac{I_t}{I_{t-1}} - 1\right)^2\right]$ is the adjustment cost function connected with this investment.

In the literature, when discussing investment, there are two possibilities. It may be assumed that households are the owners of capital, so in this case the investment decisions are equivalent to decisions about savings. This is the approximation most frequently used the capital stock comes from households' decisions about savings. On the other hand, it could be assumed that firms are the owners of the capital, in which case there would be a distinction between households on the one side and capital-producing firms on the other. Using this alternative specification, savings and investment decisions may be separated, thereby obtaining the demand for investment.

Cost of under-utilization of maximum installed capacity

An additional element, which might explain some empirical data with regard to cyclical fluctuations, is the level of utilization of installed capacity in the economy. In the basic model, all available capital is used in the production process. However, in reality, it can be seen that the intensity with which available capital is used, varies over time. This means that, in the event of a shock, not only would the level of investment be altered but also the level of utilization of installed capacity, so each of these would possess different shock transmission mechanisms.

Definition 6.1.2 (Problem of the capital-producing firm). *It is assumed that the accumulation of capital is the responsibility of a single firm that transforms a bundle of investment assets (I) into capital (K). This firm defines the quantity I to be transformed into capital, maximizing the profit earned in the transfer of capital to firms subjected to costs of investment and under-utilization of capital. Therefore, this firm should solve the following problem:*

$$\max_{U_t, K_{t+1}, I_t} E_t \sum_{t=0}^{\infty} \beta^t \lambda_{R,t} \left\{ R_t U_t K_t \right.$$

$$- \quad \underbrace{P_t K_t \left[\psi_1 (U_t - 1) + \frac{\psi_2}{2} (U_t - 1)^2 \right]}_{\text{Cost of Under-utilization of Maximum Installed Capacity*}} \quad \left. -P_t I_t \right\}$$

subject to the following law of motion of capital,

$$K_{t+1} = (1-\delta)K_t + I_t \quad \underbrace{\left[1 - \frac{\chi}{2} \left(\frac{I_t}{I_{t-1}} - 1 \right)^2 \right]}_{\text{Adjustment Cost on Investment}}$$

where $\beta^t \lambda_{R,t}$ is the stochastic discount factor used to convert expected future receipts to present value, U is the rate of capital utilization, I is investment, ψ_1 and $\psi_2 > 0$ are sensitivity parameters for the utilization of installed capacity and χ is the sensitivity parameter for the adjustment in investment.

* The cost of under-utilization of maximum installed capacity will be discussed in the following subsection.

In the literature, the reason for the variation in the utilization of installed capital offers different modeling opportunities. One way of introducing this idea is to assume that the physical rate of depreciation of capital would not be constant, but rather a function of the ratio of capital utilization. Thus, a higher level of utilization of installed capacity would give rise to a faster depreciation. The idea is a simple one: the greater the utilization of the machinery, the higher the depreciation. Therefore, the ratio of physical depreciation of capital would not be constant, but would depend rather on the level of utilization of installed capacity. This form of modeling was used by Taubman and Wilkinson (1970), Calvo (1975), Merrick (1984), Greenwood *et al.* (1988), amongst others. In this way, the law of motion of capital would be described by: $K_{t+1} = [1 - \delta(U_t)] K_t + I_t$, where $\delta(U_t)$ is a non-negative function which satisfies the following properties: $0 < \delta(U_t) < 1$, $\delta'(U_t) > 0$, $\delta''(U_t) > 0$. Greenwood *et al.* (1988) use the following specification: $\delta(U_t) = \frac{1}{\eta} U_t^{\eta}$, where $\eta > 1$. Another possibility would be $\delta(U_t) = \delta U_t^{\eta}$. Another way of introducing this friction consists of defining a cost function associated with variations in installed capacity. This form was used by Christiano, Eichenbaum and Evans (2005) and by Smets and Wouters (2003), who define a function $\Psi(U_t)$ which represents the physical cost of variations in the use of installed capacity, being an increasing, convex function: $\Psi'(U_t) > 0$ and $\Psi''(U_t) > 0$. In other words, this function shows the cost of setting a particular level of utilization of installed capacity, in units of consumption. These authors assume that, when the degree of utilization of capital is total, the cost is nil, $\Psi(1) = 0$. In this case, the net returns associated with the utilization of installed capacity would be rendered by: $R_t U_t K_t - \Psi(U_t) K_t$. The first term reflects the profitability associated with the proportion of capital utilized in production, while the second represents the costs associated with the variation in the degree of utilization of installed capacity. One possible functional form would be: $\Psi(U_t) = \Psi_1(U_t - 1) + \frac{\Psi_2}{2}(U_t - 1)^2$, where $\Psi_1, \Psi_2 > 0$.

Definition 6.1.3 (Level of utilization of installed capacity). *This deals with a firm's production limit or maximum production capacity. In other words, it is the quantity of units of product that the installed machinery and equipment are capable of producing. The level of utilization of installed capacity is given by the relationship between the volume actually produced by the firm and what could be produced if the machines were operating at full capacity.*

The model

The DSGE model presented here introduces the existence of adjustment costs on investment and the under-utilization of maximum installed capacity. This means that the process of capital accumulation will be changed, by including these costs in the budget constraints of Ricardian households. Now, for this type of household, the optimal level of utilization of installed capacity must also be chosen. Of the general assumptions, 2.2.1 and 2.2.2 remain valid.

Households

In the households group, assumptions 2.2.4, 2.2.6, 4.2.1, 4.2.2, and 5.2.1 remain valid.

Determining consumption and savings in Ricardian households

The Ricardian household maximizes its utility by choosing consumption, capital stock, level of utilization of installed capacity and investment, using the following utility function:

$$\max_{C_{R,t}, K_{R,t+1}, U_t, I_t} E_t \sum_{t=0}^{\infty} \beta^t \left[\frac{\left(C_{R,t} - \phi_c C_{R,t-1}\right)^{1-\sigma}}{1-\sigma} - \frac{L_{R,t}^{1+\varphi}}{1+\varphi} \right] \tag{6.1}$$

Assumption 6.2.1. *The functional form for the adjustment cost on investment is:*

$$\left[1 - \frac{\chi}{2} \left(\frac{I_t}{I_{t-1}} - 1 \right)^2 \right]$$

Assumption 6.2.2. *The functional form for the cost of under-utilization of maximum installed capacity is:*

$$P_t K_t \left[\Psi_1 (U_t - 1) + \frac{\Psi_2}{2} (U_t - 1)^2 \right]$$

subject to the following budget constraint:

$$P_t(C_{R,t} + I_t) = W_t L_{R,t} + R_t U_t K_t - P_t K_t \left[\Psi_1 (U_t - 1) + \frac{\Psi_2}{2} (U_t - 1)^2 \right] \tag{6.2}$$

with the law of motion of capital:

$$K_{t+1} = (1-\delta)K_t + I_t \left[1 - \frac{\chi}{2}\left(\frac{I_t}{I_{t-1}} - 1\right)^2\right] \tag{6.3}$$

where U is the level of utilization of installed capacity, ψ_1 and $\psi_2 > 0$ are sensitivity parameters for the utilization of installed capacity and χ is the sensitivity parameter for the investment adjustment.

Using the Lagrangian to solve the previous problem:

$$\mathcal{L} = E_t \sum_{t=0}^{\infty} \beta^t \left\{ \left[\frac{(C_{R,t} - \phi_c C_{R,t-1})^{1-\sigma}}{1-\sigma} - \frac{L_{R,t}^{1+\varphi}}{1+\varphi} \right] \right.$$

$$-\lambda_{R,t} \left[P_t(C_{R,t} + I_t) - W_t L_{R,t} - R_t U_t K_t + P_t K_t \right.$$

$$\left[\Psi_1(U_t - 1) + \frac{\Psi_2}{2}(U_t - 1)^2 \right] \right]$$

$$\left. -Q_t \left[K_{t+1} - (1-\delta)K_t - I_t \left[1 - \frac{\chi}{2}\left(\frac{I_t}{I_{t-1}} - 1\right)^2 \right] \right] \right\} \tag{6.4}$$

We arrive at the following first-order conditions:

$$\frac{\partial \mathcal{L}}{\partial C_{R,t}} = \left(C_{R,t} - \phi_c C_{R,t-1}\right)^{-\sigma} - \lambda_{R,t} P_t - \phi_c \beta \left(E_t C_{R,t+1} - \phi_c C_{R,t}\right)^{-\sigma} = 0 \tag{6.5}$$

$$\frac{\partial \mathcal{L}}{\partial K_{t+1}} = \beta E_t \left(\lambda_{R,t+1} R_{t+1} U_{t+1}\right) - \beta E_t \left\{\lambda_{R,t+1} P_{t+1} \left[\Psi_1(U_{t+1} - 1)\right. \right.$$

$$\left. \left. + \frac{\Psi_2}{2}(U_{t+1} - 1)^2 \right] \right\} - Q_t + \beta E_t Q_{t+1}(1-\delta) = 0 \tag{6.6}$$

where Q is the Lagrange multiplier associated with the capital stock driver. This multiplier represents the "shadow" price of capital, also known as Tobin's Q.

$$\frac{\partial \mathscr{L}}{\partial U_t} = \lambda_{R,t} R_t K_t - \lambda_{R,t} P_t K_t \Psi_1 - \lambda_{R,t} P_t K_t \Psi_2 (U_t - 1) = 0 \qquad (6.7)$$

$$\frac{\partial \mathscr{L}}{\partial I_t} = -\lambda_{R,t} P_t + \frac{\partial E_t \sum_{t=0}^{\infty} \beta^t \left\{ Q_t I_t \left[1 - \frac{\chi}{2} \left(\frac{I_t}{I_{t-1}} - 1 \right)^2 \right] \right\}}{\partial I_t} = 0$$

where,

$$\frac{\partial E_t \sum_{t=0}^{\infty} \beta^t \left[Q_t I_t - \frac{\chi}{2} Q_t I_t \left(\frac{I_t}{I_{t-1}} - 1 \right)^2 \right]}{\partial I_t} = Q_t - \frac{\chi}{2} \left\{ Q_t \left(\frac{I_t}{I_{t-1}} - 1 \right)^2 \right.$$

$$+ Q_t I_t 2 \left(\frac{I_t}{I_{t-1}} - 1 \right) \frac{1}{I_{t-1}} - \beta E_t \left[Q_{t+1} I_{t+1} 2 \left(\frac{I_{t+1}}{I_t} - 1 \right) \frac{I_{t+1}}{I_t^2} \right] \right\}$$

Then,

$$-\lambda_{R,t} P_t + Q_t \left[1 - \frac{\chi}{2} \left(\frac{I_t}{I_{t-1}} - 1 \right)^2 - \chi \frac{I_t}{I_{t-1}} \left(\frac{I_t}{I_{t-1}} - 1 \right) \right]$$

$$+ \chi \beta E_t \left[Q_{t+1} \left(\frac{I_{t+1}}{I_t} \right)^2 \left(\frac{I_{t+1}}{I_t} - 1 \right) \right] = 0 \qquad (6.8)$$

From equation (6.5),

$$\lambda_{R,t} = \frac{\left(C_{R,t} - \phi_c C_{R,t-1} \right)^{-\sigma}}{P_t} - \phi_c \beta \frac{\left(E_t C_{R,t+1} - \phi_c C_{R,t} \right)^{-\sigma}}{P_t} \qquad (6.9)$$

From equation (6.6),

$$Q_t = \beta E_t \left\{ (1 - \delta) Q_{t+1} + \lambda_{R,t+1} R_{t+1} U_{t+1} \right.$$

$$- \lambda_{R,t+1} P_{t+1} \left[\Psi_1 (U_{t+1} - 1) + \frac{\Psi_2}{2} (U_{t+1} - 1)^2 \right] \right\} \qquad (6.10)$$

From equation (6.7),

$$\frac{R_t}{P_t} = \Psi_1 + \Psi_2(U_t - 1) \tag{6.11}$$

From equation (6.8),

$$\lambda_{R,t} P_t - Q_t \left[1 - \frac{\chi}{2} \left(\frac{I_t}{I_{t-1}} - 1 \right)^2 - \chi \left(\frac{I_t}{I_{t-1}} \right) \left(\frac{I_t}{I_{t-1}} - 1 \right) \right]$$

$$= \chi \beta E_t \left[Q_{t+1} \left(\frac{I_{t+1}}{I_t} \right)^2 \left(\frac{I_{t+1}}{I_t} - 1 \right) \right] \tag{6.12}$$

Moreover, Tobin's marginal Q may be defined as the ratio between the Lagrange multipliers of the problem of the household (Q and λ_R):

$$q_t = \frac{Q_t}{\lambda_{R,t}}$$

Determination of non-Ricardian household consumption, determination of the level of wages and aggregate consumption and labor

The problem of the non-Ricardian household, the determination of wages and the way to aggregate consumption and labor remain unchanged in this chapter. Thus, we can make use of the following equations:

From equation (5.10),

$$P_t C_{NR,t} = W_t L_{NR,t} \tag{6.13}$$

From equation (5.13),

$$\lambda_{NR,t} = \frac{\left(C_{NR,t} - \phi_c C_{NR,t-1} \right)^{-\sigma}}{P_t} - \phi_c \beta \frac{\left(E_t C_{NR,t+1} - \phi_c C_{NR,t} \right)^{-\sigma}}{P_t} \tag{6.14}$$

From equations (5.18), (5.19) and (5.20),

$$W_{j,t}{}^* = \left(\frac{\psi_W}{\psi_W - 1}\right) E_t \sum_{i=0}^{\infty} (\beta\theta_W)^i \frac{L_{R,j,t+i}^{\varphi}}{\lambda_{R,t+i}} \tag{6.15}$$

$$W_{j,t}{}^* = \left(\frac{\psi_W}{\psi_W - 1}\right) E_t \sum_{i=0}^{\infty} (\beta\theta_W)^i \frac{L_{NR,j,t+i}^{\varphi}}{\lambda_{NR,t+i}} \tag{6.16}$$

$$W_t = \left[\theta_W W_{t-1}^{1-\psi_W} + (1-\theta_W) W_t^{*\,1-\psi_W}\right]^{\frac{1}{1-\psi_W}} \tag{6.17}$$

From equations (5.21) and (5.22),

$$C_t = \omega_R C_{R,t} + (1 - \omega_R) C_{NR,t} \tag{6.18}$$

$$L_t = \omega_R L_{R,t} + (1 - \omega_R) L_{NR,t} \tag{6.19}$$

Firms

The assumptions 3.2.1-3.2.6 of the firms group remain valid, so we can make use of the results in chapter 3:

Equation (3.10) has been amended slightly because of to the inclusion of installed capacity (U),

$$Y_{j,t} = A_t \left(U_t K_{j,t}\right)^{\alpha} L_{j,t}^{1-\alpha} \tag{6.20}$$

Equation (3.11),

$$\log A_t = (1 - \rho_A) \log A_{ss} + \rho_A \log A_{t-1} + \varepsilon_t \tag{6.21}$$

Equation (3.15),,

$$L_{j,t} = (1 - \alpha) MC_{j,t} \frac{Y_{j,t}}{W_t} \tag{6.22}$$

Equation (3.16),

$$U_t K_{j,t} = \alpha MC_{j,t} \frac{Y_{j,t}}{R_t} \tag{6.23}$$

Equation (3.22),

$$MC_{j,t} = \frac{1}{A_t} \left(\frac{W_t}{1-\alpha} \right)^{1-\alpha} \left(\frac{R_t}{\alpha} \right)^{\alpha} \qquad (6.24)$$

Equation (3.25),

$$P_{j,t}^* = \left(\frac{\psi}{\psi-1} \right) E_t \sum_{i=0}^{\infty} (\beta\theta)^i MC_{j,t+i} \qquad (6.25)$$

Equation (3.26),

$$P_t = \left[\theta P_{t-1}^{1-\psi} + (1-\theta) P_t^{*\,1-\psi} \right]^{\frac{1}{1-\psi}} \qquad (6.26)$$

The model's equilibrium condition

Finally, it just remains to include the equilibrium condition in the consumer goods market.

$$Y_t = C_t + I_t \qquad (6.27)$$

In summary, the model in this economy is made up of the following equations from Table 6.1.

Steady state

This section retains the procedure adopted in the previous chapters:

Households

$$\lambda_{R,ss} = \frac{C_{R,ss}^{-\sigma}(1-\phi_c)^{-\sigma}(1-\phi_c\beta)}{P_{ss}} \qquad (6.28)$$

$$\lambda_{NR,ss} = \frac{C_{NR,ss}^{-\sigma}(1-\phi_c)^{-\sigma}(1-\phi_c\beta)}{P_{ss}} \qquad (6.29)$$

$$\delta K_{ss} = I_{ss} \qquad (6.30)$$

$$\frac{R_{ss}}{P_{ss}} = \Psi_1 \qquad (6.31)$$

$$\frac{Q_{ss}}{\beta} = (1-\delta)Q_{ss} + \lambda_{R,ss}R_{ss}$$

$$R_{ss} = \left[\frac{1}{\beta} - (1-\delta)\right]\frac{Q_{ss}}{\lambda_{R,ss}} \tag{6.32}$$

$$\lambda_{R,ss}P_{ss} - Q_{ss} = 0$$

$$P_{ss} = \frac{Q_{ss}}{\lambda_{R,ss}} \tag{6.33}$$

$$W_{ss} = \left(\frac{\psi_W}{\psi_W - 1}\right)\left(\frac{1}{1 - \beta\theta_W}\right)\frac{L_{R,ss}^{\varphi}}{\lambda_{R,ss}} \tag{6.34}$$

$$W_{ss} = \left(\frac{\psi_W}{\psi_W - 1}\right)\left(\frac{1}{1 - \beta\theta_W}\right)\frac{L_{NR,ss}^{\varphi}}{\lambda_{NR,ss}} \tag{6.35}$$

where: $\sum_{i=0}^{\infty}(\beta\theta_W)^i = \frac{1}{1-\beta\theta_W}$

$$C_{ss} = \omega_R C_{R,ss} + (1 - \omega_R)C_{NR,ss} \tag{6.36}$$

$$L_{ss} = \omega_R L_{R,ss} + (1 - \omega_R)L_{NR,ss} \tag{6.37}$$

Firms

$$L_{ss} = (1-\alpha)CM_{ss}\frac{Y_{ss}}{W_{ss}} \tag{6.38}$$

$$K_{ss} = \alpha CM_{ss}\frac{Y_{ss}}{R_{ss}} \tag{6.39}$$

$$Y_{ss} = K_{ss}^{\alpha}L_{ss}^{1-\alpha} \tag{6.40}$$

$$CM_{ss} = \left(\frac{W_{ss}}{1-\alpha}\right)^{1-\alpha}\left(\frac{R_{ss}}{\alpha}\right)^{\alpha} \tag{6.41}$$

$$P_{ss} = \left(\frac{\psi}{\psi - 1}\right)\left(\frac{1}{1 - \beta\theta}\right)CM_{ss} \tag{6.42}$$

where: $\sum_{i=0}^{\infty}(\beta\theta)^i = \frac{1}{1-\beta\theta}$.

Equilibrium Condition

$$Y_{ss} = C_{ss} + I_{ss} \tag{6.43}$$

Table 6.1: Structure of the model.

Equation	(Definition)
$\lambda_{R,t} =$ $\frac{(C_{R,t}-\phi_c C_{R,t-1})^{-\sigma}}{P_t} - \phi_c \beta \frac{(E_t C_{R,t+1}-\phi_c C_{R,t})^{-\sigma}}{P_t}$	(Ricardian household Lagrangian)
$W_{j,t}^* = \left(\frac{\psi_W}{\psi_W-1}\right) E_t \sum_{i=0}^{\infty} (\beta\theta_W)^i \frac{L_{R,j,t+i}^{\varphi}}{\lambda_{R,t+i}}$	(Definition of the Ricardian household's optimal wages)
$W_t = \left[\theta_W W_{t-1}^{1-\varphi_W} + (1-\theta_W)W_t^{*\,1-\varphi_W}\right]^{\frac{1}{1-\varphi_W}}$	(Aggregate wage level)
$\pi_{W,t} = P_t/P_{t-1}$	(Gross wage inflation rate)
$Q_t = \beta \left\{ (1-\delta)E_t Q_{t+1} + E_t\lambda_{R,t+1}E_tR_{t+1}E_tU_{t+1} \right.$ $\quad - E_t\lambda_{R,t+1}E_tP_{t+1}$ $\left. \left[\Psi_1(E_tU_{t+1}-1) + \frac{\Psi_2}{2}(E_tU_{t+1}-1)^2\right] \right\}$	(Tobin's Q)
$\frac{R_t}{P_t} = \Psi_1 + \Psi_2(U_t-1)$	(Demand for installed capacity)
$\lambda_{R,t}P_t -$ $Q_t\left\{1 - \frac{\chi}{2}\left(\frac{I_t}{I_{t-1}}-1\right)^2 - \chi\left(\frac{I_t}{I_{t-1}}\right)\left(\frac{I_t}{I_{t-1}}-1\right)\right\}$ $= \chi\beta E_t Q_{t+1}\left(\frac{E_t I_{t+1}}{I_t}\right)^2\left(\frac{E_t I_{t+1}}{I_t}-1\right)$	(Demand for investment assets)
$K_{t+1} = (1-\delta)K_t + I_t\left[1 - \frac{\chi}{2}\left(\frac{I_t}{I_{t-1}}-1\right)^2\right]$	(Law of motion of capital)
$\lambda_{NR,t} = \frac{(C_{NR,t}-\phi_c C_{NR,t-1})^{-\sigma}}{P_t} -$ $\phi_c\beta\frac{(E_t C_{NR,t+1}-\phi_c C_{NR,t})^{-\sigma}}{P_t}$	(Non-Ricardian household Lagrangian)

$$W_{j,t}^* = \left(\frac{\psi_W}{\psi_W-1}\right) E_t \sum_{i=0}^{\infty} (\beta\theta_W)^i \frac{L_{NR,j,t+i}^{\varphi}}{\lambda_{NR,t+i}}$$

(Definition of the non-Ricardian household's optimal wages)

$$P_t C_{NR,t} = W_t L_{NR,t}$$

(Non-Ricardian household's budget constraint)

$$C_t = \omega_R C_{R,t} + (1-\omega_R)C_{NR,t}$$

(Aggregate consumption)

$$L_t = \omega_R L_{R,t} + (1-\omega_R)L_{NR,t}$$

(Aggregate Labor)

$$Y_t = A_t \left(U_t K_{j,t}\right)^{\alpha} L_t^{1-\alpha}$$

(Production function)

$$U_t K_t = \alpha MC_t \frac{Y_t}{R_t}$$

(Demand for capital)

$$L_t = (1-\alpha)MC_t \frac{Y_t}{W_t}$$

(Demand for labor)

$$MC_t = \frac{1}{A_t}\left(\frac{W_t}{1-\alpha}\right)^{1-\alpha}\left(\frac{R_t}{\alpha}\right)^{\alpha}$$

(Marginal cost)

$$P_t^* = \left(\frac{\psi}{\psi-1}\right) E_t \sum_{i=0}^{\infty} (\beta\theta)^i MC_{t+i}$$

(Optimal price level)

$$P_t = \left[\theta P_{t-1}^{1-\psi} + (1-\theta)P_t^{*\,1-\psi}\right]^{\frac{1}{1-\psi}}$$

(General price level)

$$\pi_t = P_t/P_{t-1}$$

(Gross inflation rate)

$$Y_t = C_t + I_t$$

(Equilibrium condition)

$$\log A_t = (1-\rho_A)\log A_{ss} + \rho_A \log A_{t-1} + \epsilon_t$$

(Productivity shock)

Firstly, the values of the prices (P_{ss}, R_{ss}, W_{ss} and CM_{ss}) must be determined. As is normal practice, the general price level is normalized ($P_{ss} = 1$), and thus R_{ss} and CM_{ss} also become known,

so, from equation (6.31),

$$R_{ss} = \Psi_1 P_{ss} \tag{6.44}$$

The remainder of the steady state is the same as in chapter 5,

$$A_{ss} = 1$$

$$U_{ss} = 1$$

$$P_{ss} = 1$$

$$R_{ss} = \Psi_1 P_{ss}$$

$$CM_{ss} = \left(\frac{\psi - 1}{\psi}\right)(1 - \beta\theta)P_{ss}$$

$$W_{ss} = (1 - \alpha)CM_{ss}^{\frac{1}{1-\alpha}}\left(\frac{\alpha}{R_{ss}}\right)^{\frac{\alpha}{1-\alpha}}$$

$$Y_{ss} = \left(\frac{R_{ss}}{R_{ss} - \delta\alpha CM_{ss}}\right)^{\frac{\sigma}{\sigma+\varphi}}\left\{(1 - \phi_c\beta)(1 - \phi_c)^{-\sigma}(1 - \beta\theta_W)\right.$$

$$\left.\left(\frac{\psi_W - 1}{\psi_W}\right)\frac{W_{ss}}{P_{ss}}\left[\frac{W_{ss}}{(1 - \alpha)CM_{ss}}\right]^{\varphi}\right\}^{\frac{1}{\sigma+\varphi}}$$

$$L_{ss} = (1 - \alpha)CM_{ss}\frac{Y_{ss}}{W_{ss}}$$

Remembering,

$$L_{ss} = L_{R,ss} = L_{NR,ss}$$

$$K_{ss} = \alpha CM_{ss}\frac{Y_{ss}}{R_{ss}}$$

$$I_{ss} = \delta K_{ss}$$

$$C_{ss} = \frac{1}{Y_{ss}^{\frac{\varphi}{\sigma}}}\left\{(1 - \phi_c\beta)(1 - \phi_c)^{-\sigma}(1 - \beta\theta_W)\left(\frac{\psi_W - 1}{\psi_W}\right)\frac{W_{ss}}{P_{ss}}\left[\frac{W_{ss}}{(1 - \alpha)CM_{ss}}\right]^{\varphi}\right\}^{\frac{1}{\sigma}}$$

Remembering,

$$C_{ss} = C_{R,ss} = C_{NR,ss}$$

The missing price was Tobin's Q,

$$Q_{ss} = \lambda_{R,ss} P_{ss}$$

Table 6.3 displays the calibrated values to be used in the simulation, while table 6.4 shows the model's steady state value.

Log-linearization (Uhlig's method)

The method developed by Uhlig continues to be used as a tool for the log-linearization of the model. The results obtained in the other chapters that concur with the results of this model will be utilized. The novelty lies in the equations related to the adjustment costs on investment and under-utilization of installed capacity. Accordingly:

From equation (5.52),

$$\widetilde{\lambda}_{R,t} = \frac{\sigma}{(1 - \phi_c)(1 - \phi_c \beta)}$$

$$\left[\phi_c \beta (E_t \widetilde{C}_{R,t+1} - \phi_c \widetilde{C}_{R,t}) - (\widetilde{C}_{R,t} - \phi_c \widetilde{C}_{R,t-1}) \right] - \widetilde{P}_t \qquad (6.45)$$

From equation (5.53),

$$\widetilde{\lambda}_{NR,t} = \frac{\sigma}{(1 - \phi_c)(1 - \phi_c \beta)}$$

$$\left[\phi_c \beta (E_t \widetilde{C}_{NR,t+1} - \phi_c \widetilde{C}_{NR,t}) - (\widetilde{C}_{NR,t} - \phi_c \widetilde{C}_{NR,t-1}) \right] - \widetilde{P}_t \qquad (6.46)$$

From equation (6.10),

$$\frac{Q_t}{\beta} = (1 - \delta) E_t Q_{t+1} + E_t \lambda_{R,t+1} E_t R_{t+1} E_t U_{t+1} - E_t \lambda_{R,t+1} E_t P_{t+1} \Psi_1 E_t U_{t+1}$$

$$+ E_t \lambda_{R,t+1} E_t P_{t+1} \Psi_1 - E_t \lambda_{R,t+1} E_t P_{t+1} \frac{\Psi_2}{2} E_t U_{t+1}^2$$

$$+ E_t \lambda_{R,t+1} E_t P_{t+1} \frac{\Psi_2}{2} E_t U_{t+1} - E_t \lambda_{R,t+1} E_t P_{t+1} \frac{\Psi_2}{2}$$

Table 6.2: Values of the structural model's parameters.

Parameter	Parameter meaning	Calibrated value
σ	Relative risk aversion o coefficient	
φ	Marginal disutility with regard to labor supply	1.5
α	Elasticity of level of production in relation to capital	0.35
β	Discount factor	0.985
δ	Depreciation rate	0.025
ρ_A	Autoregressive parameter of productivity	0.95
σ_A	Standard deviation of productivity	0.01
θ	Price stickiness parameter	0.75
ψ	Elasticity of substitution between intermediate goods	8
θ_W	Wage stickiness parameter	0.75
ψ_W	Elasticity of substitution between differentiated labor	21
ϕ_c	Habit persistence	0.8
ω_R	Share of Ricardians in consumption and labor	0.5
χ	Sensitivity of investments in relation to adjustment cost	1
Ψ_1	Sensitivity of cost of under-utilization of maximum installed capacity 1	$\frac{1}{\beta}-(1-\delta)$
Ψ_2	Sensitivity of cost of under-utilization of maximum installed capacity 2	1

Table 6.3: Values of Variables at the steady state.

Variable	Steady state
A	1
R	0.040
MC	0.229
W	0.215
Y	0.842
I	0.042
C	0.800
L	0.5814
K	1.674

$$\frac{Q_{ss}}{\beta}(1+\tilde{Q}_t) = (1-\delta)Q_{ss}(1+E_t\tilde{Q}_{t+1}) + \lambda_{R,ss}R_{ss}U_{ss}$$

$$(1+E_t\tilde{\lambda}_{R,t+1}+E_t\tilde{R}_{t+1}+E_t\tilde{U}_{t+1})$$

$$-\lambda_{R,ss}P_{ss}\Psi_1 U_{ss}(1+E_t\tilde{\lambda}_{R,t+1}+E_t\tilde{P}_{t+1}+E_t\tilde{U}_{t+1})$$

$$+\lambda_{R,ss}P_{ss}\Psi_1(1+E_t\tilde{\lambda}_{R,t+1}+E_t\tilde{P}_{t+1})$$

$$-\lambda_{R,ss}P_{ss}\frac{\Psi_2}{2}U_{ss}^2(1+E_t\tilde{\lambda}_{R,t+1}+E_t\tilde{P}_{t+1}+2E_t\tilde{U}_{t+1}) + \lambda_{R,ss}P_{ss}\Psi_2 U_{ss}$$

$$(1+E_t\tilde{\lambda}_{R,t+1}+E_t\tilde{P}_{t+1}+E_t\tilde{U}_{t+1}) - \lambda_{R,ss}P_{ss}\frac{\Psi_2}{2}(1+E_t\tilde{\lambda}_{R,t+1}+E_t\tilde{P}_{t+1})$$

$$\left(\frac{Q_{ss}}{\beta}\right)\tilde{Q}_t = (1-\delta)Q_{ss}E_t\tilde{Q}_{t+1}+\lambda_{R,ss}R_{ss}U_{ss}(E_t\tilde{\lambda}_{R,t+1}+E_t\tilde{R}_{t+1}+E_t\tilde{U}_{t+1})$$

$$-\lambda_{R,ss}P_{ss}\Psi_1 U_{ss}E_t\tilde{U}_{t+1} \tag{6.47}$$

From equation (6.11),

$$\left(\frac{R_{ss}}{P_{ss}}\right)(1+\tilde{R}_t-\tilde{P}_t) = \Psi_1 + \Psi_2 U_{ss}(1+\tilde{U}_t) - \Psi_2$$

$$\left(\frac{R_{ss}}{P_{ss}}\right)(\tilde{R}_t-\tilde{P}_t) = \Psi_2 U_{ss}\tilde{U}_t \tag{6.48}$$

From equation (6.12),

$$\lambda_{R,t}P_t - Q_t + \frac{\chi}{2}Q_t\left(\frac{I_t}{I_{t-1}}\right)^2 - \frac{\chi}{2}Q_t\left(\frac{I_t}{I_{t-1}}\right) + \frac{\chi}{2}Q_t + \chi Q_t\left(\frac{I_t}{I_{t-1}}\right)^2 - \chi Q_t\left(\frac{I_t}{I_{t-1}}\right)$$

$$= \chi\beta E_t Q_{t+1}\left(\frac{E_t I_{t+1}}{I_t}\right)^3 - \chi\beta E_t Q_{t+1}\left(\frac{E_t I_{t+1}}{I_t}\right)^2$$

$$\lambda_{R,t}P_t - \left(1 - \frac{\chi}{2}\right)Q_t + \frac{3}{2}\chi Q_t\left(\frac{I_t}{I_{t-1}}\right)^2 - 2\chi Q_t\left(\frac{I_t}{I_{t-1}}\right)$$

$$= \chi\beta E_t Q_{t+1}\left(\frac{E_t I_{t+1}}{I_t}\right)^3 - \chi\beta E_t Q_{t+1}\left(\frac{E_t I_{t+1}}{I_t}\right)^2$$

$$\lambda_{R,ss}P_{ss}(1+\tilde{\lambda}_{R,t}+\tilde{P}_t) - \left(1 - \frac{\chi}{2}\right)Q_{ss}(1+\tilde{Q}_t) + \frac{3}{2}\chi Q_{ss}[1+\tilde{Q}_t+2(\tilde{I}_t-\tilde{I}_{t-1})]$$

$$-2\chi Q_{ss}(1+\tilde{Q}_t+\tilde{I}_t-\tilde{I}_{t-1})$$
$$= \chi\beta Q_{ss}[1+E_t\tilde{Q}_t+3(E_t\tilde{I}_{t+1}-\tilde{I}_t)] - \chi\beta Q_{ss}[1+\tilde{Q}_t+2(\tilde{I}_{t+1}-\tilde{I}_t)]$$

$$\lambda_{R,ss}P_{ss}(\tilde{\lambda}_{R,t}+\tilde{P}_t) - Q_{ss}\tilde{Q}_t + \chi Q_{ss}(\tilde{I}_t-\tilde{I}_{t-1})$$
$$= \chi\beta Q_{ss}(E_t\tilde{I}_{t+1}-\tilde{I}_t) \tag{6.49}$$

$$\widetilde{\pi_W}_t = \beta E_t\widetilde{\pi_W}_{t+1} + \left[\frac{(1-\theta_W)(1-\beta\theta_W)}{\theta_W}\right](\tilde{L}_{R,t}-\tilde{\lambda}_{R,t}-\widetilde{W}_t) \tag{6.50}$$

$$\widetilde{\pi_W}_t = \beta E_t\widetilde{\pi_W}_{t+1} + \left[\frac{(1-\theta_W)(1-\beta\theta_W)}{\theta_W}\right](\tilde{L}_{NR,t}-\tilde{\lambda}_{NR,t}-\widetilde{W}_t) \tag{6.51}$$

$$C_{ss}\tilde{C}_t = \omega_R C_{R,ss}\tilde{C}_{R,ss} + (1-\omega_R)C_{NR,ss}\tilde{C}_{NR,ss} \tag{6.52}$$

$$L_{ss}\tilde{L}_t = \omega_R L_{R,ss}\tilde{L}_{R,ss} + (1-\omega_R)L_{NR,ss}\tilde{L}_{NR,ss} \tag{6.53}$$

From equation (6.3),

$$K_{t+1} = (1-\delta)K_t + I_t - \frac{\chi}{2}I_t\left(\frac{I_t}{I_{t-1}}\right)^2 + \chi I_t\left(\frac{I_t}{I_{t-1}}\right) - \frac{\chi}{2}I_t$$

$$K_{ss}(1 + \tilde{K}_{t+1}) = (1 - \delta)K_{ss}\tilde{K}_t + I_{ss}\tilde{I}_t - \frac{\chi}{2}I_{ss}(1 + 3\tilde{I}_t - 2\tilde{I}_{t-1})$$

$$+\chi I_{ss}(1 + 2\tilde{I}_t - \tilde{I}_{t-1}) - \frac{\chi}{2}I_{ss}(1 + \tilde{I}_t)$$

$$\tilde{K}_{t+1} = (1 - \delta)\tilde{K}_t + \delta\tilde{I}_t \tag{6.54}$$

The firms sector remains unaltered:

$$\tilde{Y}_t = \tilde{A}_t + \alpha\left(\tilde{U}_t + \tilde{K}_t\right) + (1 - \alpha)\tilde{L}_t \tag{6.55}$$

$$\tilde{U}_t\tilde{K}_t = \widetilde{MC}_t + \tilde{Y}_t - \tilde{R}_t \tag{6.56}$$

$$\tilde{L}_t = \widetilde{MC}_t + \tilde{Y}_t - \tilde{W}_t \tag{6.57}$$

$$\widetilde{MC}_t = [(1 - \alpha)\tilde{W}_t + \alpha\tilde{R}_t - \tilde{A}_t] \tag{6.58}$$

$$\tilde{\pi}_t = \beta E_t \tilde{\pi}_{t+1} + \left[\frac{(1 - \theta)(1 - \beta\theta)}{\theta}\right](\widetilde{MC}_t - \tilde{P}_t) \tag{6.59}$$

$$\tilde{\pi}_t = \tilde{P}_t - \tilde{P}_{t-1} \tag{6.60}$$

$$Y_{ss}\tilde{Y}_t = C_{ss}\tilde{C}_t + I_{ss}\tilde{I}_t \tag{6.61}$$

$$\tilde{A}_t = \rho_A\tilde{A}_{t-1} + \epsilon_t \tag{6.62}$$

Table 6.4 summarizes the log-linear model.

Table 6.4: Structure of the log-linear model.

Equation	(Definition)
$\tilde{\lambda}_{R,t} = \left[\dfrac{\sigma}{(1-\phi_c)(1-\phi_c\beta)} \right]$ $[\phi_c\beta(E_t\tilde{C}_{R,t+1} - \phi_c\tilde{C}_{R,t}) - (\tilde{C}_{R,t} - \phi_c\tilde{C}_{R,t-1})] - \tilde{P}_t$	(Ricardian household Lagrangian)
$\widetilde{\pi_W}_t = \beta E_t\widetilde{\pi_W}_{t+1} + \left[\dfrac{(1-\theta_W)(1-\beta\theta_W)}{\theta_W} \right](\tilde{L}_{R,t} - \tilde{\lambda}_{R,t} - \tilde{W}_t)$	(Phillips equation for Ricardian household wages)
$\widetilde{\pi_W}_t = \tilde{W}_t - \tilde{W}_{t-1}$	(Gross wage inflation rate)
$(Q_{ss}\beta)\tilde{Q}_t = E_t\big[(1-\delta)Q_{ss}\tilde{Q}_{t+1}$ $+ \lambda_{R,ss}R_{ss}U_{ss}(\tilde{\lambda}_{R,t+1} + \tilde{R}_{t+1} + \tilde{U}_{t+1})$ $- \lambda_{R,ss}P_{ss}\Psi_1 U_{ss}\tilde{U}_{t+1}\big]$	(Tobin's Q)
$\left(\dfrac{R_{ss}}{P_{ss}}\right)(\tilde{R}_t - \tilde{P}_t) = \Psi_2 U_{ss}\tilde{U}_t$	(Demand for installed capacity)
$\lambda_{R,ss}P_{ss}(\tilde{\lambda}_{R,t} + \tilde{P}_t) - Q_{ss}\tilde{Q}_t + \chi Q_{ss}(\tilde{I}_t - \tilde{I}_{t-1}) =$ $\chi\beta Q_{ss}(E_t\tilde{I}_{t+1} - \tilde{I}_t)$	(Demand for investments)
$\tilde{K}_{t+1} = (1-\delta)\tilde{K}_t + \delta\tilde{I}_t$	(Law of motion of capital)
$\tilde{\lambda}_{NR,t} = \left[\dfrac{\sigma}{(1-\phi_c)(1-\phi_c\beta)} \right]$ $[\phi_c\beta(E_t\tilde{C}_{NR,t+1} - \phi_c\tilde{C}_{NR,t}) - (\tilde{C}_{NR,t} - \phi_c\tilde{C}_{NR,t-1})]$ $- \tilde{P}_t$	(Non-Ricardian household Lagrangian)
$\widetilde{\pi_W}_t = \beta E_t\widetilde{\pi_W}_{t+1} + \left[\dfrac{(1-\theta_W)(1-\beta\theta_W)}{\theta_W} \right]$ $(\tilde{L}_{NR,t} - \tilde{\lambda}_{NR,t} - \tilde{W}_t)$	(Phillips equation for non-Ricardian household wages)
$\tilde{P}_t + \tilde{C}_{NR,t} = \tilde{W}_t + \tilde{L}_{NR,t}$	(Non-Ricardian household budget constraint)
$C_{ss}\tilde{C}_t = \omega_R C_{R,ss}\tilde{C}_{R,ss} + (1-\omega_R)C_{NR,ss}\tilde{C}_{NR,ss}$	(Aggregate consumption)
$L_{ss}\tilde{L}_t = \omega_R L_{R,ss}\tilde{L}_{R,ss} + (1-\omega_R)L_{NR,ss}\tilde{L}_{NR,ss}$	(Aggregate labor)
$\tilde{Y}_t = \tilde{A}_t + \alpha\left(\tilde{U}_t + \tilde{K}_t\right) + (1-\alpha)\tilde{L}_t$	(Production function)

$$\tilde{U}_t \tilde{K}_t = \widetilde{MC}_t + \tilde{Y}_t - \tilde{R}_t \qquad \text{(Demand for capital)}$$

$$\tilde{L}_t = \widetilde{MC}_t + \tilde{Y}_t - \tilde{W}_t \qquad \text{(Demand for labor)}$$

$$\widetilde{MC}_t = [(1-\alpha)\tilde{W}_t + \alpha\tilde{R}_t - \tilde{A}_t] \qquad \text{(Marginal cost)}$$

$$\tilde{\pi}_t = \beta E_t \tilde{\pi}_{t+1} + \left[\frac{(1-\theta)(1-\beta\theta)}{\theta}\right](\widetilde{MC}_t - \tilde{P}_t) \qquad \text{((Phillips equation)}$$

$$\tilde{\pi}_t = \tilde{P}_t - \tilde{P}_{t-1} \qquad \text{(Gross inflation rate)}$$

$$Y_{ss}\tilde{Y}_t = C_{ss}\tilde{C}_t + I_{ss}\tilde{I}_t \qquad \text{(Equilibrium condition)}$$

$$\tilde{A}_t = \rho_A \tilde{A}_{t-1} + \epsilon_t \qquad \text{(Productivity shock)}$$

Productivity Shock

This section analyzes how the presence of adjustment costs on investment and the under-utilization of maximum installed capacity has an impact on the economy, given a positive productivity shock. Qualitatively, the results are similar to those obtained in the model in the previous chapter. Figure 6.1 shows the impulse response functions for this shock. Tobin's Q only has a very short-term positive effect (2 periods), then returns to its steady state. The variable representing the level of utilization of installed capacity (U) remains above steady state for 8 periods, this being the period of time that the capital stock needs to satisfy the higher demand for this input. In other words, the positive productivity shock increases the marginal productivity of capital. Firms that produce intermediate goods respond by increasing the demand for this input. Because of the costs introduced in this chapter, the supply of capital stock takes time to respond to this higher demand. Up to the point that the capital stock responds, the economy's growth is supported by an increase in the utilization of installed capacity.

Figure 6.2 shows a comparison between the RBC, NKFR and NKIR models. The main purpose of including these costs in the DSGE model is to satisfy the "adjustment principle". It can be seen that the results of this model were smoother than the model in the previous chapter.

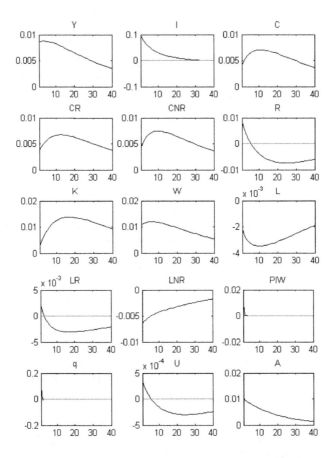

Figure 6.1: NK IRF Model with adjustment costs on investment and under-utilization of maximum installed capacity.

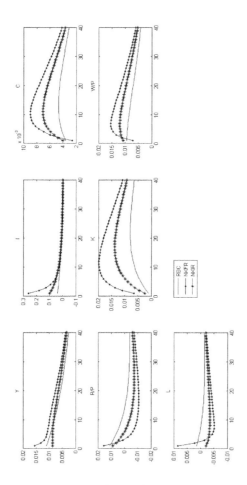

Figure 6.2: Comparison between the Impulse Response Functions for the RBC, NKFR and NKIR models.

BOX 6.1 - Log-linear NK model with rigidity in investment and in the utilization of capital on Dynare.

```
//NK Model with Rigidity in Investments
//Costs relating to investment adjustment and the
//non-utilization of maximum installed capacity
//- Chapter 6 (UNDERSTANDING DSGE MODELS)

var Y I C CR CNR R K W L LR LNR PIW P PI A LAMBDAR LAMBDANR Q U CM;
varexo e;
parameters sigma phi alpha beta delta rhoa psi theta
thetaW psiW phic omegaR Psi1 Psi2 chi;

sigma = 2;
phi = 1.5;
alpha = 0.35;
beta = 0.985;
delta = 0.025;
rhoa = 0.95;
psi = 8;
theta = 0.75;
thetaW = 0.75;
psiW = 21;
phic = 0.8;
omegaR = 0.5;
Psi1 = ((1/beta)-(1-delta));
Psi2 = 1;
chi = 1;

model(linear);
#Uss = 1;
#Pss = 1;
#Rss = Pss*Psi1;
#CMss = ((psi-1)/psi)*(1-beta*theta)*Pss;
#Wss = (1-alpha)*(CMss^(1/(1-alpha)))*((alpha/Rss)^(alpha/(1-alpha)));
#Yss = ((Rss/(Rss-delta*alpha*CMss))^(sigma/(sigma+phi)))*((1-phic*beta)
*((1-phic)^(-sigma))*(1-beta*thetaW)*((psiW-1)/psiW)*(Wss/Pss)
*(Wss/((1-alpha)*CMss))^phi)^(1/(sigma+phi)));
#Kss = alpha*CMss*(Yss/Rss);
#Iss = delta*Kss;
#Css = Yss - Iss;
#Lss = (1-alpha)*CMss*(Yss/Wss);
#CRss = Css;
#CNRss = Css;
#LRss = Lss;
#LNRss = Lss;
#LAMBDARss = (1/Pss)*(CRss^(-sigma))*((1-phic)^(-sigma))*(1-phic*beta);
#LAMBDANRss = (1/Pss)*(CNRss^(-sigma))*((1-phic)^(-sigma))*(1-phic*beta);
#Qss = Pss*LAMBDARss;
//1-Ricardian household Lagrangian
LAMBDAR = (sigma/((1-phic)*(1-phic*beta)))
*(phic*beta*(CR(+1)-phic*CR)-(CR-phic*CR(-1)))-P;
//2-Phillips equation for Ricardian household wages
PIW = beta*PIW(+1)+((1-thetaW)*(1-beta*thetaW)/thetaW)*(LR-LAMBDAR-W);
//3-Gross wage inflation rate
```

```
PIW = W - W(-1);
//4-Tobin's Q
(Qss/beta)*Q = (1-delta)*Qss*Q(+1)+LAMBDARss*Rss*Uss
*(LAMBDAR(+1)+R(+1)+U(+1))-LAMBDARss*Pss*Psi1*Uss*U(+1);
//5-Demand for Installed Capacity
(Rss/Pss)*(R-P) = Psi2*Uss*U;
//6-Demand for Investment
LAMBDARss*Pss*(LAMBDAR+P)-Qss*Q+chi*Qss*(I-I(-1))=chi*beta*Qss*(I(+1)-I);
//7-Law of Motion of Capital
K = (1-delta)*K(-1) + delta*I;
//8-Non-Ricardian household Lagrangian
LAMBDANR = (sigma/((1-phic)*(1-phic*beta)))
*(phic*beta*(CNR(+1)-phic*CNR)-(CNR-phic*CNR(-1)))-P;
//9-Phillips equation for non-Ricardian household wages
PIW = beta*PIW(+1)+((1-thetaW)*(1-beta*thetaW)/thetaW)*(LNR-LAMBDANR-W);
//10-Budget constraint of the non-Ricardian household
P+CNR=W+LNR;
//11-Aggregate consumption
Css*C = omegaR*CRss*CR + (1-omegaR)*CNRss*CNR;
//12-Aggregate labor
Lss*L = omegaR*LRss*LR + (1-omegaR)*LNRss*LNR;
//13-Production function
Y = A + alpha*(U+K(-1)) + (1-alpha)*L;
//14-Demand for capital
U + K(-1) = Y - R;
//15-Demand for labor
L = Y - W;
//16-Marginal cost
CM = ((1-alpha)*W + alpha*R - A);
//17-Phillips Equation
PI = beta*PI(+1)+((1-theta)*(1-beta*theta)/theta)*(CM-P);
//18-Gross inflation rate
PI = P - P(-1);
//19-Equilibrium condition
Yss*Y = Css*C + Iss*I;
//20-Productivity shock
A = rhoa*A(-1) + e;
end;

model_diagnostics;
steady;
check (qz_zero_threshold=1e-20);


shocks;
var e;
stderr 0.01;
end;

stoch_simul(qz_zero_threshold=1e-20)
Y I C CR CNR R K W L LR LNR PIW PI Q U A;
```

Chapter 7

New-Keynesian Model with government

Up to this point, this book has only been considering two agents (households and firms). The remainder of the book will consider another important agent, government. Thus, this chapter will examine the role of government in the DSGE models through two authorities, monetary and fiscal. The former focuses on stabilizing prices using the Taylor rule, while the fiscal authority needs to decide the composition of its spending, bearing in mind that the main role of a government is to supply public goods and services to private agents. However, some also transfer income from one group to another with the chief aim of reducing social inequality, or simply improving the welfare of the worst off. Moreover, they may invest in public capital to support the economy's production sector. This expenditure must be paid for by means of taxation, by issuing public debt or issuing currency. Generally, these three sources of funds could be considered as a form of taxation, with different costs and benefits to society.

A brief theoretical review: Government

This section will deal first with the way to introduce taxation into the DSGE models. It should be stressed that, normally, there are two distinct ways to fulfil this objective: using lump-sum taxes or using distortionary taxes. Then, the public budget will be discussed as well as the consequences of choosing to fund expenditure with taxes or via the issuance of debt. It is also shown how public investment affects the production function. Some alternative forms of government are discussed with the aim of presenting other options used in the literature for the study of fiscal policy. The section ends with a brief discussion about Taylor's rule.

Introducing taxes into the DSGE models

In general, DSGE literature considers two types of taxes. The first is known, in the literature, as a lump-sum tax, while the other is referred to as distortionary taxation, also referred to, respectively, as taxes on consumption and taxes on income from labor or capital. As they affect the price of goods and production inputs, the decisions of the economic agents will be sensitive to changes in the rates of said taxes (Torres, 2014).

Definition 7.1.1 (Lump-sum tax). *This refers to a per capita (fixed) tax. Contrary to what happens with income taxes or taxes on consumption, this type of tax does not distort the efficiency of an economy.*

Generally, the introduction of taxes into DSGE models requires modifying household budget constraints. Lump-sum taxes may be included as follows:

$$C_t + I_t = Y_t - Tr_t$$

where C_t is consumption, I_t is investment, Y_t is income and Tr_t is the lump-sum tax. One alternative is to consider distortionary taxes. Here, the assumption of a tax on income changes a household's budget constraint,

$$C_t + I_t = (1 - \tau^Y)Y_t$$

where τ^Y is the income tax rate. It is also possible to apply distortionary taxes to each source of household income. In this case, instead of considering an overall rate, tax on income from labor may be differentiated from taxes on capital.

$$C_t + I_t = (1 - \tau^l)W_t L_t + (1 - \tau^k)K_t R_t$$

where τ^l and τ^k are the rates of tax on income from labor and from capital, respectively.

As far as consumption of goods is concerned, one can think of a tax on the acquisition of consumer goods and investment assets,

$$(1 + \tau^c)(C_t + I_t) = (1 - \tau^l)W_t L_t + (1 - \tau^k)K_t R_t$$

where τ^c is the rate for the tax on the acquisition of consumer goods and investment, respectively. With the aim of having a numerical idea, table 7.1 displays these tax rates for OECD countries.

Table 7.1: Distortionary rates for OECD countries, in 2005.

	τ_c	τ_l	τ_k
Australia	0.095	0.218	0.450
Austria	0.147	0.482	0.176
Canada	0.098	0.299	0.334
Denmark	0.199	0.397	0.448
Finland	0.176	0.451	0.256
France	0.129	0.430	0.298
Germany	0.12	0.374	0.177
Italy	0.107	0.431	0.283
Japan	0.062	0.257	0.356
Netherlands	0.146	0.359	0.192
Spain	0.116	0.348	0.252
Sweden	0.166	0.523	0.301
United Kingdom	0.124	0.255	0.325
USA	0.039	0.221	0.299

Fonte: Boscá *et al.* (2009)

Government budget constraints

In this subsection, the objective is to study the limits of government involvement in DSGE modeling. To this end, it begins with a presentation of government budget constraints.

$$\underbrace{\underbrace{\frac{B_{t+1}}{R_t^B} - B_t}_{\text{Debt issuance}} + \overbrace{T_t}^{\text{Total tax revenues}} + \overbrace{M_{t+1} - M_t}^{\text{Currency issuance}}}_{\text{Total sources of funds}}$$

Current spending Public investment Income transfer

$$= \overbrace{P_t G_t} + \overbrace{P_t I_t^G} + \overbrace{P_t TRANS_t}$$

Total spending

where M the economy's stock of currency, G is the government's current spending, I^G is public investment and $TRANS$ is the transfer of income to households, the total tax revenue being as follows:

$$T_t = \underbrace{\tau_t^c P_t (C_t + I_t^P)}_{\text{Revenue from acquisition of goods}} + \underbrace{\tau_t^l W_t L_t}_{\text{Revenue from labor income}}$$

$$+ \underbrace{\tau_t^k (R_t - \delta) K_t^P}_{\text{Revenue from capital income}} + \underbrace{Tr_t}_{\text{Revenue from lump-sum taxes}}$$

where τ_t^c, τ_t^l and τ_t^k are the rates of tax on consumption and on income from labor and capital, respectively. In turn, Tr_t represents the lump-sum tax.

If the government issues B_t bonds in t-1 with just one maturity in a period[1] with a unit face value, B_t also represents the value of the stock of nominal public debt in the hands of private agents during the period t-1. In order to manage this public debt, in period t, the government issues B_{t+1} new bonds at a price of P_t^B. In practice, this operation is a loan of $P_t^B B_{t+1}$ from private agents to the government. The price of these bonds may be written as follows:

$$P_t^B = \frac{1}{R_t^B}$$

where R_t^B is the rate at which one unit of currency is discounted in the next period, and also the basic interest rate determined by the Central Bank in t.

The term $(M_{t+1} - M_t)$ measures the government funds that originate from currency being held by the agents. The literature denotes this type of fiscal resource as "seigniorage" which is, in practical terms, a tax, since if a government is not capable of obtaining revenue from other means, it can use this seigniorage. So the higher

---

[1] In reality, in each period, the Government issues bonds of different maturities. For ease of math, it is assumed that all bonds are issued to mature at the end of one period.

the rate of inflation, the greater the seigniorage obtained by the government. In many developed countries with low inflation, this type of revenue is overlooked. Therefore, in general, the DSGE models do not consider this source of public funding.

> **Definition 7.1.2** (Seigniorage). *This relates to net revenue resulting from the issuance of currency.*

Funding through taxation

Assume that in period t a permanent increase occurs of ΔG_t in government spending, funded by an increase in lump-sum taxes, ΔTr_t. Assuming $B_t = B_{t-1} = 0$ (public debt is not used to fund the variation in spending and has a starting value of zero) and $\tau_t^c, \tau_t^l, \tau_t^k$, $I_t^G, TRANS_t = 0$ (there is only one type of (current) expenditure and one type of taxation (lump-sum)) and $M_{t+1} = M_t$ (seigniorage does not exist) for all of t. Thus, the budget constraints of t-1, t and t+1 are as follows:

$$t-1: \quad G_{t-1} = Tr_{t-1}$$

$$t: \quad \underbrace{G_{t-1} + \Delta G_t}_{G_t} = \underbrace{Tr_{t-1} + \Delta Tr_t}_{Tr_t}$$

$$t+1: \quad \underbrace{G_{t-1} + \Delta G_t}_{G_{t+1}} = \underbrace{Tr_{t-1} + \Delta Tr_t}_{Tr_{t+1}}$$

In this case, if government spending sees a permanent increase of ΔG_t, then the taxes should also suffer a permanent increase (ΔTr_t) in the same amount, in order to meet the government's intertemporal budget constraint. To analyze the effects on consumption, household budget constraints should be included[2].

$$C_t = Y_t - Tr_t$$

---

[2]For the purposes of this exercise, households' acquisition of investment assets does not apply.

where Y_t is gross income which, for the purposes of simplification, is assumed to be exogenous and constant, $Y_{t-1} = Y_t = Y_{t+1}$, introducing the permanent increase in government spending in t (with the lump-sum tax growing in the same proportion). Household budget constraints for the periods t-1 and t are:

$$t-1: \quad C_{t-1} = Y_{t-1} - Tr_{t-1}$$

$$t: \quad C_t = Y_{t-1} - Tr_{t-1} - \Delta Tr_t$$

or,

$$C_t = C_{t-1} - \Delta Tr_t$$

since $Y_{t-1} = C_{t-1} + Tr_{t-1}$ and, given that $\Delta Tr_t = \Delta G_t$, we arrive at household consumption in t.

$$C_t = C_{t-1} - \Delta G_t$$

The previous expression states that the increase in government spending has a negative impact on private consumption owing to the permanent drop in income caused by the extra taxation. The result in the product is obtained by analyzing the identity of domestic income for t-1 and t:

$$t-1: \quad Y_{t-1} = C_{t-1} + G_{t-1}$$

$$t: \quad Y_t = \underbrace{C_{t-1} - \Delta G_t}_{C_t} + \underbrace{G_{t-1} + \Delta G_t}_{G_t}$$

Thus,

$$Y_t = C_{t-1} + G_{t-1}$$

Lastly, note that the fiscal stimulus is not effective in stimulating the output of the economy, since the increase in government spending is fully offset by the fall in household consumption.

Funding through the issuance of public debt

It will be assumed that the increase in spending is fully paid for using pubic bonds. The increase in debt raises public spending because of to the additional interest payments. Unlike in the previous subsection, permanent and temporary increases in government spending will be analyzed here.

Permanent increase in ΔG_t in period t
Assuming that $Tr_t = Tr_{t-1}$ (the lump-sum tribute is unaltered), $\tau_t^c, \tau_t^l, \tau_t^k, I_{g,t}, TRANS_t = 0$ (there are no distortionary taxes), $M_{t+1} = M_t$ (seigniorage does not apply), the public debt for the periods prior to the increase in government spending is zero ($B_{t-1} = B_t = 0$), Thus, the budget constraints of t-1, t, t+1, t+2 and t+n will be as follows:

$$t-1: \quad G_{t-1} = Tr_{t-1}$$

$$t: \quad G_{t-1} + \Delta G_t = \frac{B_{t+1}}{R^B} + Tr_{t-1}$$

or,

$$B_{t+1} = \Delta G_t R^B$$

$$t+1: \quad G_{t-1} + \Delta G_t = \frac{B_{t+2}}{R^B} - B_{t+1} + Tr_{t-1}$$

or,

$$B_{t+2} = \Delta G_t R^B + \Delta G_t R^{B^2}$$

$$B_{t+2} = \Delta G_t \left(R^B + R^{B^2} \right)$$

$$t+2: \quad G_{t-1} + \Delta G_t = \frac{B_{t+3}}{R^B} - B_{t+2} + Tr_{t-1}$$

or,

$$B_{t+3} = \Delta G_t R^B + \Delta G_t R^{B^2} + \Delta G_t R^{B^3}$$

$$B_{t+3} = \Delta G_t \left(R^B + R^{B^2} + R^{B^3} \right)$$

$$\vdots$$

$$B_{t+n} = \Delta G_t \left(R^B + R^{B^2} + R^{B^3} + \dots + R^{B^n} \right)$$

or,

$$B_{t+n} = \Delta G_t \sum_{s=1}^{n} R^{B^s}$$

Lastly, discounted public debt is:

$$\frac{B_{t+n}}{R^{B^n}} \approx \frac{B_{t+n}}{\sum_{s=1}^{n} R^{B^s}} = \Delta G_t$$

and,

$$\lim_{n \to \infty} \frac{B_{t+n}}{\sum_{s=1}^{n} R^{B^s}} = \Delta G_t \neq 0$$

As the discounted public debt is other than zero, it follows that this variable increases without new debt being issued. This violates the government's intertemporal budget constraint, demonstrating that a permanent increase in government spending funded by debt is not sustainable.

Temporary increase in ΔG_t in period t
The sequence of the government's intertemporal budget constraint for t-1, t, t+1 and t+n is:

$$t-1: \quad G_{t-1} = Tr_{t-1}$$

$$t: \quad G_{t-1} + \Delta G_t = \frac{B_{t+1}}{R^B} + Tr_{t-1}$$

or,

$$B_{t+1} = \Delta G_t R^B$$

$$t+1: \quad G_{t-1} = \frac{B_{t+2}}{R^B} + Tr_{t-1} - B_{t+1}$$

or,

$$B_{t+2} = \Delta G_t R^{B2}$$

$$\vdots$$

$$B_{t+n} = \Delta G_t R^{Bn}$$

and discounted public debt is:

$$\frac{B_{t+n}}{R^{Bn}} = \Delta G_t$$

and,

$$\lim_{n \to \infty} \frac{B_{t+n}}{R^{Bn}} \approx \Delta G_t \neq 0$$

As with the case of the permanent increase in public spending, this fiscal policy is unsustainable. However, suppose that the temporary change is a random shock with an average of zero, $E(\Delta G_t) = 0$ and $E(\Delta G_t \Delta G_{t+1}) = 0$. Thus, the value of average discounted public debt:

$$\lim_{n \to \infty} E\left(\frac{B_{t+n}}{R^{Bn}}\right) \approx E(\Delta G_t) = 0$$

Given this assumption, the long-term debt is not explosive. Accordingly, temporary increases in government spending represent a sustainable fiscal policy given that positive shocks in a period are offset by negative shocks in other periods. The previous mathematical expression is known in the literature as a no-Ponzi condition. In other words, this condition excludes the possibility of payment of debt interest through the issuance of new debt[3].

---

[3] A Ponzi scheme is a fraudulent financial investment transaction where the operator pays a return to its investors using investments made by new investors, instead of profits obtained from the initial investments. The operators of Ponzi schemes usually attract new investors, offering higher returns than other financial investments.

Public investment

Given an assumption of public investment, investment decisions would not only be in the hands of the private agents, but also the government. Then, public capital would be an important input in the production process. Despite the importance of the government as being responsible for public investment in infrastructure, supporting the private sector, few references to this topic can be found. Some theoretical works in the 1970s incorporate public capital in the aggregate production function (Weitzman, 1970, and Pestieau, 1974). However, it is based on the work by Barro (1990) that these incipient ideas were revived and a new sequence of studies began that considers public capital (Barro and Sala-i-Martin, 1992; Finn, 1993; Glomm and Ravikumar, 1994; Cashin, 1995; Bajo-Rubio, 2000, among others). Reflecting on these ideas, the way to consider public capital according to the DSGE literature is:

$$Y_t = A_t K_t^{P\alpha_1} L_t^{\alpha_2} K_t^{G\alpha_3}$$

where K_t^G and K_t^P are the stock of public capital and stock of private capital, respectively, α_1, α_2, α_3 represent the share of production in private capital, labor and public capital, respectively, with the capital stock having the following law of motion:

$$K_{t+1}^G = (1 - \delta_g)K_t^G + I_t^G$$

where I_t^G is the government investment and δ_g is the rate of depreciation of public capital.

Alternative forms of government in the DSGE models

The previous subsections presented the basic forms of introducing the government into the DSGE models. On the other side of the coin, there is a wealth of literature about assumptions for analyzing public policies.

Habit formation in government consumption

Following the proposition of Ravn (2006), it is assumed that government spending on a good i is carried out in a continuous grouping with $i \in (0,1)$. Thus the government's problem is to minimize its spending in each period, given a level of prices, subject to a bundle of goods and a habit formation rule, formally described as:

$$\min_{G_{i,t}} \int_0^1 p_{i,t} G_{i,t} di$$

subject to:

$$x_t^G = \left[\int_0^1 \left(G_{i,t} - \phi_G s_{i,t-1}^G \right)^{1-\frac{1}{\eta}} \right]^{\frac{1}{1-\frac{1}{\eta}}}$$

and,

$$s_{i,t}^G = \rho_{sG} s_{i,t-1}^G + (1 - \rho_{sG}) G_{i,t}$$

where η is the parameter that represents the elasticity of substitution between the different classes of goods. The variable x_t^G represents the aggregate expenditure of all goods $G_{i,t}$ with the consumption habits of each of these varieties of goods. Thus, $s_{i,t}^G$ is the government's spending habit for each good. Given that $s_{i,t}^G$ is independent of the definition of x_t^G, the intended consumption habits of the government here are external and imply that the government is sustaining levels of spending determined by the history of this variable.

Using the Lagrangian to solve this problem:

$$\mathscr{L} = \int_0^1 p_{i,t} G_{i,t} di + \lambda_t \left\{ x_t^G - \left[\int_0^1 \left(G_{i,t} - \phi_G s_{i,t-1}^G \right)^{1-\frac{1}{\eta}} \right]^{\frac{1}{1-\frac{1}{\eta}}} \right\}$$

With first-order condition:

$$\frac{\partial \mathscr{L}}{\partial G_{i,t}} = p_{i,t} - \lambda_t \left(\frac{1}{1-\frac{1}{\eta}} \right) \left[\int_0^1 \left(G_{i,t} - \phi_G s_{i,t-1}^G \right)^{1-\frac{1}{\eta}-1} \right]^{\frac{1}{1-\frac{1}{\eta}}}$$

$$\left(1 - \frac{1}{\eta} \right) \left(G_{i,t} - \phi_G s_{i,t-1}^G \right)^{1-\frac{1}{\eta}-1} = 0$$

Given that λ_t represents marginal cost, and as this is a structure of perfect competition, we get $\lambda_t = p_t$, and that $x_t^{G\frac{1}{\eta}} = \left[\int_0^1 \left(G_{i,t} - \phi_G s_{i,t-1}^G \right)^{1-\frac{1}{\eta}} \right]^{\frac{1}{\eta-1}}$, leaving the previous expression as follows:

$$p_{i,t} = p_t x_t^{G\frac{1}{\eta}} \left(G_{i,t} - \phi_G s_{i,t-1}^G \right)^{-\frac{1}{\eta}}$$

rearranging the previous expression, government demand for good i can be found:

$$G_{i,t} = \left(\frac{p_{i,t}}{p_t} \right)^{-\eta} x_t^G + \phi_G s_{i,t-1}^G$$

Public goods and services in the utility function

Public expenditure is a variable that is difficult to introduce correctly into the DSGE models. In fact, few DSGE models consider public spending as a factor that affects household utility. Nevertheless, empirical evidence shows that government spending on goods and services is relatively important in the economy's bundle of consumer goods, and these spending decisions have important implications for the drivers of other variables.

   The literature recognizes two different ways of introducing public spending into DSGE models. Firstly, it is possible to introduce it as an element of aggregate expenditure, accordingly it would not affect an individual's utility. However the assumption that public consumption does not affect an individual's utility does not appear to be the most correct one. Alternatively, the more appropriate way would be to consider that public spending is transformed into goods consumed by the private agents which would, therefore, in some way affect the household utility function (Barro, 1981, Aschauer, 1985 and Aiyagari *et al.*, 1992). Continuing this idea, the total household consumption is a linear combination of the consumption of private goods and the consumption of public goods:

$$U_t = U(C_t, L_t)$$

and

$$C_t = C_t^P + \phi_G C_t^G$$

where ϕ_G is a parameter that measures public goods as a proportion of total consumption. The specification above shows that public goods may have an impact on household utility when $\phi_G \neq 0$. The existence of DSGE models with public goods in the household utility function shows that an increase in government spending causes a negative income effect, leading the agents to reduce the supply of labor as well as the consumption of private goods (Aiyagari *et al.*, 1992; Baxter and King, 1993).

Public sector employment and wages

Assuming the introduction of public employment into the DSGE models, the government budget constraint changes to:

$$\frac{B_{t+1}}{R_t^B} - B_t + T_t + M_{t+1} - M_t$$

$$= \quad \underbrace{W_t^G L_t^G}_{\text{Spending on Public Sector Wages}} \quad + P_t G_t + P_t I_{g,t} + P_t TRANS_t$$

The production of public goods and services, C_t^G, follows the assumption that the government will combine public spending on goods and services, G_t, and public sector employment, L_t^G, using a production function,

$$C_t^G = A_t G_t^{\alpha_G} L_t^{G^{1-\alpha_G}}$$

where $0 < \alpha_G < 1$ is the share of public spending in the production of goods and services offered by the government to households.

Taylor's Rule

At the present time, the central banks are expending enormous efforts on studies into the role of monetary policy rules. This has been prompted by the fact that a wide range of studies have indicated that the performance of economic activity in the short term is significantly affected by monetary policy. In the majority of these studies, temporary price stickiness is the friction that explains the non-neutrality of monetary policy. To address this notion, the literature has used the so-called "Taylor Rule" (Taylor, 1993), whose original form was:

$$r_t = \theta + \beta \pi_t + \varphi x_t$$

where $\theta = r^* + (1 - \beta)\pi^*$, r_t is the interest rate target resulting from Taylor's rule, π_t is the average rate of inflation over the last four quarters, π^* is the target inflation rate, x_t is the output gap, r^* is the equilibrium interest rate. Note that if $\beta > 1$ and $\varphi > 0$, then the real interest rate adjusts itself so as to stabilize inflation and the product; if $\beta < 1$, a degree of inflation is admissible. The same type of reasoning applies with regard to φ, which must be non-negative for the rule to provide a stabilizing effect[4].

The model

In this section, the new-Keynesian model is solved with the inclusion of the government sector. The assumptions that continue to be valid are: 2.2.2, 2.2.4, 2.2.6, 2.2.9, 3.2.1-3.2.6, 4.2.1, 4.2.2, 5.2.1, 6.2.1 and 6.2.2. On the other hand, with the inclusion of government, assumption 2.2.1 ceases to be valid.

Households

The problem of the household is the same as in the previous chapter. The novelty is that there are now taxes that could affect the decisions of this agent. With the inclusion of the tax on consumption, the end prices in the acquisition of consumer goods and investment assets are affected. Thus, every time the government is interested in reducing household demand for these goods, it may increase the rate of this tax. There are a further two taxes that affect household decisions: taxes on income from labor and from capital. These are used to affect decisions on the supply of production inputs (labor and capital).

Assumption 7.2.1. *The taxes included in the model are distortionary and affect (Ricardian and non-Ricardian) household decisions.*

- *tax on the acquisition of consumer goods and investment assets, τ^c;*

- *tax on income from labor, τ^l; and*

- *tax on income from capital, τ^k.*

---

[4]The values defined by Taylor (1993) are $\beta = 1, 5$, $\varphi = 0, 5$, $\pi^* = 2$ and $r^* = 2$.

Assumption 7.2.2. *The government makes the transfer of net income $(TRANS_t)^5$ of the lump-sum type, to households, observing the proportion of Ricardian and non-Ricardian agents.*

Assumption 7.2.3. *Ricardian households acquire discounted bonds at the basic rate of interest ($\frac{B}{R^B}$) issued by the government in each period.*

Determining the consumption and savings of Ricardian households

Ricardian households continue to choose consumption and leisure in the same way shown in the other chapters. To this end, the following problem is solved:

$$\max_{C_{R,t},K_{t+1}^P,U_t,I_t^P,B_{t+1}} E_t \sum_{t=0}^{\infty} \beta^t \left[\frac{\left(C_{R,t} - \phi_c C_{R,t-1}\right)^{1-\sigma}}{1-\sigma} - \frac{L_{R,t}^{1+\varphi}}{1+\varphi} \right] \quad (7.1)$$

subject to,

$$P_t(1+\tau_t^c)(C_{R,t}+I_t^P) + \frac{B_{t+1}}{R_t^B} = W_t L_{R,t}(1-\tau_t^l) + R_t U_t K_t^P (1-\tau_t^k)$$

$$- P_t K_t^P \left[\Psi_1 (U_t - 1) + \frac{\Psi_2}{2}(U_t - 1)^2 \right] + B_t + \omega_R P_t TRANS_t \quad (7.2)$$

with the law of motion of capital,

$$K_{t+1}^P = (1-\delta)K_t^P + I_t^P \left[1 - \frac{\chi}{2}\left(\frac{I_t^P}{I_{t-1}^P} - 1\right)^2 \right] \quad (7.3)$$

Using the Lagrangian to solve the previous problem:

---

[5] Excluding other lump-sum taxes.

$$\mathcal{L} = E_t \sum_{t=0}^{\infty} \beta^t \left\{ \left[\frac{\left(C_{R,t} - \phi_c C_{R,t-1} \right)^{1-\sigma}}{1-\sigma} - \frac{L_{R,t}^{1+\varphi}}{1+\varphi} \right] \right.$$

$$- \lambda_{R,t} \left[P_t (1+\tau_t^c)(C_{R,t} + I_t^P) + \frac{B_{t+1}}{R_t^B} - W_t L_{R,t}(1-\tau_t^l) \right.$$

$$- R_t U_t K_t^P (1-\tau_t^k) + P_t K_t^P \left[\Psi_1 (U_t - 1) + \frac{\Psi_2}{2} (U_t - 1)^2 \right]$$

$$- B_t - \omega_R P_t TRANS_t \right]$$

$$\left. -Q_t \left[K_{t+1}^P - (1-\delta) K_t^P - I_t^P \left[1 - \frac{\chi}{2} \left(\frac{I_t^P}{I_{t-1}^P} - 1 \right)^2 \right] \right] \right\} \qquad (7.4)$$

We arrive at the following first-order conditions:

$$\frac{\partial \mathcal{L}}{\partial C_{R,t}} = \left(C_{R,t} - \phi_c C_{R,t-1} \right)^{-\sigma} - \lambda_{R,t} P_t (1+\tau_t^c)$$

$$- \phi_c \beta \left(E_t C_{R,t+1} - \phi_c C_{R,t} \right)^{-\sigma} = 0 \qquad (7.5)$$

$$\frac{\partial \mathcal{L}}{\partial K_{t+1}^P} = \beta E_t \left\{ \lambda_{R,t+1} R_{t+1} U_{t+1}(1-\tau_{t+1}^k) - \beta \lambda_{R,t+1} P_{t+1} \right.$$

$$\left[\Psi_1 (U_{t+1} - 1) + \frac{\Psi_2}{2} (U_{t+1} - 1)^2 \right]$$

$$\left. -Q_t + \beta Q_{t+1}(1-\delta) \right\} = 0 \qquad (7.6)$$

$$\frac{\partial \mathcal{L}}{\partial U_t} = \lambda_{R,t} R_t K_t^P (1-\tau_t^k) - \lambda_{R,t} P_t K_t^P \Psi_1$$

$$- \lambda_{R,t} P_t K_t^P \Psi_2 (U_t - 1) = 0 \qquad (7.7)$$

$$\frac{\partial \mathcal{L}}{\partial I_t^P} = -\lambda_{R,t} P_t (1+\tau_t^c) + Q_t \left[1 - \frac{\chi}{2} \left(\frac{I_t^P}{I_{t-1}^P} - 1 \right)^2 - \chi \frac{I_t^P}{I_{t-1}^P} \left(\frac{I_t^P}{I_{t-1}^P} - 1 \right) \right]$$

$$+ \chi \beta E_t \left[Q_{t+1} \left(\frac{I_{t+1}^P}{I_t^P} \right)^2 \left(\frac{I_{t+1}^P}{I_t^P} - 1 \right) \right] = 0 \qquad (7.8)$$

$$\frac{\partial \mathcal{L}}{\partial B_{t+1}} = -\frac{\lambda_{R,t}}{R_t^B} + \beta E_t \lambda_{R,t+1} = 0 \qquad (7.9)$$

From equation (7.5),

$$\lambda_{R,t} = \frac{\left(C_{R,t} - \phi_c C_{R,t-1} \right)^{-\sigma}}{P_t(1 + \tau_t^c)} - \phi_c \beta \frac{\left(E_t C_{R,t+1} - \phi_c C_{R,t} \right)^{-\sigma}}{P_t(1 + \tau_t^c)} \qquad (7.10)$$

From equation (7.6),

$$Q_t = \beta E_t \left\{ (1 - \delta) Q_{t+1} + \lambda_{R,t+1} R_{t+1} U_{t+1} (1 - \tau_{t+1}^k) \right.$$
$$\left. - \lambda_{R,t+1} P_{t+1} \left[\Psi_1 (U_{t+1} - 1) + \frac{\Psi_2}{2} (U_{t+1} - 1)^2 \right] \right\} \qquad (7.11)$$

From equation (7.7),

$$\frac{R_t}{P_t} = \left(\frac{1}{1 - \tau_t^k} \right) [\Psi_1 + \Psi_2 (U_t - 1)] \qquad (7.12)$$

From equation (7.8),

$$\lambda_{R,t} P_t (1 + \tau_t^c) - Q_t \left[1 - \frac{\chi}{2} \left(\frac{I_t^P}{I_{t-1}^P} - 1 \right)^2 - \chi \frac{I_t^P}{I_{t-1}^P} \left(\frac{I_t^P}{I_{t-1}^P} - 1 \right) \right]$$
$$= \chi \beta E_t \left[Q_{t+1} \left(\frac{I_{t+1}^P}{I_t^P} \right)^2 \left(\frac{I_{t+1}^P}{I_t^P} - 1 \right) \right] \qquad (7.13)$$

From equation (7.9),

$$\frac{\lambda_{R,t}}{R_t^B} = \beta E_t \lambda_{R,t+1} \qquad (7.14)$$

Determining non-Ricardian household consumption

As with the Ricardian households, this type of agent makes decisions in the same manner as in the other chapters, only now considering taxes on consumption:

$$
\max_{C_{NR,t}} E_t \sum_{t=0}^{\infty} \beta^t \left[\frac{\left(C_{NR,t} - \phi_c C_{NR,t-1}\right)^{1-\sigma}}{1-\sigma} - \frac{L_{NR,t}^{1+\varphi}}{1+\varphi} \right] \tag{7.15}
$$

subject to,

$$
P_t(1+\tau_t^c)C_{NR,t} = W_t L_{NR,t}(1-\tau_t^l) + (1-\omega_R)P_t TRANS_t \tag{7.16}
$$

Using the Lagrangian to solve the non-Ricardian household problem:

$$
\mathcal{L} = E_t \sum_{t=0}^{\infty} \beta^t \left\{ \left[\frac{\left(C_{NR,t} - \phi_c C_{NR,t-1}\right)^{1-\sigma}}{1-\sigma} - \frac{L_{NR,t}^{1+\varphi}}{1+\varphi} \right] \right.
$$
$$
- \lambda_{NR,t}\left[P_t(1+\tau_t^c)C_{NR,t} - W_t L_{NR,t}(1-\tau_t^l) \right.
$$
$$
\left. \left. - (1-\omega_R)P_t TRANS_t \right] \right\} \tag{7.17}
$$

Solving the previous problem, we arrive at the following:

$$
\frac{\partial \mathcal{L}}{\partial C_{NR,t}} = \left(C_{NR,t} - \phi_c C_{NR,t-1}\right)^{-\sigma} - \lambda_{NR,t}P_t(1+\tau_t^c)
$$
$$
- \phi_c \beta \left(E_t C_{NR,t+1} - \phi_c C_{NR,t}\right)^{-\sigma} = 0 \tag{7.18}
$$

From equation (7.18),

$$
\lambda_{NR,t} = \frac{\left(C_{NR,t} - \phi_c C_{NR,t-1}\right)^{-\sigma}}{P_t(1+\tau_t^c)} - \phi_c \beta \frac{\left(E_t C_{NR,t+1} - \phi_c C_{NR,t}\right)^{-\sigma}}{P_t(1+\tau_t^c)} \tag{7.19}
$$

Definition of wages

The problem with the definition of wages possesses the same novelty as the consumption decision, namely the inclusion of taxes. As there is no distinction between labor offered by Ricardians (R) and non-Ricardians (NR), the problem of definition of wages is singular $- x = \{R, NR\}$.

$$\max_{W_{j,t}^*} E_t \sum_{i=0}^{\infty} (\beta\theta_W)^i \left\{ -\frac{1}{1+\varphi} \left[L_{x,t+i} \left(\frac{W_{t+i}}{W_{j,t}^*} \right)^{\psi_W} \right]^{1+\varphi} \right.$$
$$\left. + \lambda_{x,t+i} \left[W_{j,t}^* L_{x,t+i} \left(\frac{W_{t+i}}{W_{j,t}^*} \right)^{\psi_W} (1-\tau_{t+i}^l) \right] \right\} \quad (7.20)$$

Resulting in the following first-order condition:

$$0 = E_t \sum_{i=0}^{\infty} (\beta\theta_W)^i \left\{ \psi_W \left[L_{x,t+i} \left(\frac{W_{t+i}}{W_{j,t}^*} \right)^{\psi_W} \right]^{\varphi} L_{x,t+i} \left(\frac{W_{t+i}}{W_{j,t}^*} \right)^{\psi_W} \frac{1}{W_{j,t}^*} \right.$$
$$\left. + (1-\psi_W)\lambda_{x,t+i} L_{x,t+i} \left(\frac{W_{t+i}}{W_{j,t}^*} \right)^{\psi_W} (1-\tau_{t+i}^l) \right\}$$

or,

$$0 = E_t \sum_{i=0}^{\infty} (\beta\theta_W)^i \left\{ \psi_W L_{x,j,t+i}^{\varphi} \frac{1}{W_{j,t}^*} + (1-\psi_W)\lambda_{x,t+i}(1-\tau_{t+i}^l) \right\}$$

With a little massaging, we arrive at the equation for the definition of optimal wages by the households chosen for this purpose:

$$W_{j,t}^* = \left(\frac{\psi_W}{\psi_W-1} \right) E_t \sum_{i=0}^{\infty} (\beta\theta_W)^i \left[\frac{L_{x,j,t+i}^{\varphi}}{\lambda_{x,t+i}(1-\tau_{t+i}^l)} \right]$$

Thus,

$$W_{j,t}^* = \left(\frac{\psi_W}{\psi_W-1} \right) E_t \sum_{i=0}^{\infty} (\beta\theta_W)^i \left[\frac{L_{R,j,t+i}^{\varphi}}{\lambda_{R,t+i}(1-\tau_{t+i}^l)} \right] \quad (7.21)$$

$$W_{j,t}^* = \left(\frac{\psi_W}{\psi_W - 1}\right) E_t \sum_{i=0}^{\infty} (\beta\theta_W)^i \left[\frac{L_{NR,j,t+i}^{\varphi}}{\lambda_{NR,t+i}(1 - \tau_{t+i}^l)}\right] \tag{7.22}$$

From the equation (4.11),

$$W_t = \left[\theta_W W_{t-1}^{1-\psi_W} + (1-\theta_W)W_t^{*\,1-\psi_W}\right]^{\frac{1}{1-\psi_W}} \tag{7.23}$$

Aggregating consumption and labor

The rule for aggregating consumption and labor remains the same as in the previous chapters:

$$C_t = \omega_R C_{R,t} + (1 - \omega_R)C_{NR,t} \tag{7.24}$$

$$L_t = \omega_R L_{R,t} + (1 - \omega_R)L_{NR,t} \tag{7.25}$$

Firms

Some of the firms group assumptions remain the same as previous chapters, but the new factor is the inclusion of stock of public capital in the production function of firms producing intermediate goods.

Assumption 7.2.4. *The production function includes labor and public and private capital as production inputs.*

Thus the production function for intermediate goods is:

$$Y_{j,t} = A_t K_{j,t}^{P\,\alpha_1} L_{j,t}^{\alpha_2} K_{j,t}^{G\,\alpha_3} \tag{7.26}$$

Productivity does not change in relation to the other chapters, hence the equation (3.11):

$$\log A_t = (1 - \rho_A)\log A_{ss} + \rho_A \log A_{t-1} + \varepsilon_t \tag{7.27}$$

The problem of the firm producing intermediate goods remains unchanged, only the new production function needs to be considered. Having said that, the first-order conditions for the problem of firms producing intermediate goods are:

$$L_{j,t} = \alpha_2 MC_{j,t} \frac{Y_{j,t}}{W_t} \tag{7.28}$$

and,

$$U_t K_{j,t}^P = \alpha_1 MC_{j,t} \frac{Y_{j,t}}{R_t} \tag{7.29}$$

Marginal cost becomes:

$$MC_{j,t} = \frac{1}{A_t K_{j,t}^{G \ \alpha_3}} \left(\frac{W_t}{\alpha_2}\right)^{\alpha_2} \left(\frac{R_t}{\alpha_1}\right)^{\alpha_1} \tag{7.30}$$

The problem of pricing the intermediate good is unchanged in this chapter. Thus, from equation (3.25):

$$P_{j,t}^* = \left(\frac{\psi}{\psi-1}\right) E_t \sum_{i=0}^{\infty} (\beta\theta)^i MC_{j,t+i} \tag{7.31}$$

And from equation (3.26):

$$P_t = \left[\theta P_{t-1}^{1-\psi} + (1-\theta) P_t^{*\,1-\psi}\right]^{\frac{1}{1-\psi}} \tag{7.32}$$

Government

In this section, the government is represented by two authorities, fiscal and monetary. The former is responsible for steering the model's fiscal policy, while the latter represents price stability via the Taylor rule.

Fiscal authority

The fiscal authority is considered to be the agent that taxes households and issues debt to fund its expenses, as follows: current expenditure, G_t; public investment, I_t^G; and transfer of income to households, $TRANS_t$.

Assumption 7.2.5. *It is supposed that the government is unable to obtain funds via seigniorage. In other words, the government does not issue currency, so assumption 2.2.2 remains valid.*

Accordingly, the government's budget constraint is:

$$\frac{B_{t+1}}{R_t^B} - B_t + T_t = P_t G_t + P_t I_t^G + P_t TRANS_t \tag{7.33}$$

And total tax revenue is:

$$T_t = \tau_t^c P_t (C_t + I_t^P) + \tau_t^l W_t L_t + \tau_t^k (R_t - \delta) K_t^P \tag{7.34}$$

The government possesses three fiscal policy instruments on the expenditure side: G_t; I_t^G; and $TRANS_t$. On the revenue side, the instruments used are: τ_t^c; τ_t^l; and τ_t^k. All the instruments follow the same fiscal policy rule:

$$\frac{Z_t}{Z_{ss}} = \left(\frac{Z_{t-1}}{Z_{ss}}\right)^{\gamma_Z} \left(\frac{B_t}{Y_{t-1}P_{t-1}} \frac{Y_{ss}P_{ss}}{B_{ss}}\right)^{(1-\gamma_Z)\phi_Z} S_t^Z \tag{7.35}$$

where $Z = \{G_t, I_t^G, TRANS_t, \tau_t^c, \tau_t^l, \tau_t^k\}$.

The fiscal shock is represented by:

$$\log S_t^Z = (1 - \rho_Z)\log S_{ss}^Z + \rho_Z \log S_{t-1}^Z + \varepsilon_{Z,t} \tag{7.36}$$

And the rule for the motion of stock of public capital is represented by:

$$K_{t+1}^G = (1 - \delta_G)K_t^G + I_t^G \tag{7.37}$$

Monetary authority

The central bank follows a simple Taylor rule with a twofold objective: price stability and economic growth.

$$\frac{R_t^B}{R_{ss}^B} = \left(\frac{R_{t-1}^B}{R_{ss}^B}\right)^{\gamma_R} \left[\left(\frac{\pi_t}{\pi_{ss}}\right)^{\gamma_\pi} \left(\frac{Y_t}{Y_{ss}}\right)^{\gamma_Y}\right]^{(1-\gamma_R)} S_t^m \tag{7.38}$$

where γ_Y and γ_π are the sensitivities of the basic interest rate in relation to the product and the inflation rate, respectively, and γ_R is the smoothing parameter. S_t^m is the monetary shock, represented by:

$$\log S_t^m = (1 - \rho_m)\log S_{ss}^m + \rho_m \log S_{t-1}^m + \varepsilon_{m,t} \qquad (7.39)$$

Model's equilibrium condition

The equilibrium condition now includes government, represented by public investment (I_t^G) and current expenditure (G_t).

$$Y_t = C_t + I_t^P + I_t^G + G_t \qquad (7.40)$$

The model for this economy is composed of the following equations from Table 7.2.

Table 7.2: Model structure

Equation	(Definition)
$\lambda_{R,t} = \dfrac{(C_{R,t}-\phi_c C_{R,t-1})^{-\sigma}}{P_t(1+\tau_t^c)} - \phi_c\beta\dfrac{(E_t C_{R,t+1}-\phi_c C_{R,t})^{-\sigma}}{P_t(1+\tau_t^c)}$	(Ricardian household Lagrangian)
$W_{j,t}^* = \left(\dfrac{\psi_W}{\psi_W-1}\right)E_t\sum_{i=0}^{\infty}(\beta\theta_W)^i\left[\dfrac{L_{R,j,t+i}^{\varphi}}{\lambda_{R,t+i}(1-\tau_{t+i}^l)}\right]$	(Ricardian household optimal wage definition)
$W_t = \left[\theta_W W_{t-1}^{1-\psi_W} + (1-\theta_W)W_t^{*\,1-\psi_W}\right]^{\frac{1}{1-\psi_W}}$	(Overall wage level)
$\pi_{W,t} = W_t/W_{t-1}$	(Gross wage inflation rate)
$P_t(1+\tau_t^c)(C_{R,t}+I_t^P) + \dfrac{B_{t+1}}{R_t^B} =$ $W_t L_{R,t}(1-\tau_t^l) + R_t U_t K_t^P(1-\tau_t^k)$ $-P_t K_t^P\left[\Psi_1(U_t-1)+\dfrac{\Psi_2}{2}(U_t-1)^2\right]$ $+B_t + \omega_R P_t TRANS_t$	(Ricardian household budget constraint)
$Q_t = \beta E_t\left\{(1-\delta)Q_{t+1} + \lambda_{R,t+1}R_{t+1}U_{t+1}(1-\tau_{t+1}^k)\right.$ $\left.-\lambda_{R,t+1}P_{t+1}\left[\Psi_1(U_{t+1}-1)+\dfrac{\Psi_2}{2}(U_{t+1}-1)^2\right]\right\}$	(Tobin's Q)

$$\frac{R_t}{P_t} = \left(\frac{1}{1-\tau_t^k}\right)[\Psi_1 + \Psi_2(U_t - 1)]$$

(Demand for installed capacity)

$$\lambda_{R,t} P_t (1 + \tau_t^c) -$$
$$Q_t \left[1 - \frac{\chi}{2}\left(\frac{I_t^P}{I_{t-1}^P} - 1\right)^2 - \chi \frac{I_t^P}{I_{t-1}^P}\left(\frac{I_t^P}{I_{t-1}^P} - 1\right)\right] =$$
$$\chi \beta E_t \left[Q_{t+1}\left(\frac{I_{t+1}^P}{I_t^P}\right)^2\left(\frac{I_{t+1}^P}{I_t^P} - 1\right)\right]$$

(Demand for investments)

$$K_{t+1}^P = (1-\delta)K_t^P + I_t^P\left[1 - \frac{\chi}{2}\left(\frac{I_t^P}{I_{t-1}^P} - 1\right)^2\right]$$

(Law of motion of private capital)

$$\frac{\lambda_{R,t}}{R_t^B} = \beta E_t \lambda_{R,t+1}$$

(Euler equation (Public bond))

$$\lambda_{NR,t} =$$
$$\frac{(C_{NR,t} - \phi_c C_{NR,t-1})^{-\sigma}}{P_t(1+\tau_t^c)} - \phi_c \beta \frac{(E_t C_{NR,t+1} - \phi_c C_{NR,t})^{-\sigma}}{P_t(1+\tau_t^c)}$$

(Non-Ricardian household Lagrangian)

$$W_{j,t}^* = \left(\frac{\psi_W}{\psi_W - 1}\right) E_t \sum_{i=0}^{\infty} (\beta\theta_W)^i \left[\frac{L_{NR,j,t+i}^{\varphi}}{\lambda_{NR,t+i}(1-\tau_{t+i}^l)}\right]$$

(Non-Ricardian household optimal wage definition)

$$C_t = \omega_R C_{R,t} + (1-\omega_R)C_{NR,t}$$

(Aggregate consumption)

$$L_t = \omega_R L_{R,t} + (1-\omega_R)L_{NR,t}$$

(Aggregate Labor)

$$Y_{j,t} = A_t\left(U_t K_{j,t}^P\right)^{\alpha_1} L_{j,t}^{\alpha_2} K_{j,t}^{G\ \alpha_3}$$

(Production function)

$$\frac{L_{j,t}}{U_t K_{j,t}^P} = \left(\frac{\alpha_2}{\alpha_1}\right)\frac{R_t}{W_t}$$

(Problem of the firm trade-off (MRS=Relative price))

$$CM_{j,t} = \frac{1}{A_t K_{j,t}^{G\ \alpha_3}}\left(\frac{W_t}{\alpha_2}\right)^{\alpha_2}\left(\frac{R_t}{\alpha_1}\right)^{\alpha_1}$$

(Marginal Cost)

$$P_{j,t}^* = \left(\frac{\psi}{\psi - 1}\right) E_t \sum_{i=0}^{\infty} (\beta\theta)^i CM_{j,t+i}$$

(Optimal price level)

$$P_t = \left[\theta P_{t-1}^{1-\psi} + (1-\theta)P_t^{*\ 1-\psi}\right]^{\frac{1}{1-\psi}}$$

(General price level)

$$\pi_t = P_t/P_{t-1}$$

(Gross inflation rate)

$$\frac{B_{t+1}}{R_t^B} - B_t + T_t = P_t G_t + P_t I_t^G + P_t TRANS_t$$

(Government budget constraint)

$$T_t = \tau_t^c P_t (C_t + I_t^P) + \tau_t^l W_t L_t + \tau_t^k (R_t - \delta) K_t^P$$

(Total government revenue)

$$\frac{Z_t}{Z_{ss}} = \left(\frac{Z_{t-1}}{Z_{ss}}\right)^{\gamma_Z} \left(\frac{B_t}{Y_{t-1} P_{t-1}} \frac{Y_{ss} P_{ss}}{B_{ss}}\right)^{(1-\gamma_Z)\phi_Z} S_t^Z,$$

$$where \quad Z = \{\tau_t^c, \tau_t^l, \tau_t^k\}$$

(Fiscal policy rule)

$$K_{t+1}^G = (1 - \delta_G) K_t^G + I_t^G$$

(Law of motion of public capital)

$$\frac{R_t^B}{R_{ss}^B} = \left(\frac{R_{t-1}^B}{R_{ss}^B}\right)^{\gamma_R} \left[\left(\frac{\pi_t}{\pi_{ss}}\right)^{\gamma_\pi} \left(\frac{Y_t}{Y_{ss}}\right)^{\gamma_Y}\right]^{(1-\gamma_R)} S_t^m$$

(Taylor's rule)

$$Y_t = C_t + I_t^P + I_t^G + G_t$$

(Equilibrium condition)

$$\log A_t = (1 - \rho_A) \log A_{ss} + \rho_A \log A_{t-1} + \varepsilon_t$$

(Productivity shock)

$$\log S_t^Z = (1 - \rho_Z) \log S_{ss}^Z + \rho_Z \log S_{t-1}^Z + \varepsilon_{Z,t}$$

(Fiscal policy shocks)

$$\log S_t^m = (1 - \rho_m) \log S_{ss}^m + \rho_m \log S_{t-1}^m + \varepsilon_{m,t}$$

(Monetary shock)

Steady state

This section retains the procedure adopted in the other chapters for the resolution of the steady state:

Households

$$I_{ss}^P = \delta K_{ss}^P \tag{7.41}$$

$$\lambda_{R,ss} = \frac{C_{R,ss}^{-\sigma}(1 - \phi_c)^{-\sigma}(1 - \phi_c \beta)}{P_{ss}(1 + \tau_{ss}^c)} \tag{7.42}$$

$$\frac{Q_{ss}}{\beta} = (1 - \delta) Q_{ss} + \lambda_{R,ss} R_{ss}(1 - \tau_{ss}^k) \tag{7.43}$$

$$\frac{R_{ss}}{P_{ss}} = \frac{\Psi_1}{1 - \tau_{ss}^k} \tag{7.44}$$

$$\frac{Q_{ss}}{\lambda_{R,ss}} = P_{ss}(1 + \tau_{ss}^c) \tag{7.45}$$

$$R_{ss}^B = \frac{1}{\beta} \tag{7.46}$$

$$\lambda_{NR,ss} = \frac{C_{NR,ss}^{-\sigma}(1 - \phi_c)^{-\sigma}(1 - \phi_c\beta)}{P_{ss}(1 + \tau_{ss}^c)} \tag{7.47}$$

$$W_{ss} = \left(\frac{\psi_W}{\psi_W - 1}\right)\left(\frac{1}{1 - \beta\theta_W}\right)\left[\frac{L_{R,ss}^\varphi}{\lambda_{R,ss}(1 - \tau_{ss}^l)}\right] \tag{7.48}$$

$$W_{ss} = \left(\frac{\psi_W}{\psi_W - 1}\right)\left(\frac{1}{1 - \beta\theta_W}\right)\left[\frac{L_{NR,ss}^\varphi}{\lambda_{NR,ss}(1 - \tau_{ss}^l)}\right] \tag{7.49}$$

where $\sum_{i=0}^{\infty}(\beta\theta_W)^i = \frac{1}{1-\beta\theta_W}$

$$C_{ss} = C_{R,ss} = C_{NR,ss} \tag{7.50}$$

$$L_{ss} = L_{R,ss} = L_{NR,ss} \tag{7.51}$$

Firms

$$L_{ss} = \alpha_2 CM_{ss}\frac{Y_{ss}}{W_{ss}} \tag{7.52}$$

$$K_{ss} = \alpha_1 CM_{ss}\frac{Y_{ss}}{R_{ss}} \tag{7.53}$$

$$Y_{ss} = K_{ss}^{P\,\alpha_1} L_{ss}^{\alpha_2} K_{ss}^{G\,\alpha_3} \tag{7.54}$$

$$CM_{ss} = \frac{1}{K_{ss}^{G\,\alpha_3}}\left(\frac{W_{ss}}{\alpha_2}\right)^{\alpha_2}\left(\frac{R_{ss}}{\alpha_1}\right)^{\alpha_1} \tag{7.55}$$

$$P_{ss} = \left(\frac{\psi}{\psi - 1}\right)\left(\frac{1}{1 - \beta\theta}\right)CM_{ss} \tag{7.56}$$

where $\sum_{i=0}^{\infty}(\beta\theta)^i = \frac{1}{1-\beta\theta}$.

Government

$$B_{ss}\left(\frac{1}{R_{ss}^B} - 1\right) + \tau_{ss}^c P_{ss}(C_{ss} + I_{ss}^P) + \tau_{ss}^l W_{ss}L_{ss} + \tau_{ss}^k(R_{ss} - \delta)K_{ss}^P$$

$$= P_{ss}G_{ss} + P_{ss}I_{ss}^G + P_{ss}TRANS_{ss} \tag{7.57}$$

$$I_{ss}^G = \delta_G K_{ss}^G \tag{7.58}$$

Equilibrium Condition

$$Y_{ss} = C_{ss} + I_{ss}^P + I_{ss}^G + G_{ss} \tag{7.59}$$

Beginning with the determination of price values (R_{ss}^B, P_{ss}, R_{ss}, W_{ss}, Q_{ss} eand MC_{ss}). By normalizing the general price level ($P_{ss} = 1$),), then R_{ss} and MC_{ss} are also found.

From equations (7.43) and (7.45),

$$R_{ss} = P_{ss}\left(\frac{1 + \tau_{ss}^c}{1 - \tau_{ss}^k}\right)\left[\frac{1}{\beta} - (1 - \delta)\right] \tag{7.60}$$

Given that from equation (7.44),

$$R_{ss} = P_{ss}\left(\frac{\Psi_1}{1 - \tau_{ss}^k}\right)$$

in which,

$$\Psi_1 = (1 + \tau_{ss}^c)\left[\frac{1}{\beta} - (1 - \delta)\right]$$

and from equation (7.56),

$$MC_{ss} = \left(\frac{\psi - 1}{\psi}\right)(1 - \beta\theta)P_{ss} \tag{7.61}$$

Knowing R_{ss} and MC_{ss}, the value of W_{ss} is also known, and from the equation (7.55)[6],

$$W_{ss}^{\alpha_2} = MC_{ss}K_{ss}^{G\alpha_3}(\alpha_2)^{\alpha_2}\left(\frac{\alpha_1}{R_{ss}}\right)^{\alpha_1}$$

---

[6]It is assumed that to determine marginal cost in steady state, $K_{ss}^{G\alpha_3} = 0,2^{\alpha_3}$.

$$W_{ss} = \alpha_2 \left(MC_{ss} K_{ss}^{G\,\alpha_3} \right)^{\frac{1}{\alpha_2}} \left(\frac{\alpha_1}{R_{ss}} \right)^{\frac{\alpha_1}{\alpha_2}} \tag{7.62}$$

Having determined the prices, the next step is to obtain the variables that make up aggregate demand (C_{ss}, I_{ss}^P, I_{ss}^G and G_{ss}). Consumption and private investment are obtained from the convergence of the supply and demand for production inputs (labor and capital). So, by substituting the equation (7.53) in equation (7.41),

$$I_{ss}^P = \left(\frac{\delta \alpha_1 MC_{ss}}{R_{ss}} \right) Y_{ss} \tag{7.63}$$

and substituting equations (7.42) and (7.52) in equation (7.48),

$$W_{ss} = \left(\frac{\psi_W}{\psi_W - 1} \right) \left(\frac{1}{1 - \beta\theta_W} \right) \left\{ \frac{\left[\alpha_2 MC_{ss} \frac{Y_{ss}}{W_{ss}} \right]^{\varphi}}{\frac{C_{ss}^{-\sigma}(1 - \phi_c\beta)(1 - \phi_c)^{-\sigma}}{P_{ss}(1 + \tau_{ss}^c)}(1 - \tau_{ss}^l)} \right\}$$

$$C_{ss}^{\sigma} Y_{ss}^{\varphi} = (1 - \phi_c\beta)(1 - \phi_c)^{-\sigma}(1 - \beta\theta_W)$$

$$\left(\frac{\psi_W - 1}{\psi_W} \right) \left(\frac{1 - \tau_{ss}^l}{1 + \tau_{ss}^c} \right) \frac{W_{ss}}{P_{ss}} \left[\frac{W_{ss}}{\alpha_2 MC_{ss}} \right]^{\varphi}$$

$$C_{ss} = \frac{1}{Y_{ss}^{\frac{\varphi}{\sigma}}} \left\{ (1 - \phi_c\beta)(1 - \phi_c)^{1-\sigma}(1 - \beta\theta_W) \right.$$

$$\left. \left(\frac{\psi_W - 1}{\psi_W} \right) \left(\frac{1 - \tau_{ss}^l}{1 + \tau_{ss}^c} \right) \frac{W_{ss}}{P_{ss}} \left[\frac{W_{ss}}{\alpha_2 MC_{ss}} \right]^{\varphi} \right\}^{\frac{1}{\sigma}} \tag{7.64}$$

It simply remains to find the value of government spending in steady state, G_{ss}. This value is obtained from the government budget constraint (Figure 7.1). It is assumed that, in steady state, the ratio for the level of public debt/GDP is $B_{ss} = \phi_{B_{ss}} Y_{ss}$, that the public investment/GDP $I_{ss}^G = \phi_{I_{ss}^G} Y_{ss}$ and that the level of transfer of income to households/GDP is $TRANS_{ss} = \phi_{TRANS_{ss}} Y_{ss}$. So by solving (7.57) for G_{ss}, and substituting the result in (7.59), we arrive at:

$$G_{ss} = \tau_{ss}^c(C_{ss} + I_{ss}^P) + \tau_{ss}^l \frac{W_{ss}}{P_{ss}} L_{ss} + \tau_{ss}^k \frac{(R_{ss} - \delta)}{P_{ss}} K_{ss}$$

$$+ Y_{ss} \frac{\phi_{B_{ss}}}{P_{ss}} \left(\frac{1}{R_{ss}^B} - 1 \right) - \phi_{TRANS_{ss}} Y_{ss} - \phi_{I_{ss}^G} Y_{ss}$$

$$Y_{ss} = C_{ss} + I_{ss}^P + \phi_{I_{ss}^G} Y_{ss} + \tau_{ss}^c(C_{ss} + I_{ss}) + \tau_{ss}^l \frac{W_{ss}}{P_{ss}} L_{ss} + \tau_{ss}^k \frac{(R_{ss} - \delta)}{P_{ss}} K_{ss}$$

$$+ Y_{ss} \frac{\phi_{B_{ss}}}{P_{ss}} \left(\frac{1}{R_{ss}^B} - 1 \right) - \phi_{TRANS_{ss}} Y_{ss} - \phi_{IG} Y_{ss}$$

$$Y_{ss} = (1 + \tau_{ss}^c)(C_{ss} + I_{ss}^P) + \tau_{ss}^l \frac{W_{ss}}{P_{ss}} L_{ss} + \tau_{ss}^k \frac{(R_{ss} - \delta)}{P_{ss}} K_{ss}$$

$$+ Y_{ss} \frac{\phi_{B_{ss}}}{P_{ss}} \left(\frac{1}{R_{ss}^B} - 1 \right) - \phi_{TRANS_{ss}} Y_{ss} \tag{7.65}$$

Now, substituting (7.52) and (7.53) in (7.65),

$$Y_{ss} = (1 + \tau_{ss}^c)(C_{ss} + I_{ss}^P) + \tau_{ss}^l \frac{\alpha_2 MC_{ss}}{P_{ss}} Y_{ss}$$

$$+ \tau^k \frac{(R_{ss} - \delta)\alpha_1 MC_{ss}}{P_{ss} R_{ss}} Y_{ss} + Y_{ss} \frac{\phi_{B_{ss}}}{P_{ss}} \left(\frac{1}{R_{ss}^B} - 1 \right) - \phi_{TRANS_{ss}} Y_{ss}$$

$$\left[1 - \tau_{ss}^l \frac{\alpha_2 MC_{ss}}{P_{ss}} - \tau_{ss}^k \frac{(R_{ss} - \delta)\alpha_1 MC_{ss}}{P_{ss} R_{ss}} - \frac{\phi_B}{P_{ss}} \left(\frac{1}{R_{ss}^B} - 1 \right) \right.$$

$$\left. + \phi_{TRANS_{ss}} \right] Y_{ss} = (1 + \tau_{ss}^c)(C_{ss} + I_{ss}^P)$$

$$\left[1 - \tau_{ss}^l \frac{\alpha_2 MC_{ss}}{P_{ss}} - \tau_{ss}^k \frac{(R_{ss} - \delta)\alpha_1 MC_{ss}}{P_{ss} R_{ss}} - \frac{\phi_{B_{ss}}}{P_{ss}} \left(\frac{1}{R_{ss}^B} - 1 \right) \right.$$

$$\left. + \phi_{TRANS} \right] \left(\frac{1}{1 + \tau_{ss}^c} \right) Y_{ss} = C_{ss} + I_{ss}^P \tag{7.66}$$

And substituting (7.63) and (7.64) in (7.66),

$$
\left[1 - \tau_{ss}^l \frac{\alpha_2 MC_{ss}}{P_{ss}} - \tau_{ss}^k \frac{(R_{ss} - \delta)\alpha_1 MC_{ss}}{P_{ss} R_{ss}} - \frac{\phi_{B_{ss}}}{P_{ss}} \left(\frac{1}{R_{ss}^B} - 1 \right) \right.
$$
$$
\left. + \phi_{TRANS_{ss}} \right] \left(\frac{1}{1 + \tau_{ss}^c} \right) Y_{ss} = \frac{1}{Y_{ss}^{\frac{\varphi}{\sigma}}} \left\{ (1 - \phi_c \beta)(1 - \phi_c)^{-\sigma} \right.
$$
$$
(1 - \beta \theta_W) \left(\frac{\psi_W - 1}{\psi_W} \right) \left(\frac{1 - \tau_{ss}^l}{1 + \tau_{ss}^c} \right) \frac{W_{ss}}{P_{ss}} \left[\frac{W_{ss}}{\alpha_2 MC_{ss}} \right]^{\varphi} \left. \right\}^{\frac{1}{\sigma}}
$$
$$
+ \left(\frac{\delta \alpha_1 MC_{ss}}{R_{ss}} \right) Y_{ss}
$$

$$
\left[\frac{R_{ss}(P_{ss} - \tau^l \alpha_2 MC_{ss}) - \tau^k (R_{ss} - \delta)\alpha_1 MC_{ss}}{P_{ss} R_{ss}(1 + \tau_{ss}^c)} - \left(\frac{\delta \alpha_1 MC_{ss}}{R_{ss}} \right) \right.
$$
$$
\left. - \frac{\phi_{B_{ss}}}{P_{ss}} \left(\frac{1}{R_{ss}^B} - 1 \right) + \phi_{TRANS_{ss}} \right] Y_{ss} = \frac{1}{Y_{ss}^{\frac{\varphi}{\sigma}}}
$$
$$
\left\{ (1 - \phi_c \beta)(1 - \phi_c)^{-\sigma}(1 - \beta \theta_W) \left(\frac{\psi_W - 1}{\psi_W} \right) \left(\frac{1 - \tau_{ss}^l}{1 + \tau_{ss}^c} \right) \right.
$$
$$
\frac{W_{ss}}{P_{ss}} \left[\frac{W_{ss}}{\alpha_2 MC_{ss}} \right]^{\varphi} \left. \right\}^{\frac{1}{\sigma}}
$$

$$
A_1 = \left[(1 - \phi_c \beta)(1 - \phi_c)^{-\sigma}(1 - \beta \theta_W) \left(\frac{\psi_W - 1}{\psi_W} \right) \left(\frac{1 - \tau_{ss}^l}{1 + \tau_{ss}^c} \right) \right.
$$
$$
\left. \frac{W_{ss}}{P_{ss}} \left[\frac{W_{ss}}{\alpha_2 MC_{ss}} \right]^{\varphi} \right]^{\frac{1}{\sigma}}
$$

$$A_2 = \left[\frac{R_{ss}(P_{ss} - \tau^l_{ss}\alpha_2 MC_{ss}) - \tau^k_{ss}(R_{ss} - \delta)\alpha_1 MC_{ss}}{P_{ss}R_{ss}(1 + \tau^C_{ss})} \right.$$

$$\left. - \left(\frac{\delta\alpha_1 MC_{ss}}{R_{ss}}\right) - \frac{\phi_{B_{ss}}}{P_{ss}}\left(\frac{1}{R^B_{ss}} - 1\right) + \phi_{TRANS_{ss}} \right]$$

$$Y_{ss}^{\frac{\sigma+\varphi}{\sigma}} = \frac{A_1}{A_2}$$

Thus, the output in steady state is:

$$Y_{ss} = \left(\frac{A_1}{A_2}\right)^{\frac{\sigma}{\sigma+\varphi}} \tag{7.67}$$

The previous procedures are summarized in the steady state presentation below:

$$A_{ss} = 1$$

$$P_{ss} = 1$$

$$R^B_{ss} = \frac{1}{\beta}$$

$$R_{ss} = P_{ss}\left(\frac{1+\tau^C_{ss}}{1-\tau^k_{ss}}\right)\left[\frac{1}{\beta} - (1-\delta)\right]$$

$$MC_{ss} = \left(\frac{\psi-1}{\psi}\right)(1-\beta\theta)P_{ss}$$

$$W_{ss} = (1-\alpha)MC_{ss}^{\frac{1}{1-\alpha}}\left(\frac{\alpha}{R_{ss}}\right)^{\frac{\alpha}{1-\alpha}}$$

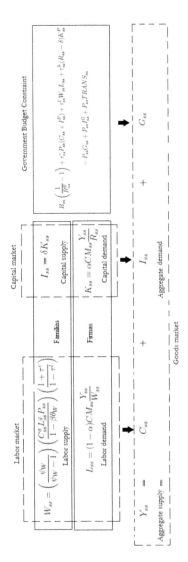

Figure 7.1: Steady state market adjustment structure with government. The dashed lines represent the labor, capital goods and consumer goods markets.

$$A_1 = \left[(1 - \phi_c \beta)(1 - \phi_c)^{-\sigma} (1 - \beta \theta_W) \left(\frac{\psi_W - 1}{\psi_W} \right) \left(\frac{1 - \tau_{ss}^l}{1 + \tau_{ss}^c} \right) \right.$$

$$\left. \frac{W_{ss}}{P_{ss}} \left[\frac{W_{ss}}{\alpha_2 MC_{ss}} \right]^{\varphi} \right]^{\frac{1}{\sigma}}$$

$$A_2 = \left[\frac{R_{ss}(P_{ss} - \tau_{ss}^l \alpha_2 MC_{ss}) - \tau_{ss}^k (R_{ss} - \delta) \alpha_1 MC_{ss}}{P_{ss} R_{ss}(1 + \tau_{ss}^c)} \right.$$

$$\left. - \left(\frac{\delta \alpha_1 MC_{ss}}{R_{ss}} \right) - \frac{\phi_{B_{ss}}}{P_{ss}} \left(\frac{1}{R_{ss}^B} - 1 \right) + \phi_{TRANS_{ss}} \right]$$

$$Y_{ss} = \left(\frac{A_1}{A_2} \right)^{\frac{\sigma}{\sigma + \varphi}}$$

$$B_{ss} = \phi_{B_{ss}} Y_{ss}$$

$$I_{ss}^G = \phi_{I_{ss}^G} Y_{ss}$$

$$K_{ss}^G = \frac{I_{ss}^G}{\delta_G}$$

$$TRANS_{ss} = \phi_{TRANS_{ss}} Y_{ss}$$

$$L_{ss} = \alpha_2 MC_{ss} \frac{Y_{ss}}{W_{ss}}$$

$$K_{ss} = \alpha_1 MC_{ss} \frac{Y_{ss}}{R_{ss}}$$

$$I_{ss}^P = \delta K_{ss}^P$$

$$C_{ss} = \frac{A_1}{Y_{ss}^{\frac{\varphi}{\sigma}}}$$

$$G_{ss} = \tau_{ss}^c(C_{ss} + I_{ss}) + \tau_{ss}^l \frac{W_{ss}}{P_{ss}} L_{ss} + \tau_{ss}^k \frac{(R_{ss} - \delta)}{P_{ss}} K_{ss}$$

$$+ Y_{ss} \frac{\phi_B}{P_{ss}} \left(\frac{1}{R_{ss}^B} - 1 \right) - \phi_{TRANS} Y_{ss} - \phi_{IG} Y_{ss}$$

$$Q_{ss} = \lambda_{R,ss} P_{ss}(1 + \tau_{ss}^c)$$

$$C_{ss} = C_{R,ss} = C_{NR,ss}$$

$$L_{ss} = L_{R,ss} = L_{NR,ss}$$

Tables 7.3 and 7.4 show the calibrated values to be used in the simulation and the model's steady state value, respectively.

Table 7.3: Structural model parameter values.

Parameter	Parameter meaning	Calibrated value
σ	Relative risk aversion coefficient	2
φ	Marginal disutility with regard to supply of labor	1.5
α_1	Elasticity of level of production in relation to private capital	0.3
α_2	Elasticity of level of production in relation to labor	0.6
α_3	Elasticity of level of production in relation to public capital	0.05
β	Discount factor	0.985
δ	Depreciation rate	0.025
θ	Price stickiness parameter	0.75
ψ	Elasticity of substitution among intermediate goods	8
θ_W	Wage stickiness parameter	0.75
ψ_W	Elasticity of substitution between differentiated labor	21

τ_{ss}^c	Rate of tax on consumption in steady state	0.16
τ_{ss}^l	Rate of tax on income from labor in steady state	0.17
τ_{ss}^k	Rate of tax on income from capital in steady state	0.08
ω_R	Participation of Ricardians in consumption and labor in the economy	0.5
ϕ_c	Habit persistence	0.8
χ	Sensitivity of investments in relation to adjustment cost	1
Ψ_1	Sensitivity of cost of under-utilization maximum installed capacity 1	$\frac{1}{\beta} - (1-\delta)$
Ψ_2	Sensitivity of cost of under-utilization maximum installed capacity 2	1
δ_G	Rate of depreciation of public capital	0.025
γ_R	Interest rate persistence	0.79
γ_Y	Sensitivity of interest rate in relation to GDP	0.16
γ_π	Sensitivity of interest rate in relation to inflation	2.43
$\phi_{TRANS_{ss}}$	Proportion of transfers in relation to GDP	0.01
$\phi_{B_{ss}}$	Proportion of public debt in relation to GDP	1
$\phi_{I_{ss}^G}$	Proportion of public investment in relation to GDP	0.02
γ_G	Public spending persistence	0
γ_{I^G}	Persistence of public investment	0.1
γ_{TRANS}	Persistence of income transfer	0.1
γ_{τ^c}	Persistence of tax on consumption	0
γ_{τ^l}	Persistence of tax on labor income	0
γ_{τ^k}	Persistence of tax on capital income	0
ϕ_G	Public spending over debt	0

ϕ_{IG}	Public investment over debt	-0.1
ϕ_{TRANS}	Income transfer over debt	-0.1
ϕ_{τ^c}	Tax on consumption over debt	0
ϕ_{τ^l}	Tax on labor income over debt	0
ϕ_{τ^k}	Tax on capital income over debt	0

Table 7.4: Variable values in steady state.

Variable	Steady state
RB	1.015
R	0.051
MC	0.229
W	0.135
Y	0.5926
B	0.5926
L	0.654
K^P	0.801
K^G	0.474
I^P	0.020
I^G	0.012
C	0.490
G	0.070

Log-linearization (Uhlig's Method)

The method developed by Uhlig continues to be used as a tool for the log-linearization of the model. The results of the other chapters that concur with this model will be reused. The new element is the log-linearization of the problem of the household and the government sector.

Defining the following auxiliary variables:

$$T_t^c = 1 + \tau_t^c \qquad (7.68)$$

$$T_t^l = 1 - \tau_t^l \qquad (7.69)$$

$$T_t^k = 1 - \tau_t^k \tag{7.70}$$

$$CC_{R,t} = C_{R,t} - \phi_c C_{R,t-1} \tag{7.71}$$

$$CC_{R,t+1} = C_{R,t+1} - \phi_c C_{R,t} \tag{7.72}$$

And the log-linearizations of equations (7.68), (7.69), (7.70), (7.71) and (7.72),

$$T_{ss}^c(1 + \widetilde{T}_t^c) = 1 + \tau_{ss}^c(1 + \widetilde{\tau}_t^c)$$

$$T_{ss}^c + T_{ss}^c \widetilde{T}_t^c = 1 + \tau_{ss}^c + \tau_{ss}^c \widetilde{\tau}_t^c$$

Given that at the steady state, $T_{ss}^c = 1 + \tau_{ss}^c$, results in:

$$T_{ss}^c \widetilde{T}_t^c = \tau_{ss}^c \widetilde{\tau}_t^c$$

$$\widetilde{T}_t^c = \left(\frac{\tau_{ss}^c}{1 + \tau_{ss}^c}\right) \widetilde{\tau}_t^c \tag{7.73}$$

$$\widetilde{T}_t^k = -\left(\frac{\tau_{ss}^k}{1 - \tau_{ss}^k}\right) \widetilde{\tau}_t^k \tag{7.74}$$

$$\widetilde{T}_t^l = -\left(\frac{\tau_{ss}^l}{1 - \tau_{ss}^l}\right) \widetilde{\tau}_t^l \tag{7.75}$$

The log-linearizations for (7.71) and (7.72) are as follows:

$$\widetilde{CC}_{R,t} = \left(\frac{1}{1 - \phi_c}\right)(\widetilde{C}_{R,t} - \phi_c \widetilde{C}_{R,t-1}) \tag{7.76}$$

and,

$$\widetilde{CC}_{R,t+1} = \left(\frac{1}{1 - \phi_c}\right)(\widetilde{C}_{R,t+1} - \phi_c \widetilde{C}_{R,t}) \tag{7.77}$$

Beginning with the Euler equation for public bonds,

$$\frac{\lambda_{R,t}}{R_t^B} = \beta E_t \lambda_{R,t+1}$$

$$\frac{\lambda_{R,ss}}{R_{ss}^B}(1 + \tilde{\lambda}_{R,t} - \tilde{R}_t^B)$$

$$= \beta \lambda_{R,ss}(1 + E_t \tilde{\lambda}_{R,t+1})$$

Remembering that in steady state, $R_{ss}^B = \frac{1}{\beta}$,

$$\tilde{\lambda}_{R,t} - \tilde{R}_t^B = E_t \tilde{\lambda}_{R,t+1} \tag{7.78}$$

Log-linearizing the Lagrangian of the Ricardian household (equation (7.10)),

$$\lambda_{R,t} = \frac{\left(C_{R,t} - \phi_c C_{R,t-1}\right)^{-\sigma}}{P_t(1 + \tau_t^c)}$$

$$-\phi_c \beta \frac{\left(E_t C_{R,t+1} - \phi_c C_{R,t}\right)^{-\sigma}}{P_t(1 + \tau_t^c)}$$

Substituting equations (7.68), (7.71) and (7.72) in the previous expression,

$$\lambda_{R,t} = \frac{CC_{R,t}^{-\sigma}}{P_t T_t^c} - \phi_c \beta \frac{E_t CC_{R,t+1}^{-\sigma}}{P_t T_t^c}$$

$$\lambda_{R,t} P_t T_t^c = CC_{R,t}^{-\sigma} - \phi_c \beta E_t CC_{R,t+1}^{-\sigma}$$

$$\lambda_{R,ss} P_{ss} T_{ss}^c (1 + \tilde{\lambda}_{R,t} + \tilde{P}_t + \tilde{T}_t^c)$$

$$= CC_{R,ss}^{-\sigma}(1 - \sigma \widetilde{CC}_{R,t}) - \phi_c \beta CC_{R,ss}^{-\sigma}(1 - \sigma E_t \widetilde{CC}_{R,t+1})$$

At the steady state, $\lambda_{R,ss} P_{ss} T_{ss}^c = CC_{R,ss}^{-\sigma}(1 - \phi_c)$,

$$\lambda_{R,ss} P_{ss} T_{ss}^c (\tilde{\lambda}_{R,t} + \tilde{P}_t + \tilde{T}_t^c)$$

$$= \sigma CC_{R,ss}^{-\sigma}(\phi_c \beta E_t \widetilde{CC}_{R,t+1} - \widetilde{CC}_{R,t})$$

$$\lambda_{R,ss} P_{ss} (\tilde{\lambda}_{R,t} + \tilde{P}_t + \tilde{T}_t^c)$$

$$= \sigma \frac{CC_{R,ss}^{-\sigma}}{T_{ss}^c}(\phi_c \beta E_t \widetilde{CC}_{R,t+1} - \widetilde{CC}_{R,t})$$

Given that $\lambda_{R,ss} P_{ss} = \frac{C_{R,ss}^{-\sigma}(1-\phi_c)^{-\sigma}(1-\phi_c\beta)}{(1+\tau_{ss}^c)}$, $CC_{R,ss}^{-\sigma} = C_{R,ss}^{-\sigma}(1-\phi_c)^{-\sigma}$
e $T_{ss}^c = (1+\tau_{ss}^c)$,

$$\left[\frac{C_{R,ss}^{-\sigma}(1-\phi_c)^{-\sigma}(1-\phi_c\beta)}{(1+\tau_{ss}^c)}\right](\tilde{\lambda}_{R,t} + \tilde{P}_t + \tilde{T}_t^c)$$

$$= \left[\frac{\sigma(1-\phi_c)^{-\sigma}C_{R,ss}^{-\sigma}}{(1+\tau_{ss}^c)}\right](\phi_c\beta E_t\widetilde{CC}_{R,t+1} - \widetilde{CC}_{R,t})$$

$$\tilde{\lambda}_{R,t} + \tilde{P}_t + \tilde{T}_t^c = \frac{\sigma}{(1-\phi_c\beta)}(\phi_c\beta E_t\widetilde{CC}_{R,t+1} - \widetilde{CC}_{R,t})$$

Substituting (7.73), (7.76) and (7.77) in the previous expression,

$$\tilde{\lambda}_{R,t} + \tilde{P}_t + \left(\frac{\tau_{ss}^c}{1+\tau_{ss}^c}\right)\tilde{\tau}_t^c = \left[\frac{\sigma}{(1-\phi_c\beta)(1-\phi_c)}\right]$$

$$\left[\phi_c\beta(E_t\tilde{C}_{R,t+1} - \phi_c\tilde{C}_{R,t}) - (\tilde{C}_{R,t} - \phi_c\tilde{C}_{R,t-1})\right] \tag{7.79}$$

Equivalent to the Lagrangian of the non-Ricardian households,

$$\tilde{\lambda}_{NR,t} + \tilde{P}_t + \left(\frac{\tau_{ss}^c}{1+\tau_{ss}^c}\right)\tilde{\tau}_t^c = \left[\frac{\sigma}{(1-\phi_c\beta)(1-\phi_c)}\right]$$

$$\left[\phi_c\beta(E_t\tilde{C}_{NR,t+1} - \phi_c\tilde{C}_{NR,t}) - (\tilde{C}_{NR,t} - \phi_c\tilde{C}_{NR,t-1})\right] \tag{7.80}$$

Log-linearizing the Tobin Q equation:
From equation (7.13),

$$Q_t = \beta E_t\left\{(1-\delta)Q_{t+1} + \lambda_{R,t+1}R_{t+1}U_{t+1}(1-\tau_{t+1}^k)\right.$$
$$\left. - \lambda_{R,t+1}P_{t+1}\left[\Psi_1(U_{t+1}-1) + \frac{\Psi_2}{2}(U_{t+1}-1)^2\right]\right\}$$

Substituting (7.70) in the previous equation,

$$Q_t = \beta E_t\left\{(1-\delta)Q_{t+1} + \lambda_{R,t+1}R_{t+1}U_{t+1}T_{t+1}^k\right.$$
$$\left. - \lambda_{R,t+1}P_{t+1}\left[\Psi_1(U_{t+1}-1) + \frac{\Psi_2}{2}(U_{t+1}-1)^2\right]\right\}$$

$$\frac{Q_{ss}}{\beta}(1+\widetilde{Q}_t) = E_t\left\{(1-\delta)Q_{ss}(1+\widetilde{Q}_{t+1}) + \lambda_{R,ss}R_{ss}U_{ss}T_{ss}^k\right.$$

$$(1+\widetilde{\lambda}_{R,t+1}+\widetilde{R}_{t+1}+\widetilde{U}_{t+1}+\widetilde{T}_{t+1}^k)$$

$$-\lambda_{R,ss}P_{ss}\Psi_1 U_{ss}(1+\widetilde{\lambda}_{R,t+1}+\widetilde{P}_{t+1}+\widetilde{U}_{t+1}) + \lambda_{R,ss}P_{ss}\Psi_1(1+\widetilde{\lambda}_{R,t+1}+\widetilde{P}_{t+1})$$

$$-\lambda_{R,ss}P_{ss}\frac{\Psi_2}{2}U_{ss}^2(1+\widetilde{\lambda}_{R,t+1}+\widetilde{P}_{t+1}+2\widetilde{U}_{t+1}) + \lambda_{R,ss}P_{ss}\Psi_2 U_{ss}(1+\widetilde{\lambda}_{R,t+1}$$

$$\left.+\widetilde{P}_{t+1}+\widetilde{U}_{t+1}) - \lambda_{R,ss}P_{ss}\frac{\Psi_2}{2}(1+\widetilde{\lambda}_{R,t+1}+\widetilde{P}_{t+1})\right\}$$

$$\left(\frac{Q_{ss}}{\beta}\right)\widetilde{Q}_t = E_t\left\{(1-\delta)Q_{ss}\widetilde{Q}_{t+1} + \lambda_{R,ss}R_{ss}U_{ss}T_{ss}^k\right.$$

$$\left.(\widetilde{\lambda}_{R,t+1}+\widetilde{R}_{t+1}+\widetilde{U}_{t+1}+\widetilde{T}_{t+1}^k) - \lambda_{R,ss}P_{ss}\Psi_1 U_{ss}\widetilde{U}_{t+1}\right\}$$

Remembering that $T_{ss}^k = (1-\tau_{ss}^k)$, and substituting (7.74) in the previous equation,

$$\left(\frac{Q_{ss}}{\beta}\right)\widetilde{Q}_t = E_t\left\{(1-\delta)Q_{ss}\widetilde{Q}_{t+1} + \lambda_{R,ss}R_{ss}U_{ss}(1-\tau_{ss}^k)\right.$$

$$\left[\widetilde{\lambda}_{R,t+1}+\widetilde{R}_{t+1}+\widetilde{U}_{t+1}-\left(\frac{\tau_{ss}^k}{1-\tau_{ss}^k}\right)\widetilde{\tau}_{t+1}^k\right]$$

$$\left.-\lambda_{R,ss}P_{ss}\Psi_1 U_{ss}\widetilde{U}_{t+1}\right\} \qquad (7.81)$$

Log-linearizing the demand for installed capacity:
From equation (7.12),

$$\frac{R_t}{P_t} = \left(\frac{1}{1-\tau_t^k}\right)[\Psi_1 + \Psi_2(U_t-1)]$$

Replacing (7.70) in the previous equation,

$$\frac{R_t}{P_t} = \left(\frac{1}{T_t^k}\right)[\Psi_1 + \Psi_2(U_t-1)]$$

$$\frac{R_t T_t^k}{P_t} = \Psi_1 + \Psi_2(U_t - 1)$$

$$\frac{R_{ss} T_{ss}^k}{P_{ss}}(1 + \widetilde{R}_t - \widetilde{P}_t + \widetilde{T}_t^k) = \Psi_1 + \Psi_2 U_{ss}(1 + \widetilde{U}_t) - \Psi_2$$

At the steady state $\frac{R_{ss} T_{ss}^k}{P_{ss}} = \Psi_1$,

$$\frac{R_{ss} T_{ss}^k}{P_{ss}}(\widetilde{R}_t - \widetilde{P}_t + \widetilde{T}_t^k) = \Psi_2 U_{ss} \widetilde{U}_t$$

Remembering that $T_{ss}^k = (1 - \tau_{ss}^k)$, and substituting (7.74) in the previous equation,

$$(1 - \tau_{ss}^k)\frac{R_{ss}}{P_{ss}}\left[\widetilde{R}_t - \widetilde{P}_t - \left(\frac{\tau_{ss}^k}{1 - \tau_{ss}^k}\right)\widetilde{\tau}_t^k\right] = \Psi_2 U_{ss} \widetilde{U}_t \qquad (7.82)$$

Log-linearizing demand for investments:
From equation (7.13),

$$\lambda_{R,t} P_t(1 + \tau_t^c) - Q_t\left\{1 - \frac{\chi}{2}\left(\frac{I_t}{I_{t-1}} - 1\right)^2 - \chi Q_t \frac{I_t}{I_{t-1}}\left(\frac{I_t}{I_{t-1}} - 1\right)\right\}$$

$$= \chi \beta E_t Q_{t+1}\left(\frac{E_t I_{t+1}}{I_t}\right)^2\left(\frac{E_t I_{t+1}}{I_t} - 1\right)$$

Substituting (7.68) in the previous equation,

$$\lambda_{R,t} P_t T_t^c - Q_t\left\{1 - \frac{\chi}{2}\left(\frac{I_t}{I_{t-1}} - 1\right)^2 - \chi Q_t \frac{I_t}{I_{t-1}}\left(\frac{I_t}{I_{t-1}} - 1\right)\right\}$$

$$= \chi \beta E_t Q_{t+1}\left(\frac{E_t I_{t+1}}{I_t}\right)^2\left(\frac{E_t I_{t+1}}{I_t} - 1\right)$$

$$\lambda_{R,t} P_t T_t^c - Q_t + \frac{\chi}{2}Q_t\left(\frac{I_t}{I_{t-1}}\right)^2 - \frac{\chi}{2}Q_t\left(\frac{I_t}{I_{t-1}}\right)$$

$$+ \frac{\chi}{2}Q_t + \chi Q_t\left(\frac{I_t}{I_{t-1}}\right)^2 - \chi Q_t\left(\frac{I_t}{I_{t-1}}\right)$$

$$= \chi \beta E_t Q_{t+1}\left(\frac{E_t I_{t+1}}{I_t}\right)^3 - \chi \beta E_t Q_{t+1}\left(\frac{E_t I_{t+1}}{I_t}\right)^2$$

$$\lambda_{R,t} P_t T_t^c - \left(1 - \frac{\chi}{2}\right) Q_t + \frac{3}{2}\chi Q_t \left(\frac{I_t}{I_{t-1}}\right)^2 - 2\chi Q_t \left(\frac{I_t}{I_{t-1}}\right)$$

$$= \chi\beta E_t Q_{t+1} \left(\frac{E_t I_{t+1}}{I_t}\right)^3 - \chi\beta E_t Q_{t+1} \left(\frac{E_t I_{t+1}}{I_t}\right)^2$$

$$\lambda_{R,ss} P_{ss} T_{ss}^c (1 + \tilde{\lambda}_{R,t} + \tilde{P}_t + \tilde{T}_t^c) - \left(1 - \frac{\chi}{2}\right) Q_{ss} (1 + \tilde{Q}_t)$$

$$+ \frac{3}{2}\chi Q_{ss} [1 + \tilde{Q}_t + 2(\tilde{I}_t - \tilde{I}_{t-1})]$$

$$-2\chi Q_{ss}(1 + \tilde{Q}_t + \tilde{I}_t - \tilde{I}_{t-1}) = \chi\beta Q_{ss}[1 + \tilde{Q}_t + 3(E_t \tilde{I}_{t+1} - \tilde{I}_t)]$$

$$- \chi\beta Q_{ss}[1 + \tilde{Q}_t + 2(E_t \tilde{I}_{t+1} - \tilde{I}_t)]$$

$$\lambda_{R,ss} P_{ss} T_{ss}^c (\tilde{\lambda}_{R,t} + \tilde{P}_t + \tilde{T}_t^c) - Q_{ss}\tilde{Q}_t + \chi Q_{ss}(\tilde{I}_t - \tilde{I}_{t-1})$$

$$= \chi\beta Q_{ss}(E_t \tilde{I}_{t+1} - \tilde{I}_t)$$

Given that $T_{ss}^c = (1 + \tau_{ss}^c)$ and substituting equation (7.69) in the previous equation,

$$(1 + \tau_{ss}^c)\lambda_{R,ss} P_{ss} \left[\tilde{\lambda}_{R,t} + \tilde{P}_t + \left(\frac{\tau_{ss}^c}{1 + \tau_{ss}^c}\right)\tilde{\tau}_t^c\right] - Q_{ss}\tilde{Q}_t + \chi Q_{ss}(\tilde{I}_t - \tilde{I}_{t-1})$$

$$= \chi\beta Q_{ss}(E_t \tilde{I}_{t+1} - \tilde{I}_t) \qquad (7.83)$$

Non-Ricardian household budget constraint:
From equation (7.16),

$$P_t(1 + \tau_t^c)C_{NR,t} = W_t L_{NR,t}(1 - \tau_t^l)$$

Substituting (7.68) and (7.69) in the previous expression,

$$P_t T_t^c C_{NR,t} = W_t L_{NR,t} T_t^l$$

$$P_{ss} T_{ss}^c C_{NR,ss}(1 + \tilde{P}_t + \tilde{T}_t^c + \tilde{C}_{NR,t}) = W_{ss} L_{NR,ss} T_{ss}^l(1 + \tilde{W}_t + \tilde{L}_{NR,t} + \tilde{T}_t^l)$$

At the steady state $P_{ss} T_{ss}^c C_{NR,ss} = W_{ss} L_{NR,ss} T_{ss}^l$,

$$\tilde{P}_t + \tilde{T}_t^c + \tilde{C}_{NR,t} = \tilde{W}_t + \tilde{L}_{NR,t} + \tilde{T}_t^l$$

Substituting (7.73) and (7.75) in the previous expression,

$$\widetilde{P}_t + \widetilde{C}_{NR,t} + \left(\frac{\tau^c_{ss}}{1+\tau^c_{ss}}\right)\widetilde{\tau}^c_t = \widetilde{W}_t + \widetilde{L}_{NR,t} - \left(\frac{\tau^l_{ss}}{1-\tau^l_{ss}}\right)\widetilde{\tau}^l_t \qquad (7.84)$$

Determining the Phillips equation for wages for Ricardian agents,

$$W^*_t = \left(\frac{\psi_W}{\psi_W - 1}\right)E_t \sum_{i=0}^{\infty}(\beta\theta_W)^i \left[\frac{L^{\varphi}_{R,t+i}}{\lambda_{R,t+i}(1-\tau^l_{t+i})}\right]$$

Substituting (7.69) in the previous equation,

$$W^*_t = \left(\frac{\psi_W}{\psi_W - 1}\right)E_t \sum_{i=0}^{\infty}(\beta\theta_W)^i \left(\frac{L^{\varphi}_{R,t+i}}{\lambda_{R,t+i}\,T^l_{t+i}}\right)$$

$$W_{ss}(1+\widetilde{W}^*_t) = \left(\frac{\psi_W}{\psi_W - 1}\right)\left(\frac{1-\beta\theta_W}{1-\beta\theta_W}\right)\left(\frac{L^{\varphi}_{R,ss}}{\lambda_{R,ss}\,T^l_{ss}}\right)$$

$$E_t \sum_{i=0}^{\infty}(\beta\theta_W)^i(1+\varphi\widetilde{L}_{R,t+i}-\widetilde{\lambda}_{R,t+i}-\widetilde{T}^l_{t+i})$$

Given that in steady state, $W_{ss} = \left(\frac{\psi_W}{\psi_W-1}\right)\left(\frac{1}{1-\beta\theta_W}\right)\left(\frac{L^{\varphi}_{R,ss}}{\lambda_{R,ss}\,T^l_{ss}}\right)$,

$$\widetilde{W}^*_t = (1-\beta\theta_W)E_t \sum_{i=0}^{\infty}(\beta\theta_W)^i(\varphi\widetilde{L}_{R,t+i}-\widetilde{\lambda}_{R,t+i}-\widetilde{T}^l_{t+i}) \qquad (7.85)$$

Substituting (7.85) in the log-linear wage level, $\widetilde{W}_t = \theta_W\widetilde{W}_{t-1} + (1-\theta_W)\widetilde{W}^*_t$ (equation (4.46)),

$$\widetilde{W}_t = \theta_W\widetilde{W}_{t-1}+(1-\theta_W)(1-\beta\theta_W)E_t \sum_{i=0}^{\infty}(\beta\theta_W)^i(\varphi\widetilde{L}_{R,t+i}-\widetilde{\lambda}_{R,t+i}-\widetilde{T}^l_{t+i})$$

Using the quasi-differencing procedure, by multiplying both sides of the previous equation by $(1-L^{-1}\beta\theta_W)$,

$$\widetilde{W}_t - \beta\theta_W E_t\widetilde{W}_{t+1} = \theta_W\widetilde{W}_{t-1} + (1-\theta_W)(1-\beta\theta_W)$$

$$E_t \sum_{i=0}^{\infty}(\beta\theta_W)^i(\varphi\widetilde{L}_{R,t+i}-\widetilde{\lambda}_{R,t+i}-\widetilde{T}^l_{t+i})$$

$$-\beta\theta_W\theta_W\widetilde{W}_t - (1-\theta_W)(1-\beta\theta_W)\beta\theta_W$$

$$E_t \sum_{i=0}^{\infty} (\beta\theta_W)^i (\varphi\widetilde{L}_{R,t+1+i} - \widetilde{\lambda}_{R,t+1+i} - \widetilde{T}_{t+1+i}^l)$$

Resulting in:

$$\widetilde{W}_t - \beta\theta_W E_t \widetilde{W}_{t+1} = \theta_W \widetilde{W}_{t-1} - \beta\theta_W\theta_W \widetilde{W}_t$$

$$+ (1-\theta_W)(1-\beta\theta_W)(\varphi\widetilde{L}_{R,t} - \widetilde{\lambda}_{R,t} - \widetilde{T}_t^l)$$

Adding and subtracting $\widetilde{W}_t(1-\theta_W)(1-\beta\theta_W) = \widetilde{W}_t - \theta_W \widetilde{W}_t - \beta\theta_W \widetilde{W}_t + \beta\theta_W\theta_W \widetilde{W}_t$, in the previous equation,

$$\widetilde{W}_t - \beta\theta_W E_t \widetilde{W}_{t+1} = \theta_W \widetilde{W}_{t-1} - \beta\theta_W\theta_W \widetilde{W}_t + \widetilde{W}_t - \theta_W \widetilde{W}_t - \beta\theta_W \widetilde{W}_t$$

$$+ \beta\theta_W\theta_W \widetilde{W}_t + (1-\theta_W)(1-\beta\theta_W)(\varphi\widetilde{L}_{R,t} - \widetilde{\lambda}_{R,t} - \widetilde{T}_t^l)$$

$$\theta_W(\widetilde{W}_t - \widetilde{W}_{t-1}) = \beta(E_t \widetilde{W}_{t+1} - \widetilde{W}_t) + (1-\theta_W)(1-\beta\theta_W)(\varphi\widetilde{L}_{R,t} - \widetilde{\lambda}_{R,t} - \widetilde{T}_t^l)$$

Dividing both sides of the previous equation by θ_W, and using the gross wage inflation rates for t and t+1, $\widetilde{\pi}_{Wt} = \widetilde{W}_t - \widetilde{W}_{t-1}$, $\widetilde{\pi}_{Wt+1} = \widetilde{W}_{t+1} - \widetilde{W}_t$, results in the Phillips equation for wages:

$$\widetilde{\pi}_{Wt} = \beta E_t \widetilde{\pi}_{Wt+1} + \left[\frac{(1-\theta_W)(1-\beta\theta_W)}{\theta_W}\right](\varphi\widetilde{L}_{R,t} - \widetilde{\lambda}_{R,t} - \widetilde{T}_t^l)$$

Substituting (7.75) in the previous expression:

$$\widetilde{\pi}_{Wt} = \beta E_t \widetilde{\pi}_{Wt+1} + \left[\frac{(1-\theta_W)(1-\beta\theta_W)}{\theta_W}\right]$$

$$\left[\varphi\widetilde{L}_{R,t} - \widetilde{\lambda}_{R,t} + \left(\frac{\tau_{ss}^l}{1-\tau_{ss}^l}\right)\widetilde{\tau}_t^l\right] \tag{7.86}$$

Comparatively for the non-Ricardian households,

$$\widetilde{\pi}_{Wt} = \beta E_t \widetilde{\pi}_{Wt+1} + \left[\frac{(1-\theta_W)(1-\beta\theta_W)}{\theta_W}\right]$$

$$\left[\varphi\widetilde{L}_{NR,t} - \widetilde{\lambda}_{NR,t} + \left(\frac{\tau_{ss}^l}{1-\tau_{ss}^l}\right)\widetilde{\tau}_t^l\right] \tag{7.87}$$

Log-linearizing the law of motion of private capital (equation (7.3)),

$$K_{t+1} = (1-\delta)K_t + I_t - \frac{\chi}{2}I_t\left(\frac{I_t}{I_{t-1}}\right)^2 + \chi I_t\left(\frac{I_t}{I_{t-1}}\right) - \frac{\chi}{2}I_t$$

$$K_{ss}(1+\tilde{K}_{t+1}) = (1-\delta)K_{ss}\tilde{K}_t + I_{ss}\tilde{I}_t - \frac{\chi}{2}I_{ss}(1+3\tilde{I}_t - 2\tilde{I}_{t-1})$$

$$+\chi I_{ss}(1+2\tilde{I}_t - \tilde{I}_{t-1}) - \frac{\chi}{2}I_{ss}(1+\tilde{I}_t)$$

$$\tilde{K}_{t+1} = (1-\delta)\tilde{K}_t + \delta\tilde{I}_t \tag{7.88}$$

The equations resulting from the problem of the firm are the same as those in the previous chapter[7]:

$$\tilde{Y}_t = \tilde{A}_t + \alpha_1\left(\tilde{U}_t + \tilde{K}_t^P\right) + \alpha_2\tilde{L}_t + \alpha_3\tilde{K}_t^G \tag{7.89}$$

$$\left(\tilde{U}_t + \tilde{K}_t^P\right) = \widetilde{MC}_t + \tilde{Y}_t - \tilde{R}_t \tag{7.90}$$

$$\tilde{L}_t = \widetilde{MC}_t + \tilde{Y}_t - \tilde{W}_t \tag{7.91}$$

$$\widetilde{MC}_t = \alpha_2\tilde{W}_t + \alpha_1\tilde{R}_t - \tilde{A}_t - \alpha_3\tilde{K}_t^G \tag{7.92}$$

$$\tilde{\pi}_t = \beta E_t\tilde{\pi}_{t+1} + \left[\frac{(1-\theta)(1-\beta\theta)}{\theta}\right](\widetilde{MC}_t - \tilde{P}_t) \tag{7.93}$$

$$\tilde{\pi}_t = \tilde{P}_t - \tilde{P}_{t-1} \tag{7.94}$$

Aggregate consumption and labor:

$$C_{ss}\tilde{C}_t = \omega_R C_{R,ss}\tilde{C}_{R,ss} + (1-\omega_R)C_{NR,ss}\tilde{C}_{NR,ss} \tag{7.95}$$

$$L_{ss}\tilde{L}_t = \omega_R L_{R,ss}\tilde{L}_{R,ss} + (1-\omega_R)L_{NR,ss}\tilde{L}_{NR,ss} \tag{7.96}$$

---

[7]Assuming the introduction of public capital

Log-linearization of the government budget constraint:

$$\frac{B_{ss}}{R_{ss}^B}(1+\tilde{B}_{t+1}-\tilde{R}_t^B)-B_{ss}(1+\tilde{B}_t)+T_{ss}(1+\tilde{T}_t)$$

$$=P_{ss}G_{ss}(1+\tilde{G}_t+\tilde{P}_t)+P_{ss}I_{ss}^G(1+\tilde{I}_t^G+\tilde{P}_t)+P_{ss}TRANS_{ss}(1+\widetilde{TRANS}_t+\tilde{P}_t)$$

in steady state, $B_{ss}\left(\frac{1}{R_{ss}^B}-1\right)+T_{ss}=P_{ss}G_{ss}+P_{ss}I_{ss}^G+P_{ss}TRANS_{ss}$,

$$\frac{B_{ss}}{R_{ss}^B}(\tilde{B}_{t+1}-\tilde{R}_t^B)-B_{ss}\tilde{B}_t+T_{ss}\tilde{T}_t=P_{ss}G_{ss}(\tilde{G}_t+\tilde{P}_t)+P_{ss}I_{ss}^G(\tilde{P}_t+\tilde{I}_t^G)$$

$$+P_{ss}TRANS_{ss}(\tilde{P}_t+\widetilde{TRANS}_t) \tag{7.97}$$

Total government revenue,

$$T_{ss}(1+\tilde{T}_t)=\tau^c C_{ss}P_{ss}(1+\tilde{C}_t+\tilde{P}_t)+\tau^c I_{ss}^P P_{ss}(1+\tilde{I}_t^P+\tilde{P}_t)$$

$$+\tau^l W_{ss}L_{ss}(1+\tilde{W}_t+\tilde{L}_t)+\tau^k R_{ss}K_{ss}^P(1+\tilde{R}_t+\tilde{K}_t^P)-\tau^k\delta K_{ss}^P(1+\tilde{K}_t^P)$$

in steady state, $T_{ss}=\tau^c C_{ss}P_{ss}+\tau^c I_{ss}^P P_{ss}+\tau^l W_{ss}L_{ss}+\tau^k R_{ss}K_{ss}^P-\tau^k\delta K_{ss}^P$,

$$T_{ss}\tilde{T}_t=\tau^c P_{ss}\left[C_{ss}(\tilde{C}_t+\tilde{P}_t)+I_{ss}^P(\tilde{I}_t^P+\tilde{P}_t)\right]+\tau^l W_{ss}L_{ss}(\tilde{W}_t+\tilde{L}_t)$$

$$+\tau^k K_{ss}^P\left[R_{ss}(\tilde{R}_t+\tilde{K}_t^P)-\delta\tilde{K}_t^P\right] \tag{7.98}$$

Log-linear fiscal policy rule,

$$\tilde{Z}_t=\gamma_Z\tilde{Z}_{t-1}+(1-\gamma_Z)\phi_Z(\tilde{B}_t-\tilde{Y}_{t-1}-\tilde{P}_{t-1})+\tilde{S}_t^Z \tag{7.99}$$

Fiscal policy shock:

$$\tilde{S}_t^Z=\rho_Z\tilde{S}_{t-1}^Z+\varepsilon_{Z,t} \tag{7.100}$$

Log-linearization of the Taylor Rule,

$$\frac{R_{ss}}{R_{ss}}(1+\tilde{R}_t)=\left(\frac{R_{ss}}{R_{ss}}\right)^{\gamma_R}\left(\frac{\pi_{ss}}{\pi_{ss}}\right)^{\gamma_\pi(1-\gamma_R)}\left(\frac{Y_{ss}}{Y_{ss}}\right)^{\gamma_Y(1-\gamma_R)}$$

$$[1+\gamma_R\tilde{R}_{t-1}+\gamma_\pi(1-\gamma_R)\tilde{\pi}_t+\gamma_Y(1-\gamma_R)\tilde{Y}_t+\tilde{S}_t^m]$$

$$1+\tilde{R}_t=1+\gamma_R\tilde{R}_{t-1}+\gamma_\pi(1-\gamma_R)\tilde{\pi}_t+\gamma_Y(1-\gamma_R)\tilde{Y}_t+\tilde{S}_t^m$$

$$\widetilde{R}_t = \gamma_R \widetilde{R}_{t-1} + (1 - \gamma_R)(\gamma_\pi \widetilde{\pi}_t + \gamma_Y \widetilde{Y}_t) + \widetilde{S}_t^m \tag{7.101}$$

The log-linearization for the monetary shock is:

$$\widetilde{S}_t^m = \rho_m \widetilde{S}_{t-1}^m + \epsilon_{m,t} \tag{7.102}$$

Lastly, the equilibrium condition and productivity shock:

$$Y_{ss}\widetilde{Y}_t = C_{ss}\widetilde{C}_t + I_{ss}^P \widetilde{I}_t^P + I_{ss}^G \widetilde{I}_t^G + G_{ss}\widetilde{G}_t \tag{7.103}$$

and the productivity shock:

$$\widetilde{A}_t = \rho_A \widetilde{A}_{t-1} + \epsilon_t \tag{7.104}$$

Table 7.5 summarizes the log-linear model.

Table 7.5: Structure of the log-linear model.

Equation	(Definition)
$\widetilde{\lambda}_{R,t} + \widetilde{P}_t + \left(\dfrac{\tau_{ss}^C}{1+\tau_{ss}^C}\right)\widetilde{\tau}_t^c = \left[\dfrac{\sigma}{(1-\phi_c\beta)(1-\phi_c)}\right]$ $[\phi_c\beta(E_t\widetilde{C}_{R,t+1} - \phi_c\widetilde{C}_{R,t}) - (\widetilde{C}_{R,t} - \phi_c\widetilde{C}_{R,t-1})]$	(Ricardian household Lagrangian)
$\widetilde{\pi}_{W\,t} = \beta E_t\widetilde{\pi}_{W\,t+1} +$ $\left[\dfrac{(1-\theta_W)(1-\beta\theta_W)}{\theta_W}\right]\left[\varphi\widetilde{L}_{R,t} - \widetilde{\lambda}_{R,t} + \left(\dfrac{\tau_{ss}^l}{1-\tau_{ss}^l}\right)\widetilde{\tau}_t^l\right]$	(Phillips equation for the Ricardian household)
$\widetilde{\pi}_{W,t} = \widetilde{W}_t - \widetilde{W}_{t-1}$	(Gross wage inflation rate)
$P_{ss}C_{R,ss}\left[(\widetilde{P}_t + \widetilde{C}_{R,t})(1+\tau_{ss}^c) + \tau_{ss}^c\widetilde{\tau}_t^c\right] +$ $P_{ss}I_{ss}^P\left[\left(\widetilde{P}_t + \widetilde{I}_t^P\right)(1+\tau_{ss}^c) + \tau_{ss}^c\widetilde{\tau}_t^c\right]$ $+ \dfrac{B_{ss}}{R_{ss}^B}\left(\widetilde{B}_{t+1} - \widetilde{R}_t^B\right) =$ $W_{ss}L_{R,ss}\left[(\widetilde{W}_t + \widetilde{L}_{R,t})(1-\tau_{ss}^l) - \tau_{ss}^l\widetilde{\tau}_t^l\right] + R_{ss}K_{ss}^P$ $\left[\left(\widetilde{R}_t + \widetilde{K}_t^P\right)(1-\tau_{ss}^k) - \tau_{ss}^k\widetilde{\tau}_t^k\right]$ $+ B_{ss}\widetilde{B}_t + \omega_R TRANS_{ss}\widetilde{TRANS}_t$	(Ricardian household budget constraint)

$$\left(\frac{Q_{ss}}{\beta}\right)\widetilde{Q}_t = E_t\left\{(1-\delta)Q_{ss}\widetilde{Q}_{t+1} + \lambda_{R,ss}R_{ss}U_{ss}(1-\tau_{ss}^k)\right.$$

$$\left[\widetilde{\lambda}_{R,t+1} + \widetilde{R}_{t+1} + \widetilde{U}_{t+1} - \left(\frac{\tau_{ss}^k}{1-\tau_{ss}^k}\right)\widetilde{\tau}_{t+1}^k\right] \qquad \text{(Tobin's Q)}$$

$$\left. -\lambda_{R,ss}P_{ss}\Psi_1 U_{ss}\widetilde{U}_{t+1}\right\}$$

$$(1-\tau_{ss}^k)\frac{R_{ss}}{P_{ss}}\left[\widetilde{R}_t - \widetilde{P}_t - \left(\frac{\tau_{ss}^k}{1-\tau_{ss}^k}\right)\widetilde{\tau}_t^k\right] = \Psi_2 U_{ss}\widetilde{U}_t \qquad \begin{array}{r}\text{(Demand for}\\\text{installed capacity)}\end{array}$$

$$(1+\tau_{ss}^c)\lambda_{R,ss}P_{ss}\left[\widetilde{\lambda}_{R,t} + \widetilde{P}_t + \left(\frac{\tau_{ss}^c}{1+\tau_{ss}^c}\right)\widetilde{\tau}_t^c\right] - \qquad \begin{array}{r}\text{(Demand for}\\\text{investments)}\end{array}$$

$$Q_{ss}\widetilde{Q}_t + \chi Q_{ss}(\widetilde{I}_t^P - \widetilde{I}_{t-1}^P) = \chi\beta Q_{ss}(E_t\widetilde{I}_{t+1}^P - \widetilde{I}_t^P)$$

$$\widetilde{K}_{t+1}^P = (1-\delta)\widetilde{K}_t^P + \delta\widetilde{I}_t^P \qquad \begin{array}{r}\text{(Law of motion of}\\\text{private capital)}\end{array}$$

$$\widetilde{\lambda}_{R,t} - \widetilde{R}_t^B = \widetilde{\lambda}_{R,t+1} \qquad \begin{array}{r}\text{(Euler equation}\\\text{(Public bond))}\end{array}$$

$$\widetilde{\lambda}_{NR,t} + \widetilde{P}_t + \left(\frac{\tau_{ss}^c}{1+\tau_{ss}^c}\right)\widetilde{\tau}_t^c = \left[\frac{\sigma}{(1-\phi_c\beta)(1-\phi_c)}\right] \qquad \begin{array}{r}\text{(Non-Ricardian}\\\text{household}\\\text{Lagrangian)}\end{array}$$

$$[\phi_c\beta(E_t\widetilde{C}_{NR,t+1} - \phi_c\widetilde{C}_{NR,t}) - (\widetilde{C}_{NR,t} - \phi_c\widetilde{C}_{NR,t-1})]$$

$$\widetilde{\pi_W}_t = \beta E_t\widetilde{\pi_W}_{t+1} + \left[\frac{(1-\theta_W)(1-\beta\theta_W)}{\theta_W}\right]$$

$$\left[\varphi\widetilde{L}_{NR,t} - \widetilde{\lambda}_{NR,t} + \left(\frac{\tau_{ss}^l}{1-\tau_{ss}^l}\right)\widetilde{\tau}_t^l\right] \qquad \begin{array}{r}\text{(Phillips equation}\\\text{for non-Ricardian}\\\text{household}\\\text{wagesa)}\end{array}$$

$$C_{ss}\widetilde{C}_t = \omega_R C_{R,ss}\widetilde{C}_{R,ss} + (1-\omega_R)C_{NR,ss}\widetilde{C}_{NR,ss} \qquad \begin{array}{r}\text{(Aggregate}\\\text{consumption)}\end{array}$$

$$L_{ss}\widetilde{L}_t = \omega_R L_{R,ss}\widetilde{L}_{R,ss} + (1-\omega_R)L_{NR,ss}\widetilde{L}_{NR,ss} \qquad \text{(Aggregate Labor)}$$

$$\widetilde{Y}_t = \widetilde{A}_t + \alpha_1\left(\widetilde{U}_t + \widetilde{K}_t^P\right) + \alpha_2\widetilde{L}_t + \alpha_3\widetilde{K}_t^G \qquad \begin{array}{r}\text{(Production}\\\text{function)}\end{array}$$

$$\widetilde{L}_t - \widetilde{U}_t - \widetilde{K}_t^P = \widetilde{R}_t - \widetilde{W}_t \qquad \begin{array}{r}\text{(Problem of the}\\\text{firm trade-}\\\text{off(MRS=Relative}\\\text{price))}\end{array}$$

$$\widetilde{MC}_t = \alpha_2\widetilde{W}_t + \alpha_1\widetilde{R}_t - \widetilde{A}_t - \alpha_3\widetilde{K}_t^G \qquad \text{(Marginal cost)}$$

$$\widetilde{\pi}_t = \beta E_t\widetilde{\pi}_{t+1} + \left[\frac{(1-\theta)(1-\beta\theta)}{\theta}\right](\widetilde{MC}_t - \widetilde{P}_t) \qquad \text{(Phillips equation)}$$

$$\tilde{\pi}_t = \tilde{P}_t - \tilde{P}_{t-1}$$ (Gross inflation rate)

$$\frac{B_{ss}}{R_{ss}^B}(\tilde{B}_{t+1} - \tilde{R}_t^B) - B_{ss}\tilde{B}_t + T_{ss}\tilde{T}_t = P_{ss}G_{ss}(\tilde{G}_t + \tilde{P}_t) +$$
$$P_{ss}I_{ss}^G(\tilde{P}_t + \tilde{I}_t^G) + P_{ss}TRANS_{ss}(\tilde{P}_t + \widetilde{TRANS}_t)$$ (Government budget constraint)

$$T_{ss}\tilde{T}_t = \tau^c P_{ss}\left[C_{ss}(\tilde{C}_t + \tilde{P}_t) + I_{ss}^P(\tilde{I}_t^P + \tilde{P}_t)\right] +$$
$$\tau^l W_{ss}L_{ss}(\tilde{W}_t + \tilde{L}_t) + \tau^k K_{ss}^P\left[R_{ss}(\tilde{R}_t + \tilde{K}_t^P) - \delta\tilde{K}_t^P\right]$$ (Government tax revenues)

$$\tilde{K}_{t+1}^G = (1 - \delta_G)\tilde{K}_t^G + \delta\tilde{I}_t^G$$ (Law of motion of public capital)

$$\tilde{Z}_t = \gamma_Z\tilde{Z}_{t-1} + (1 - \gamma_Z)\phi_Z(\tilde{B}_t - \tilde{Y}_{t-1} - \tilde{P}_{t-1}) + \tilde{S}_t^Z$$ (Fiscal policy rule1)

$$\tilde{R}_t^B = \gamma_R\tilde{R}_{t-1}^B + (1 - \gamma_R)(\gamma_\pi\tilde{\pi}_t + \gamma_Y\tilde{Y}_t) + \tilde{S}_t^m$$ (Taylor's rule)

$$Y_{ss}\tilde{Y}_t = C_{ss}\tilde{C}_t + I_{ss}^P\tilde{I}_t^P + I_{ss}^G\tilde{I}_t^G + G_{ss}\tilde{G}_t$$ (Equilibrium condition)

$$\tilde{A}_t = \rho_A\tilde{A}_{t-1} + \epsilon_t$$ (Productivity shock)

$$\tilde{S}_t^Z = \rho_Z\tilde{S}_{t-1}^Z + \epsilon_{Z,t}$$ (Fiscal policy shocks)

$$\tilde{S}_t^m = \rho_m\tilde{S}_{t-1}^m + \epsilon_{m,t}$$ (Monetary policy shock)

Monetary and fiscal policy productivity shocks and analysis of the Laffer curve

This section begins with a discussion about productivity shocks in monetary and fiscal policy. Then, an analysis will be performed of the use of taxation to stabilize the economy, finishing with a discussion of Laffer curves for three distortionary taxes in this model.

Before analyzing each shock, it is important to highlight a number of assumptions with regard to the behavior of the fiscal authority. Owing to empirical evidence related to greater rigidity of current government spending, amongst the fiscal policy variables (G, I^G and TRANS on the expenditure side and τ^c, τ^l and τ^k on the rev-

enue side) only public investment (I^G) and the transfer of income
are adjusted to stabilize the level of public debt as a proportion of
the GDP[8].

Productivity and monetary shocks

Figure 7.2 displays the results for the productivity shock. This shock
raises the marginal productivity of labor and capital, firms react by
increasing demand for these inputs. With regard to labor, Ricardian
households increase the supply (substitution effect), while non-Ricardians diminish supply (income effect), with a negative net result
on the aggregate supply of labor. Because of to the increase in productivity, nominal tax revenues rise, permitting an improvement in
the government accounts: by reducing public debt and increasing
government investment. With this increase in public investment,
capital requirements are easily satisfied and private capital diminishes. As a result, in the composition of inputs, the supply of labor and of capital diminishes, while the supply of public capital increases, a result which extends beyond the period of this study.

In summary, the growth in productivity improves the quality of
the public budget. The carrying cost of the public debt is reduced
for two reasons: the first is related to the reduction in the stock of
debt and the other the fall in interest rates. As mentioned in the
introduction, it is assumed that current government spending remains unchanged. Finally, the transfer of income to the households is reduced because of to the improvement in productivity,
economic activity in general and the situation of households.

The expansionist monetary shock (figure 7.3) reduces the ba-
sic interest rate which raises the price of government bonds ($P_t^B = \frac{1}{R_t^B}$). This brings down the demand for these bonds by Ricardian
households that adjust their budgets by acquiring consumer goods
and private investment. If, on the one hand, the lower demand for
government bonds helped to broaden private capital, on the other
hand, the lower demand for public bonds has forced an adjustment
in the government budget through a fall in public investment. As far
as the supply of labor is concerned, Ricardian households reduce
their supply, while the non-Ricardians increase theirs, however the

---

[8]Table 7.3 shows the parameter values used in this model simulation.

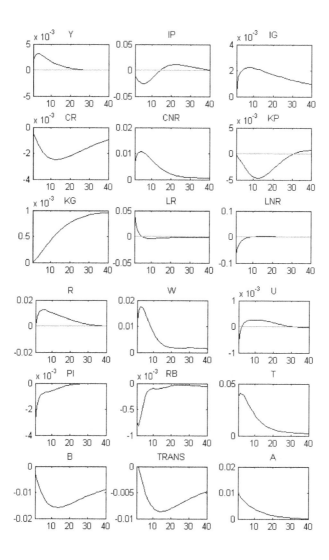

Figure 7.2: Productivity shock.

end result, in terms of the supply of labor, is nil. However, private investment was sufficiently robust to sustain, by itself, an increase in output growth.

Fiscal policy shocks

In this subsection, the possibility of fiscal policy shocks will be discussed. It begins with spending shocks and moves on to a discussion of shocks in terms of the rates of taxation.

Spending shocks (G, I^G and TRANS)

Figure 7.4 shows the impulse-response functions for the government's spending policies. A shock in current expenditure raises aggregate demand, which puts pressure on the general price levels. The central bank (through the Taylor rule) raises the basic rate of interest, something which "pushes down" the price of government bonds, thus increasing demand for these bonds. So in this new household budget composition, it can be seen that the demand for goods (consumer goods and private investment) by households is reduced, owing to the crowding out effect, having a negative impact on the government's tax revenues. The solution for the government with regard to this negative result in the public coffers (higher spending and lower revenue) is to raise funds through new debt issues. Private investment recovers in five periods. Tax revenue follows the same trend, though the cost of having a higher public debt causes the government to adjust the composition of its spending, and public investment falls. The result for production inputs is a reduction in public and private capital and an increase in the supply of labor both for Ricardian and non-Ricardian households (having a negative impact on the welfare of households).

> **Definition 7.3.1** (Crowding out effect). *This happens when the increase in the rate of interest on account of an expansionist fiscal policy, reduces private spending on investment, an occurrence which weakens the effect of growth in economic activity.*

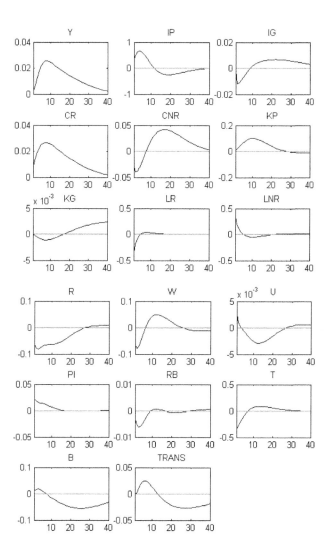

Figure 7.3: Expansionist monetary shock.

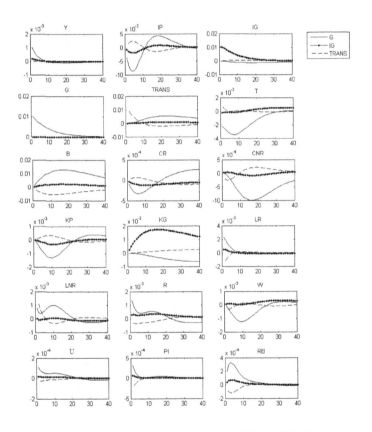

Figure 7.4: Government spending shock (G, IG and TRANS).

The shock in public investment does not cause significant changes in the model's variables. Only the stock of public capital rises, but the result on the aggregate supply is not significant. On the other hand, the shock in terms of the transfer of income to the households increases the net income of these agents. This increases the demand of Ricardians for goods and reduces the supply of labor for these two groups of households. In other words, the Ricardians increase the demand for consumption and leisure, while the non-Ricardians only demand more leisure. The higher demand from Ricardian households for private investment assets (increase in the supply of private capital) is more than offset by the increase in the demand for private capital by firms producing intermediate goods, which reduces the return on capital (firms' cost of capital). Thus marginal cost is reduced together with the level of prices. The central bank reacts by reducing the basic rate of interest and the cost of public debt is lower, as there is no need to adjust the composition of the government budget.

Taxation rate shocks (τ^c, τ^l and τ^k)

Figure 7.5 displays the shocks of fiscal relaxation. The result for the shock in the rate of tax on consumption is very similar to the shock on current government spending. The increase in demand for goods by both Ricardians and non-Ricardians, puts pressure the general price levels (initially the Ricardians increase their demand for private investment assets and then replace demand for this type of asset with consumer goods, the central bank raises the basic rate of interest and the demand for government bonds rises. The result to the public coffers is a fall in revenue (because of to the relaxation) offset by a reduction in public investment and an increase in government debt. The non-Ricardians do not change their supply of labor, even with a rise in wages, on the other hand the Ricardians increase it (substitution effect). The result, in respect of production inputs, is a slight increase in the supply of labor and private capital, while the supply of public capital diminishes.

The relaxation of the labor income tax increases the supply of labor of Ricardian agents (substitution effect) while that of the non-Ricardians diminishes (income effect), but the result on the aggregate supply of labor is positive. The main result of this relaxation is

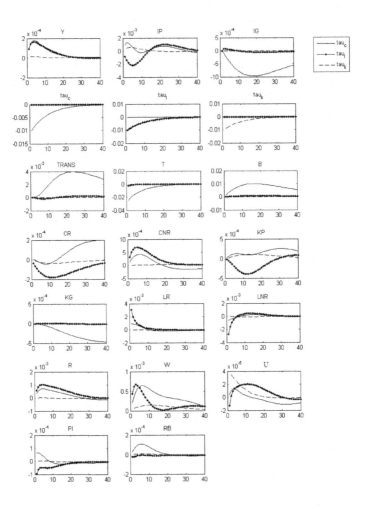

Figure 7.5: Tax rate shocks (τ^c, τ^l and τ^k).

a change in the composition of production inputs, increased supply of labor, and fall in public capital. Finally, the relaxation in terms of capital does not result in significant changes in economic activity.

Using taxation for fiscal adjustment

In this section, a counterfactual analysis will be performed of a positive shock on productivity by analyzing the involvement of taxation in fiscal adjustment. To this end, the following parameters will be assumed as the fiscal policy values: $\gamma_G, \gamma_{IG}, \gamma_{TRANS}, \gamma_{\tau^c}, \gamma_{\tau^l}, \gamma_{\tau^k} = 0, 1; \phi_G, \phi_{IG}, \phi_{TRANS} = -0, 1$ and $\phi_{\tau^c}, \phi_{\tau^l}, \phi_{\tau^k} = \{0; 0, 1; 1; 10\}$.

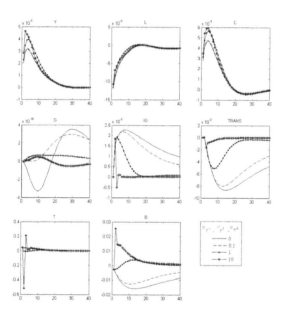

Figure 7.6: Share of taxes in the adjustment of the economy given a positive productivity shock.

Given a positive productivity shock, it can be seen that as involvement of taxation for fiscal adjustment increases, the positive effect on economic activity rises. When $\phi_{\tau^c}, \phi_{\tau^l}, \phi_{\tau^k} = 0$ the adjustments occur in the spending variables – current spending and transfer of income to households is reduced – with a fall in public debt. With $\phi_{\tau^c}, \phi_{\tau^l}, \phi_{\tau^k} = 10$, the adjustment ceases to occur with the spending variables but switches to taxes, and public debt grows to conclude the fiscal adjustment.

The Laffer curve

One interesting analytical tool with regard to taxation is the Laffer curve (Laffer, 1981). The relevance of this concept lies in the fact that to know the position of the rate of a given tax is important in determining if this rate should be raised or lowered to achieve greater tax collection efficiency. In other words, if the current rate is below (above) the rate which generates maximum tax revenue, the fiscal authority should increase (decrease) this rate.

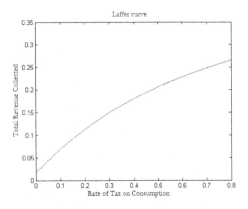

Figure 7.7: Laffer curve for tax on consumption.

The exercise here is to reproduce the concept of the Laffer curve on the three forms of taxation in this model. Figure 7.7 shows the Laffer curve for the tax on consumer goods. The model's steady state was calculated using rates between 0 and 1; a particular fact of this tax is that the rate may exceed 1 as it is an ad-valorem tax. However, in order to maintain a conformity with rates actually set by governments, the study is limited to the domain from 0 to 1. Note that as the curve is always positive, the tax's elasticity of revenue is always greater than 1, and there would be no maximum. The logic for this outcome is that this tax does not affect economic activity via production factors. Thus, an increase in the tax rate raises tax revenue and could offset this higher cost for households by increasing spending on goods and services, which raises income. In other words, the tax on consumption merely introduces a "premium" on the price of goods and services acquired by households.

Figure 7.8 demonstrates the result of the Laffer curve analysis for income tax. The result is a parabola, in accordance with the concept presented in definition 7.3.1. This figure shows the points of the rate used in the simulation and the rate which results in maximum tax revenues (τ^{l^*}), noting that the total tax collected could rise if an increase in the rate of this tax were to occur.

> **Definition 7.3.2** (Laffer curve). *This is a theoretical representation of the relationship between total taxes collected, at different rates, for a given tax. It is a tool used to illustrate the concept of "elasticity of taxable revenue". The main idea that underpins the Laffer curve is that if a tax rate is zero, the government receives no tax revenue, the same applying in the case of a tax rate of 100%, though here the reason would be different since, at this rate, there would be no incentive for the individual liable to this tax obligation to perform the fact that generates this tax (e.g. there is no incentive for an individual to work if the tax on his labor is 100%). Thus, if there is no tax collection for these extreme values (0% and 100%) it may be concluded that there must be a rate at which maximum tax revenue collection is attained. Accordingly, the Laffer curve is typically represented by a parabola. The theoretical result of the Laffer curve is that by increasing rates beyond a certain point, tax revenue begins to diminish.*

The third Laffer curve exercise involves the tax on capital income (figure 7.9). This result is different from the other two exercises. Note that this curve is decreasing for all rates for this tax. This behavior is the result of the distortionary effect of this tax on the accumulation of capital, and so it acts on the level of economic activity as the aggregate supply is a function of the level of capital.

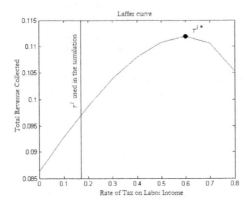

Figure 7.8: Laffer curve for tax on labor income.

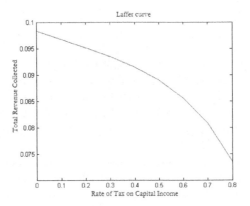

Figure 7.9: Laffer curve for the tax on capital income.

BOX 7.1 - NK model with log-linear government on Dynare.

```
//NK model with Government - Chapter 7 (UNDERSTANDING DSGE MODELS)

var Y IP IG C CR CNR G
KP KG L LR LNR
R W CM P PI PIW Q RB LAMBDAR LAMBDANR
T tau_c tau_k tau_l TRANS B
A Sm SG SIG STRANS Stau_c Stau_l Stau_k U;

varexo e e_m e_G e_IG e_TRANS e_tau_c e_tau_l e_tau_k;

parameters sigma phi alpha1 alpha2 alpha3 beta delta
deltaG rhoa psi theta thetaW psiW
rhoG rhoIG rhoTRANS rhotau_c rhotau_l rhotau_k rhom
gammaG gammaIG gammaTRANS gammatau_c gammatau_l gammatau_k
phiG phiIG phiTRANS phitau_c phitau_l phitau_k
gammaR gammaPI gammaY tau_css tau_lss tau_kss phic omegaR Psi1 Psi2 chi;

alpha1 = 0.3;
alpha2 = 0.65;
alpha3 = 0.05;
beta = 0.985;
delta = 0.025;
deltaG = 0.025;
theta = 0.75;
thetaW = 0.75;
sigma = 2;
phi = 1.5;
psi = 8;
psiW = 21;
tau_css = 0.16;
tau_lss = 0.17;
tau_kss = 0.08;
phic = 0.8;
omegaR = 0.5;
Psi2 = 1;
chi = 1;
//Fiscal Policy Parameters
gammaG = 0;
gammaIG = 0.1;
gammaTRANS = 0.1;
gammatau_c = 0;
gammatau_l = 0;
gammatau_k = 0;
phiG = 0;
phiIG = -0.1;
phiTRANS = -0.1;
phitau_c = 0;
phitau_l = 0;
phitau_k = 0;
//Taylor's Rule Parameters
gammaR = 0.8;
gammaY = 0.5;
gammaPI = 1.5;
//Autoregressive Shock Parameters
rhoa = 0.9;
rhoG = 0.9;
```

```
rhoIG = 0.9;
rhoTRANS = 0.9;
rhotau_c = 0.9;
rhotau_l = 0.9;
rhotau_k = 0.9;
rhom = 0.9;
//
Psi1 = (1+tau_css)*((1/beta)-(1-delta));

model(linear);
#phiB = 1;
#phi_TRANS=0.01;
#phi_IG=0.02;
#Uss = 1;
#Pss = 1;
#PIss = 1;
#RBss = 1/beta;
#Rss = Pss*((1+tau_css)/(1-tau_kss))*((1/beta)-(1-delta));
#CMss = ((psi-1)/psi)*(1-beta*theta)*Pss;
#Wss = alpha2*((CMss*0.2^alpha3)^(1/alpha2))*(alpha1/Rss)^(alpha1/alpha2));
#A1 = ((1-phic*beta)*((1-phic)^(-sigma))*(1-beta*thetaW)*((psiW-1)/psiW)
*((1-tau_lss)/(1+tau_css))*(Wss/Pss)*(Wss/(alpha2*CMss))^phi)^(1/sigma);
#A2 = (((Rss*(Pss-tau_lss*(1-alpha1)*CMss)-tau_kss*(Rss-delta)
*alpha1*CMss)/(Pss*Rss*(1+tau_css)))-(delta*alpha1*CMss/Rss)
-(phiB/Pss)*((1/RBss)-1)+phi_TRANS);
#Yss = (A1/A2)^(sigma/(sigma+phi));
#Bss = phiB*Yss;
#Lss = alpha2*CMss*(Yss/Wss);
#LRss = Lss;
#LNRss = Lss;
#KPss = alpha1*CMss*(Yss/Rss);
#IPss = delta*KPss;
#IGss = phi_IG*Yss;
#KGss = IGss/deltaG;
#Css = (1/(Yss^(phi/sigma)))*A1;
#CRss = Css;
#CNRss = Css;
#Gss = Yss - IPss - IGss - Css;
#TRANSss = phiTRANS*Yss;
#Tss = Pss*Gss + Pss*IGss + Pss*TRANSss - Bss*((1/RBss)-1);
#LAMBDARss = ((CRss^(-sigma))*(1-phic*beta)
*(1-phic)^(-sigma))/((1+tau_css)*Pss);
#LAMBDANRss = ((CNRss^(-sigma))*(1-phic*beta)
*(1-phic)^(-sigma))/((1+tau_css)*Pss);
#Qss = LAMBDARss*Pss*(1+tau_css);
//1-Ricardian Lagrangian household
LAMBDAR + P + (tau_css/(1+tau_css))*tau_c = (sigma/((1-phic)
*(1-phic*beta)))*(phic*beta*(CR(+1)-CR)-(CR-CR(-1)));
//2-Phillips equation for Ricardian household wages
PIW = beta*PIW(+1)+((1-thetaW)*(1-beta*thetaW)/thetaW)
*(phi*LR-LAMBDAR+(tau_lss/(1-tau_lss))*tau_l);
//3-Gross wage inflations
PIW = W - W(-1);
//4-Ricardian household budget constraint
Pss*CRss*((P+CR)*(1+tau_css)+tau_css*tau_c) + Pss*IPss*((P+IP)
*(1+tau_css)+tau_css*tau_c) + (Bss/RBss)*(B-RB)  = Wss*LRss
*((W+LR)*(1-tau_lss)-tau_lss*tau_l)+Rss*KPss*((R+KP(-1))
*(1-tau_kss)-tau_kss*tau_k) + Bss*B(-1) + omegaR*TRANSss*TRANS;
//5-Tobin's Q
(Qss/beta)*Q = (1-delta)*Qss*Q(+1) + LAMBDARss*Rss*Uss
*(1-tau_kss)*(LAMBDAR(+1)+R(+1)+U(+1)-(tau_kss/(1-tau_kss))
```

```
*tau_k(+1))-LAMBDARss*Pss*Uss*Psi1*U(+1);
//6-Demand for installed capacity
(1-tau_kss)*(Rss/Pss)*(R-P-(tau_kss/(1-tau_kss))*tau_k)=Psi2*Uss*U;
//7-Demand for investments
(1+tau_css)*LAMBDARss*Pss*(LAMBDAR+P+(tau_css/(1+tau_css))*tau_c)
-Qss*Q+chi*Qss*(IP-IP(-1))=chi*beta*Qss*(IP(+1)-IP);
//8-Law of motion of private capital
KP = (1-delta)*KP(-1) + delta*IP;
//9-Euler's equation (Public bond)
LAMBDAR - RB = LAMBDAR(+1);
//10-Non-Ricardian household Lagrangian
LAMBDANR + P + (tau_css/(1+tau_css))*tau_c
= (sigma/((1-phic)*(1-phic*beta)))*(phic*beta*(CNR(+1)-CNR)-(CNR-CNR(-1)));
//11-Phillips equation for non-Ricardian household wages
PIW = beta*PIW(+1)+((1-thetaW)*(1-beta*thetaW)/thetaW)
*(phi*LNR-LAMBDANR+(tau_lss/(1-tau_lss))*tau_l);
//12-Aggregate consumption
Css*C = omegaR*CRss*CR + (1-omegaR)*CNRss*CNR;
//13-Aggregate labor
Lss*L = omegaR*LRss*LR + (1-omegaR)*LNRss*LNR;
//14-Production Function
Y = A + alpha1*(U+KP(-1)) + alpha2*L + alpha3*KG(-1);
//15- Problem of the firm trade-off (MRS=Relative price)
L - U - KP(-1) = R - W;
//16-Marginal Cost
CM = alpha2*W + alpha1*R - A - alpha3*KG(-1);
//17-Phillips Equation
PI = beta*PI(+1) + ((1-theta)*(1-beta*theta)/theta)*(CM-P);
//18-Gross Inflation Rate
PI(+1) = P(+1) - P;
//19-Government budget constraint
(Bss/RBss)*(B-RB)-Bss*B(-1) + Tss*T = Pss*Gss*(P+G)
+ Pss*IGss*(P+IG) + Pss*TRANSss*(P+TRANS);
//20-Government tax revenue
Tss*T = tau_css*Pss*(Css*(C+P+tau_c)+IPss*(IP+P+tau_c))
+tau_lss*Wss*Lss*(W+L+tau_l)
+tau_kss*KPss*(Rss*(R+KP(-1)+tau_k)-delta*(KP(-1)+tau_k));
//21-Rule for the movement of public capital
KG = (1-deltaG)*KG(-1) + deltaG*IG;
//22-Rule for the movement of public spending
G = gammaG*G(-1) + (1-gammaG)*phiG*(B(-1)-Y(-1)-P(-1))+SG;
//23-Rule for the movement of public investment
IG = gammaIG*IG(-1) + (1-gammaIG)*phiIG*(B(-1)-Y(-1)-P(-1))+SIG;
//24-Rule for the movement of transfer of income
TRANS = gammaTRANS*TRANS(-1) + (1-gammaTRANS)
*phiTRANS*(B(-1)-Y(-1)-P(-1))+STRANS;
//25-Rule for the movement of tax on consumption
tau_c = gammatau_c*tau_c(-1) + (1-gammatau_c)
*phitau_c*(B(-1)-Y(-1)-P(-1))+Stau_c;
//26-Rule for the movement of tax on labor Income
tau_l = gammatau_l*tau_l(-1) + (1-gammatau_l)
*phitau_l*(B(-1)-Y(-1)-P(-1))+Stau_l;
//27-Rule for the movement of tax on consumption
tau_k = gammatau_k*tau_k(-1) + (1-gammatau_k)
*phitau_k*(B(-1)-Y(-1)-P(-1))+Stau_k;
//28-Taylor's rule
RB = gammaR*RB(-1)+(1-gammaR)*(gammaPI*PI + gammaY*Y)+Sm;
//29-Equilibrim condition
Yss*Y = Css*C + IPss*IP + IGss*IG + Gss*G;
//30-Productivity shock
A = rhoa*A(-1) + e;
```

```
//31 - Shock in Public Spending
SG = rhoG*SG(-1) + e_G;
//32 - Shock in Public Investment
SIG = rhoIG*SIG(-1) + e_IG;
//33 - Shock in Transfer of Income
TRANS = rhoTRANS*STRANS(-1) + e_TRANS;
//34 - Shock in tax on Consumption
Stau_c = rhotau_c*Stau_c(-1) - e_tau_c;
//35 - Shock in tax on Labor Income
Stau_l = rhotau_l*Stau_l(-1) - e_tau_l;
//36 - Shock in tax on Capital Income
Stau_k = rhotau_k*Stau_k(-1) - e_tau_k;
//37- Monetary Shock
Sm = rhom*Sm(-1)-e_m;
end;

steady;
check(qz_zero_threshold=1e-20);

shocks;
var e; stderr 0.01;
var e_G; stderr 0.01;
var e_IG; stderr 0.01;
var e_TRANS; stderr 0.01;
var e_tau_c; stderr 0.01;
var e_tau_l; stderr 0.01;
var e_tau_k; stderr 0.01;
var e_m; stderr 0.01;
end;

stoch_simul(periods=1000,qz_zero_threshold=1e-20)
Y IP IG CR CNR G KP KG LR LNR R W U PI RB T B tau_c tau_k tau_l TRANS A;
```

References

Abel, A. B. (1990). **Asset prices under habit formation and catching up with the Joneses**. The American Economic Review, 80(2), 38-42.

Abel, A., & Blanchard, O. (1983). **An intertemporal equilibrium model of savings and investment**. Econometrica, 51, 675-692.

Aiyagari, S. R., Christiano, L. J., & Eichenbaum, M. (1992). **The output, employment, and interest rate effects of government consumption**. Journal of Monetary Economics, 30(1), 73-86.

Akerlof, G. A., & Yellen, J. L. (1990). **The fair wage-effort hypothesis and unemployment**. The Quarterly Journal of Economics, 255-283.

Aschauer, D. A. (1985). **Fiscal policy and aggregate demand**. The American Economic Review, 75(1), 117-127.

Bajo-Rubio, O. (2000). **A further generalization of the Solow growth model: the role of the public sector**. Economics Letters, 68(1), 79-84.

Barro, R. J. (1981). **Output Effects of Government Purchases**. The Journal of Political Economy, 1086-1121.

———. (1990). **Government Spending in a Simple Model of Endogenous Growth**. Journal of Political Economy, 98(5 pt 2).

————. (1997). **Macroeconomics**. Cambridge: The MIT Press.

Barro, R., & i-Martin, X. S. (1992). **Economic growth**. London, England: MIT Press.

Barron, J. M., Ewing, B. T., & Lynch, G. J. (2006). **Understanding macroeconomic theory**. Routledge.

Baxter, M., & King, R. G. (1993). **Fiscal policy in general equilibrium**. The American Economic Review, 315-334.

Benassy, J. (2011). **Macroeconomic Theory**. OUP Catalogue, Oxford University Press.

Blanchard, O. J., & Fischer, S. (1989). **Lectures on Macroeconomics**. Cambridge: MIT Press.

Blanchard, O. J., & Kahn, C. M. (1980). **The Solution of Linear Difference Models under Rational Expectations**. Econometrica, Econometric Society, vol. 48(5), pages 1305-11, July.

Blanchard, O. J., & Kiyotaki, N. (1987). **Monopolistic competition and effects of aggregate demand**. American Economic Review, 77:647-66.

Blog AC3L, 2013. Available in http://aconscienciadetres/liberais.blogspot.com.br/2013/04/macroeconomia-identificacao.html.

Boldrin, M., Christiano, L., & Fisher, J. (2001). **Habit persistence, asset returns, and the business cycle**. American Economic Review, 91(1), 149-166.

Boscá, J., García, J., & Taguas, D. (2009). **Taxation in the OECD: 1965-2004**. Ministerio de Economía y Hacienda, Spain. Working paper.

Calvo, G. (1975). **Efficient and optimal utilization of capital services**. American Economic Review, 65, 181-186.

————. (1983). **Staggered prices in a utility-maximizing frame-work**. Journal of Monetary Economics, 12:383-98.

Campbell, J., & Mankiw, N. (1989). **Consumption, income, and interest rates: Reinterpreting the time series evidence**. NBER Macroeconomics Annual, MIT Press. Cambridge.

Canova, F., (2007). **Methods for Applied Macroeconomic Research**. New Jersey: Princeton University Press. 492 p.

Carroll, C., Overland, J., & Weil, D. (2000). **Saving and growth with habit formation**. American Economic Review, 90(3), 341-355.

Cashin, P. (1995). **Government spending, taxes, and economic growth**. International Monetary Fund Staff Papers, 42 , 237-269.

Chari, V., Kehoe, P., & McGrattan, E. (2009). **New Keynesian Models: Not Yet Useful for Policy Analysis**. American Economic Journal: Macroeconomics, American Economic Association, vol. 1(1), pages 242-66, January.

Chiang, A. C., & Wainwright, K. (2005). **Fundamental methods of mathematical economics**. McGraw-Hill, New York.

Christiano, L., Eichenbaum, M., & Evans, C. (2005). **Nominal Rigidities and the Dynamic Effects of a Shock to Monetary Policy**. Journal of Political Economy 113, 1-45.

Christoffel, K., & Kuester, K. (2008). **Resuscitating the wage channel in models with unemployment fluctuations**. Journal of Monetary Economics, 55:865-887.

Christoffel, K., Kuester, K., & Linzert, T. (2009). **The role of labor markets for euro area monetary policy**. European Economic Review, 53:908-936.

Clarida, R., Galí, J., & Gertler, M. (2002). **A simple framework for international monetary policy analysis**. Journal of Monetary Economics, 49:879-904.

Constantinides, G. (1990). **Habit formation: A resolution of the equity premium puzzle**. Journal of Political Economy, 98(3), 519-543.

Deaton, A. (1992). **Understanding consumption**. Clarendon Lectures in Economics, Clarendon Press: Oxford.

DeJong, D., N., & Dave, C. (2007). **Structural Macroeconometrics**. New Jersey: Princeton University Press.

Dixit, A. K., & Stiglitz, J. E. (1977). **Monopolistic Competition and Optimum Product Diversity**. American Economic Review, American Economic Association, vol. 67(3), pages 297-308, June.

Duesenberry, J. S. (1949). **Income, Saving, and the Theory of Consumer Behavior**. Harvard University Press, Cambridge,Mass.

Ehrenberg, R. G., & Smith, R. S. (2000). **Modern Labor Economics: Theory and Public Policy**. Prentice Hall.

Finn, M. (1993). **Is all government capital productive?** Federal Reserve Bank of Richmond Economic Quarterly, 79 , 53-80.

Friedman, M. (1957). **A theory of the consumption function (Vol. 63)**. Princeton: princeton university press.

Galí, J. (2008). **Monetary Policy, Inflaction, and the Business Cycle: An Introduction to the New Keynesian Framework**. New Jersey: Princeton University Press. 203 p.

Galí, J., & Monacelli, T. (2005). **Monetary policy and exchange rate volatility in a small open economy**. Review of Economic Studies, 72:707-734.

Galí, J., López-Salido, J., & Vallés, J. (2007). **Understanding the effects of government spending on consumption**. Journal of the European Economic Association, 5(1), 227-270.

Gertler, M., & Karadi, P. (2011). **A model of unconventional monetary policy**. Journal of monetary Economics, 58(1), 17-34.

Glomm, G., & Ravikumar, B. (1994). **Public investment in infrastructure in a sumple growth model**. Journal of Economic Dynamics and Control , 18 , 1173-1187.

Greenwood, J., Hercowitz, Z., & Huffman, G. (1988). **Investment, capacity utilisation and the real business cycle**. American Economic Review, 78(3), 402-417.

Griffoli, T. M. (2011). **Dynare 4: User Guide**.

Hansen, G. D. (1985). **Indivisible labor and the business cycle**. Journal of Monetary Economics, Elsevier, vol. 16(3), pages 309-327, November.

Hayashi, F. (1982). **Tobin's marginal q and average q: A neoclassical interpretation**. Econometrica, 50(1), 213-224.

Johnson, D., Parker, J. & Souleles, N. (2006). **Household expenditure and the income tax rebates of 2001**. American Economic Review, 96(5), 1589-1610.

Jorgenson, D. (1963). **Capital theory and investment behavior**. American Economic Review, 53(2), 247-259.

Juillard, M., Karam, P., Laxton, D., & Pesenti, P. (2006). **Welfare-based monetary policy rules in an estimated DSGE model of the us economy**. ECB, Working Paper, 613.

Klein, P. (2000). **Using the Generalized Schur Form to Solve a Multivariate Linear Rational Expectations Model**. Journal of Economic Dynamics and Control, 24, 1, 405-23.

Kocherlakota, N. R. (2007). **Model fit and model selection**. Review-Federal Reserve Bank of Saint Louis, 89(4), 349.

Kydland, F., & Prescott, E. (1982). **Time to build and aggregate fluctuations**. Econometrica, v. 50 , p. 1350-1372.

Laffer, A. (1981). **Government exactions and revenue deficiencies**. Cato Journal, 1, 1-21.

Lim, G. C., & McNelis, P. D. (2008). **Computational Macroeconomics for The Open Economy**. Cambridge: The MIT Press..

Lindenberg, E., & Ross, S. (1981). **Tobin's Q Ration and Insdustrial Organization**. Journal of Business, v. 54.

Lucas, R. (1976). **Econometric Policy Evaluation: A Critique**. In Brunner, K.; Meltzer, A. The Phillips Curve and Labor Markets. Carnegie-Rochester Conference Series on Public Policy 1. New York: American Elsevier. pp. 19-46.

Mankiw, N. (2000). **The savers-spenders theory of fiscal policy**. American Economic Review, 90(2), 120-125.

McCandless, G. (2008). **The ABCs of RBCs: An Introduction to Dynamic Macroeconomic Models**. London: Harvard University Press. 421 p.

Merrick, J. (1984). **The anticipated real interest rate, capital utilization and the cyclical pattern of real wages**. Journal of Monetary Economics, 13, 17-30.

Pestieau, P. (1974). **Optimal taxation and discount rate for public investment in a growth setting**. Journal of Public Economics, 3 , 217-235.

Pollak, R. (1970). **Habit formation and dynamic demand functions**. Journal of Political Economy, 78(4), 745-763.

Raff, D., & Summers, L. (1987). **Did Henry Ford pay efficiency wages?**. Journal of Labor Economics, Oct 1987.

Ravenna, F., & Walsh, C. E. (2006). **Optimal monetary policy with the cost channel**. Journal of Monetary Economics, 53(2): 199-216.

Ravn, M., Schmitt-Grohé, S., & Uribe, M. (2006). **Deep Habits**. Review of Economic Studies. 73(1): 195-218.

Reinhart, W. J. (1977). **The Theoretical Development and Empirical Investigation of a Relative Valuation Concept.** Ph. D. Dissertation. Chapel Hill: University of North Carolina.

Romer, D. (2012). **Advanced Macroeconomics.** 4th ed. New York: McGraw-Hill.

Rotemberg, J. (1982). **Sticky prices in the United States.** Journal of Political Economy, 90:1187-211.

Rotemberg, J., & Woodford, M. (1997). **An optimization-based econometric framework for the evaluation of monetary policy.** In NBER Macroeconomics Annual 1997, Volume 12 (pp. 297-361). MIT Press.

Schmitt-Grohé, S., & Uribe, M. (2012). **What's news in business cycles.** Econometrica, 80(6), 2733-2764.

Shapiro, M. (1986). **The dynamic demand for capital and labor.** Quarterly Journal of Economics, 101, 512-542.

Simon, C. P., & Blume, L. (1994). **Mathematics for economists (Vol. 7).** New York: Norton.

Sims, C. A. (2001). **Solving Linear Rational Expectations Models.** Computational Economics, 20, 1-20.

Smets, F., & Wouters, R. (2003). **An estimated dynamic stochastic general equilibrium model of the euro area**. Journal of the European Economic Association, 1:5 (September), 1123-1175.

———. (2007). **Shocks and frictions in U.S. business cycle: a Bayesian DSGE approach**. Amerian Economic Review, 97:586-606.

Souleles, N. (1999). **The response of household consumption to income tax refunds.** American Economic Review, 89(4), 947-958.

Taubman, P., & Wilkinson, M. (1970). **User cost, capital utilization and investment theory**. International Economic Review, 11, 209-215.

Taylor, J. B. (1993). **Discretion versus policy rules in practice.** In Carnegie-Rochester conference series on public policy (Vol. 39, pp. 195-214). North-Holland.

Tobin, J. (1969). **A general equilibrium approach to monetary theory.** Journal of Money, Credit and Banking, 1(1), 15-29.

Torres, J. L. (2014). **Introduction to Dynamic Macroeconomia General Equilibrium Models.** Malaga: Vernon Press, p. 246.

Uhlig, H. (1999). **A Toolkit for Analysing Nonlinear Dynamic Stochastic Models Easily.** in Marion, R. e Scott, A. eds, Computational Methods for the Study of Dynamic Economies, Oxford University Press, New York, 30-61.

Varian, H. R. (1992). **Microeconomics Analysis.** Norton & Company, Inc. 3rd edition.

Vereda, L., & Cavalcanti, M. A. F. H. (2010). **Modelo dinâmico estocástico de equilíbrio geral (DSGE) para a economia brasileira.** Ipea, Texto para Discussão, 1479.

Weitzman, M. (1970). **Optimal growth with scale economies in the creation of overhead capital.** Review of Economic Studies, 37, 556-570.

Wickens, M. (2011). **Macroeconomic Theory.** Princeton University Press, second edition.

Williamson, S. D. (2008). **Macroeconomics.** Third Edition, Pearson International Edition.

Wolff, M. (1998). **Recent trends in the size distribution of household wealth.** Journal of Economic Perspectives, 12, 131-150.

Appendices

Mathematical Tools

Lagrange Optimization

Consider the following problem of optimization with constraints. There is a function $f(x, y)$ whose objective is to find the values for x and y that maximize $f(x, y)$ and satisfy the relationship $g(x, y) = 0$. The Lagrange method for dealing with this problem goes as follows: define an auxiliary variable λ that is known as the Lagrange multiplier (or Lagrangian). Then set up the so-called Lagrange function:

$$\mathscr{L}(x, y, \lambda) = f(x, y) + \lambda g(x, y) \qquad (105)$$

In other words, the Lagrange function ($\mathscr{L}$) is formed by two components: the objective function $f(x, y)$ which is maximized; and λ times the constraint function $g(x, y)$.

The next step is to calculate the partial derivatives of $\mathscr{L}$ as a function of the three arguments (x, y, λ) and define that each expression is equal to zero. The three expressions are:

$$\frac{\partial \mathscr{L}}{\partial x} = \frac{\partial f(x, y)}{\partial x} + \lambda \frac{\partial g(x, y)}{\partial x} = 0 \qquad (106)$$

$$\frac{\partial \mathscr{L}}{\partial y} = \frac{\partial f(x, y)}{\partial y} + \lambda \frac{\partial g(x, y)}{\partial y} = 0 \qquad (107)$$

$$\frac{\partial \mathscr{L}}{\partial \lambda} = g(x, y) = 0 \qquad (108)$$

These three equations are the first-order conditions of the problem of optimization with constraints. So this system of first-order conditions is composed of three equations for three variables.

From equations (A.2) and (A.3), it is known that:

$$\lambda = -\frac{\frac{\partial f(x,y)}{\partial x}}{\frac{\partial g(x,y)}{\partial x}} \tag{109}$$

$$\lambda = -\frac{\frac{\partial f(x,y)}{\partial y}}{\frac{\partial g(x,y)}{\partial y}} \tag{110}$$

So by combining equations (A.5) and (A.6),

$$\frac{\frac{\partial f(x,y)}{\partial x}}{\frac{\partial g(x,y)}{\partial x}} = \frac{\frac{\partial f(x,y)}{\partial y}}{\frac{\partial g(x,y)}{\partial y}} \tag{111}$$

Equation (A.7) is the optimal solution to the proposed problem.

Example

Suppose that it is required to discover the point at which the function $f(x, y) = x^2 + y^2$ subject to the constraint $x + y = 2$. Classify the maximum point.

Firstly construct the Lagrange function:

$$\mathcal{L}(x, y, \lambda) = x^2 + y^2 - \lambda(x + y - 2) \tag{112}$$

Now, obtaining the first-order conditions:

$$\frac{\partial \mathcal{L}}{\partial x} = 2x + \lambda = 0 \tag{113}$$

$$\frac{\partial \mathcal{L}}{\partial y} = 2y + \lambda = 0 \tag{114}$$

$$\frac{\partial \mathcal{L}}{\partial \lambda} = x + y - 2 = 0 \tag{115}$$

Resolving equations (A.9) and (A.10) for ? and by combining the results,

$$\lambda = -2x$$

$$\lambda = -2y$$

$$x = y \tag{116}$$

Substituting the equation (A.12) in (A.11),

$$y + y = 2$$

$$y = 1 \tag{117}$$

Substituting (A.13) in (A.10),

$$\lambda = -2 \tag{118}$$

Therefore the maximum point for this problem is $(x, y, \lambda) = (1, 1, -2)$.

Operations with matrices and eigenvalues

Adding and subtracting matrices

The operation to add matrices is defined only between matrices that have the same dimension. Thus,

$$\text{Let } A = \begin{bmatrix} a_{11} & \cdots & a_{1m} \\ \vdots & \ddots & \vdots \\ a_{n1} & \cdots & a_{nm} \end{bmatrix} \text{ and } B = \begin{bmatrix} b_{11} & \cdots & b_{1m} \\ \vdots & \ddots & \vdots \\ b_{n1} & \cdots & b_{nm} \end{bmatrix}$$

two matrices $n \times m$.

The sum of the matrices A and B, represented by A+B, is defined by:

$$(A + B) = \begin{bmatrix} (a_{11} + b_{11}) & \cdots & (a_{1m} + b_{1m}) \\ \vdots & \ddots & \vdots \\ (a_{n1} + b_{n1}) & \cdots & (a_{nm} + b_{nm}) \end{bmatrix}$$

In other words, each element of the matrix (A+B), corresponding to the ith line and j^{th} column, is equal to $(a_{ij} + b_{ij})$.

In turn, the operation to subtract matrix B from matrix A, represented by (A-B), is defined by:

$$(A - B) = \begin{bmatrix} (a_{11} - b_{11}) & \cdots & (a_{1m} - b_{1m}) \\ \vdots & \ddots & \vdots \\ (a_{n1} - b_{n1}) & \cdots & (a_{nm} - b_{nm}) \end{bmatrix}$$

Multiplication of matrices

The operation to multiply a matrix A by a matrix B is only defined if the number of columns in matrix A is equal to the number of lines in matrix B.

Thus, if A is a matrix with m columns, B must have m lines.

$$\text{Let } A = \begin{bmatrix} a_{11} & \cdots & a_{1m} \\ \vdots & \ddots & \vdots \\ a_{n1} & \cdots & a_{nm} \end{bmatrix} \text{ and } B = \begin{bmatrix} b_{11} & \cdots & b_{1q} \\ \vdots & \ddots & \vdots \\ b_{m1} & \cdots & b_{mq} \end{bmatrix}$$

two matrices $n \times m$.

So, multiplying A by B, represented by $A * B$, is defined by:

$$(A*B) = \begin{bmatrix} (a_{11}b_{11} + \ldots + a_{1m}b_{m1}) & \cdots & (a_{11}b_{1q} + \ldots + a_{1m}b_{mq}) \\ \vdots & \ddots & \vdots \\ (a_{n1}b_{11} + \ldots + a_{nm}b_{m1}) & \cdots & (a_{n1}b_{1q} + \ldots + a_{nm}b_{mq}) \end{bmatrix}$$

Calculation of the inverse matrix

Given a square matrix A of dimension nxn, such that $|A| \neq 0$,

$$A^{-1} = \frac{1}{|A|} adj(A) = \frac{1}{|A|} C^t \tag{119}$$

where $adj(A) = C^t$ is called the adjoint matrix of

$$A.C = \begin{bmatrix} |C_{11}| & \cdots & |C_{1n}| \\ \vdots & \ddots & \vdots \\ |C_{n1}| & \cdots & |C_{nn}| \end{bmatrix}, C^t \text{ being the transposed matrix of}$$

C (cofactor matrix). As cofactor $|C_{ij}| = (-1)^{i+j}|M_{ij}|$, where $|M_{ij}|$ is the determinant of the "smaller" matrix, resulting from the removal of the ith line and the jth column of matrix A.

Example: inverse matrix

Let,

$$A = \begin{bmatrix} 1 & 3 & 1 \\ 2 & 0 & 1 \\ 0 & 0 & 1 \end{bmatrix}$$

Calculating the determinant of matrix A:

$$|A| = (0 + 0 + 0) - (0 + 6 + 0) = -6|$$

As $|A| \neq 0$ A is invertible. The next step is to construct the cofactor matrix of B.

$|C_{11}| = (-1)^{1+1} \begin{bmatrix} 0 & 1 \\ 0 & 1 \end{bmatrix} = 0; \qquad |C_{12}| = (-1)^{1+2} \begin{bmatrix} 2 & 1 \\ 0 & 1 \end{bmatrix} = -2;$

$|C_{13}| = (-1)^{1+3} \begin{bmatrix} 2 & 0 \\ 0 & 0 \end{bmatrix} = 0;$

$|C_{21}| = (-1)^{2+1} \begin{bmatrix} 3 & 1 \\ 0 & 1 \end{bmatrix} = -3; \qquad |C_{22}| = (-1)^{2+2} \begin{bmatrix} 1 & 1 \\ 0 & 1 \end{bmatrix} = 0;$

$|C_{23}| = (-1)^{2+3} \begin{bmatrix} 1 & 3 \\ 0 & 0 \end{bmatrix} = 0;$

$|C_{31}| = (-1)^{3+1} \begin{bmatrix} 3 & 1 \\ 0 & 1 \end{bmatrix} = 3; \qquad |C_{32}| = (-1)^{3+2} \begin{bmatrix} 1 & 1 \\ 2 & 1 \end{bmatrix} = 1;$

$|C_{33}| = (-1)^{3+3} \begin{bmatrix} 1 & 3 \\ 2 & 0 \end{bmatrix} = -6.$

So:

$$C = \begin{bmatrix} 0 & -2 & 0 \\ -3 & 1 & 0 \\ 3 & 1 & -6 \end{bmatrix}$$

and,

$$C^{-1} = \begin{bmatrix} 0 & -3 & 3 \\ -2 & 1 & 1 \\ 0 & 0 & -6 \end{bmatrix}$$

Thus,

$$A^{-1} = \begin{bmatrix} 0 & \frac{1}{2} & -\frac{1}{2} \\ \frac{1}{3} & -\frac{1}{6} & -\frac{1}{6} \\ 0 & 0 & 1 \end{bmatrix}$$

Eigenvalues

In order to find the eigenvalues of a matrix A, it is necessary to employ the following equation:

$$|A - \lambda I| = 0 \qquad (120)$$

Let,

$$V = \begin{bmatrix} a_{11} & \cdots & a_{1m} \\ \vdots & \ddots & \vdots \\ a_{n1} & \cdots & a_{nm} \end{bmatrix} - \lambda \begin{bmatrix} 1 & \cdots & 0 \\ \vdots & \ddots & \vdots \\ 0 & \cdots & 1 \end{bmatrix} =$$

$$\begin{bmatrix} a_{11} & \cdots & a_{1m} \\ \vdots & \ddots & \vdots \\ a_{n1} & \cdots & a_{nm} \end{bmatrix} - \begin{bmatrix} \lambda & \cdots & 0 \\ \vdots & \ddots & \vdots \\ 0 & \cdots & \lambda \end{bmatrix} =$$

$$\begin{bmatrix} a_{11} - \lambda & \cdots & a_{1m} \\ \vdots & \ddots & \vdots \\ a_{n1} & \cdots & a_{nm} - \lambda \end{bmatrix}$$

Lastly, it is required to find the determinant of matrix V.

Example: eigenvalues

To find the eigenvalues of matrix $A = \begin{bmatrix} 2 & 2 \\ 1 & 3 \end{bmatrix}$, the following equation must first be solved:

$$|A - \lambda I| = \begin{bmatrix} 2 - \lambda & 2 \\ 1 & 3 - \lambda \end{bmatrix} = (2 - \lambda)(3 - \lambda) - 2 = 0$$

Thus,

$$\lambda^2 - 5\lambda + 4 = 0$$

The eigenvalues of matrix A are the roots of the previous equation: $\lambda_1 = 4$ and $\lambda_2 = 1$.

Appendix B

Basic ideas about DSGE

Calibration

For the purposes of the numerical implementation of the model, it is necessary to assign values to the parameters. Generally speaking, the most recommended course of action is to estimate them. On the other hand, calibration is still quite popular among researchers working with DSGE, but to talk in depth about the methods used in DSGE model estimation is not within the realms of this book. So, in short, calibration will be discussed using the RBC model as an example.

The rate of depreciation of capital stock (δ), is usually estimated using a database and an equation representing the movement of capital stock intertemporally, such as the equation (2.26), $I_{ss} = \delta K_{ss}$. For quarterly data, the literature works with values between 0.02 and 0.03. In the case of annual data, it would be between 0.04 and 0.1. In this book, the data are considered to be quarterly, so the equation $\delta = 0.025$ will be assumed.

The parameter β is called the discount factor, representing how the agents assess future utility versus present utility. The literature assumes that this parameter falls between 0.97 for annual data and 0.99 for quarterly data. On the other hand, its value may be obtained from the equation (2.25). Assuming an average quarterly nominal interest rate of four percent $(R_{ss} = 4\%)$[9]:

$$\beta = \frac{1}{R_{ss} + (1 - \delta)} = 0.985$$

---

[9]As in this model there is no financial bond, the interest rate may be used as a proxy for return on capital.

The proportion of capital used in the production process, α, is obtained from data in the domestic accounts. International literature works with values between 0.3 and 0.4. In this work, it is being adopted $\alpha = 0.35$. The value of the autoregressive parameter, ρ_A, is normally greater than 0.9. However, it is possible to obtain an estimation of the total productivity of factors like the production function residual (known as the Solow Residual), and then estimate this parameter.

There is little consensus over the values for the relative risk aversion coefficient[10], σ. Vereda and Cavalcanti (2010) conducted parameterizations in a quest to determine the parameter limits of a DSGE model for Brazil, and the value found by the authors was between 1 and 3. In this book, the average of this study has been assumed, $\sigma = 2$. The same problem occurs with the marginal disutility of labor[11], φ. The result from the Vereda and Cavalcanti (2010) study is between 0 and 3. The choice for this parameter was also the average of the result of these authors, namely $\varphi = 1.5$.

In summary, to calibrate for DSGE modeling means assigning values to the parameters, in some form. No one form is more correct than the other, but it is always necessary to proceed with caution and common sense.

Blanchard-Kahn (BK) unique solution and stability condition

The model, in linearized form, may be expressed in state-space form as:

$$E\left[\begin{array}{c} z_t \\ E_t x_{t+1} \end{array}\right] = A_0 \left[\begin{array}{c} z_{t-1} \\ x_t \end{array}\right] + D r_{n,t} + G \varepsilon_t \qquad (121)$$

where z_t is a vector of predetermined variables in time t, x_t is a vector of forward-looking variables. E, A_0, D and G are matrices and ε_t is a shock vector, and

---

[10]Christiano, Eichenbaum and Evans (2005), Juillard *et al.* (2006) and Rotemberg and Woodford (1997), assign 1, 1.25 and 6.25, respectively.

[11]Christiano, Eichenbaum and Evans (2005) and Juillard *et al.* (2006), define as 1 and 3, respectively.

$$r_{n,t} = K \begin{bmatrix} z_{t-1} \\ x_t \end{bmatrix}$$

where K is defined depending on the model.

So the equation (B.1) is:

$$E \begin{bmatrix} z_t \\ E_t x_{t+1} \end{bmatrix} = [A_0 + DK] \begin{bmatrix} z_{t-1} \\ x_t \end{bmatrix} + G\varepsilon_t$$

or,

$$E \begin{bmatrix} z_t \\ E_t x_{t+1} \end{bmatrix} = A \begin{bmatrix} z_{t-1} \\ x_t \end{bmatrix} + G\varepsilon_t$$

resulting in,

$$\begin{bmatrix} z_t \\ E_t x_{t+1} \end{bmatrix} = \bar{A} \begin{bmatrix} z_{t-1} \\ x_t \end{bmatrix} + \bar{G}\varepsilon_t \qquad (122)$$

where $\bar{A} = E^{-1}A$ and $\bar{G} = E^{-1}G$.

Thus rational expectations are formed using a set of information $\{z_s, x_{s+1}, \varepsilon_s\}$, with $s \leq t$.

The condition for unique equilibrium and stability depends on the magnitude of the eigenvalues of the matrix $(A_0 + DK)$. If the number of eigenvalues with an absolute value greater than 1 (unstable root) is equal to the number of forward-looking variables, the system has a unique solution and is also stable on a saddle path (Blanchard and Kahn, 1980). On the other hand, indeterminacy occurs when the number of eigenvalues of the matrix $(A_0 + DK)$ with an absolute value greater than 1 is lower than the number of forward-looking variables (many stable roots). This means that when the shock shifts the economy out of its steady state, many paths exist that lead to equilibrium, in other words, there are multiple solutions to the model. The possibility also exists of the number of unstable roots being greater than the number of forward-looking variables (many unstable roots). In this case, the system has no solution and all paths are explosive (Figure B.1).

Blanchard-Kahn Satisfied

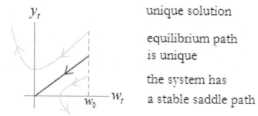

unique solution

equilibrium path
is unique

the system has
a stable saddle path

Many Stable Roots

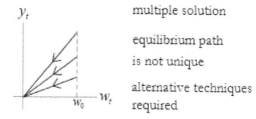

multiple solution

equilibrium path
is not unique

alternative techniques
required

Many Unstable Roots

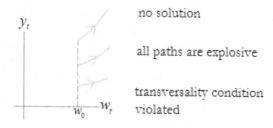

no solution

all paths are explosive

transversality condition
violated

Figure 10: Examples of positive results for the BK analysis.

An example from the book: RBC model in Chapter 2

The log-linear system of the RBC model developed in chapter 2 is as follows:

$$\sigma \widetilde{C}_t + \varphi \widetilde{L}_t = \widetilde{W}_t \tag{123}$$

$$\frac{\sigma}{\beta}(E_t \widetilde{C}_{t+1} - \widetilde{C}_t) = R_{ss} E_t \widetilde{R}_{t+1} \tag{124}$$

$$\widetilde{K}_{t+1} = (1 - \delta)\widetilde{K}_t + \delta \widetilde{I}_t \tag{125}$$

$$\widetilde{Y}_t = \widetilde{A}_t + \alpha \widetilde{K}_t + (1 - \alpha)\widetilde{L}_t \tag{126}$$

$$\widetilde{K}_t = \widetilde{Y}_t - \widetilde{R}_t \tag{127}$$

$$\widetilde{L}_t = \widetilde{Y}_t - \widetilde{W}_t \tag{128}$$

$$Y_{ss}\widetilde{Y}_t = C_{ss}\widetilde{C}_t + I_{ss}\widetilde{I}_t \tag{129}$$

$$\widetilde{A}_t = \rho_A \widetilde{A}_{t-1} + \epsilon_t \tag{130}$$

The first step to facilitating the BK analysis is to simplify the previous system:

Substituting equation (B.8) in equation (B.3), the equation (B.7) in equation (B.4) and equation (B.9) in equation (B.5), leaves the system with three fewer equations (and three fewer variables) than the initial system.

$$\sigma \widetilde{C}_t + (1 + \varphi)\widetilde{L}_t = \widetilde{Y}_t \tag{131}$$

$$\frac{\sigma}{\beta}(E_t \widetilde{C}_{t+1} - \widetilde{C}_t) = R_{ss} E_t (\widetilde{Y}_{t+1} - \widetilde{K}_{t+1}) \tag{132}$$

$$\widetilde{K}_{t+1} = (1 - \delta)\widetilde{K}_t + \delta \left[\left(\frac{Y_{ss}}{I_{ss}}\right)\widetilde{Y}_t - \left(\frac{C_{ss}}{I_{ss}}\right)\widetilde{C}_t \right] \tag{133}$$

$$\widetilde{Y}_t = \widetilde{A}_t + \alpha \widetilde{K}_t + (1 - \alpha)\widetilde{L}_t \tag{134}$$

$$\widetilde{A}_t = \rho_A \widetilde{A}_{t-1} + \epsilon_t \tag{135}$$

In this system, there are two forward-looking variables, $E_t \tilde{C}_{t+1}$ and $E_t \tilde{Y}_{t+1}$, and two predetermined variables, $\tilde{A}_t$ and $\tilde{K}_{t+1}$ [12].

This type of system may be represented in state-space form:

$$E \begin{bmatrix} \tilde{A}_t \\ \tilde{K}_{t+1} \\ E_t \tilde{C}_{t+1} \\ E_t \tilde{Y}_{t+1} \end{bmatrix} = A_0 \begin{bmatrix} \tilde{A}_{t-1} \\ \tilde{K}_t \\ \tilde{C}_t \\ \tilde{Y}_t \end{bmatrix} + D L_t + G \epsilon_t \qquad (136)$$

In order to help with the construction of the matrices, it is better to write the model in a form that is consistent with the state-space:

$$A: \tilde{A}_t = \rho_A \tilde{A}_{t-1} + \epsilon_t$$

$$K: \tilde{K}_{t+1} = (1-\delta)\tilde{K}_t + \delta \left[\left(\frac{Y_{ss}}{I_{ss}}\right)\tilde{Y}_t - \left(\frac{C_{ss}}{I_{ss}}\right)\tilde{C}_t \right]$$

$$C: \frac{\sigma}{\beta} E_t \tilde{C}_{t+1} - R_{ss} E_t \tilde{Y}_{t+1} + R_{ss} E_t \tilde{K}_{t+1} = \frac{\sigma}{\beta} \tilde{C}_t$$

Owing to the variable $E_t \tilde{Y}_{t+1}$ only appearing in the previous equation, it is necessary to use a dummy equation to represent it:

$$YY: R_{ss} E_t \tilde{Y}_{t+1} = R_{ss} E_t \tilde{Y}_{t+1}$$

$$Y: \tilde{Y}_t = \tilde{A}_t + \alpha \tilde{K}_t + (1-\alpha)\tilde{L}_t$$

$$L: \sigma \tilde{C}_t + (1+\varphi)\tilde{L}_t - \tilde{Y}_t = 0$$

The next step is to find the matrices E, A_0, D and L_t:

$$E = \begin{bmatrix} 1 & 0 & 0 & 0 \\ 0 & 1 & 0 & 0 \\ 0 & R_{ss} & \frac{\sigma}{\beta} & -R_{ss} \\ 0 & 0 & 0 & R_{ss} \end{bmatrix} \qquad (137)$$

[12] Remembering that, as per the convention adopted in this book, the stock-variables have period opening values, thus when writing the simulation program, each stock-variable should be postponed by one period.

$$A_0 = \begin{bmatrix} \rho_A & 0 & 0 & 0 \\ 0 & (1-\delta) & -\delta\frac{C_{ss}}{I_{ss}} & \delta\frac{Y_{ss}}{I_{ss}} \\ 0 & 0 & \frac{\sigma}{\beta} & 0 \\ -1 & \alpha & 0 & 1 \end{bmatrix} \tag{138}$$

$$D = \begin{bmatrix} 0 \\ 0 \\ 0 \\ (1-\alpha) \end{bmatrix} \tag{139}$$

$$L_t = \begin{bmatrix} 0 & 0 & \frac{\sigma}{1+\varphi} & -\frac{1}{1+\varphi} \end{bmatrix} * \begin{bmatrix} \tilde{A}_{t-1} \\ \tilde{K}_t \\ \tilde{C}_t \\ \tilde{Y}_t \end{bmatrix}$$

$$= K * \begin{bmatrix} \tilde{A}_{t-1} \\ \tilde{K}_t \\ \tilde{C}_t \\ \tilde{Y}_t \end{bmatrix} \tag{140}$$

where:

$$K = \begin{bmatrix} 0 & 0 & \frac{\sigma}{1+\varphi} & -\frac{1}{1+\varphi} \end{bmatrix}$$

Thus, DK is obtained:

$$DK = \begin{bmatrix} 0 \\ 0 \\ 0 \\ (1-\alpha) \end{bmatrix} * \begin{bmatrix} 0 & 0 & \frac{\sigma}{1+\varphi} & -\frac{1}{1+\varphi} \end{bmatrix} =$$

$$\begin{bmatrix} 0 & 0 & 0 & 0 \\ 0 & 0 & 0 & 0 \\ 0 & 0 & 0 & 0 \\ 0 & 0 & \frac{(1-\alpha)\sigma}{1+\varphi} & \frac{(1-\alpha)}{1+\varphi} \end{bmatrix} \tag{141}$$

The next step is to obtain matrix A:

$$A = A_0 + DK = \begin{bmatrix} \rho_A & 0 & 0 & 0 \\ 0 & (1-\delta) & -\delta\frac{C_{ss}}{I_{ss}} & \delta\frac{Y_{ss}}{I_{ss}} \\ 0 & 0 & \frac{\sigma}{\beta} & 0 \\ -1 & \alpha & 0 & 1 \end{bmatrix}$$

$$+ \begin{bmatrix} 0 & 0 & 0 & 0 \\ 0 & 0 & 0 & 0 \\ 0 & 0 & 0 & 0 \\ 0 & 0 & \frac{(1-\alpha)\sigma}{1+\varphi} & \frac{(1-\alpha)}{1+\varphi} \end{bmatrix}$$

$$= \begin{bmatrix} \rho_A & 0 & 0 & 0 \\ 0 & (1-\delta) & -\delta\frac{C_{ss}}{I_{ss}} & \delta\frac{Y_{ss}}{I_{ss}} \\ 0 & 0 & \frac{\sigma}{\beta} & 0 \\ -1 & \alpha & \frac{(1-\alpha)\sigma}{1+\varphi} & 1-\frac{(1-\alpha)}{1+\varphi} \end{bmatrix} \qquad (142)$$

Finally, the aim is to analyze the eigenvalues of the matrix $\bar{A}$, where:

$$\bar{A} = E^{-1} A \qquad (143)$$

Table 6: Values of the structural model's parameters.

Parameter	Parameter meaning	Calibrated value
σ	Relative risk aversion coefficient	2
φ	Marginal disutility with regard to supply of labor	1.5
α	Elasticity of level of production in relation to capital	0.35
β	Discount factor	0.985
δ	Depreciation rate	0.025
ρ_A	Autoregressive parameter - productivity	0.95
σ_A	Standard deviation of productivity	0.01

By finding the eigenvalues for the matrix $\bar{A}$ it is possible to analyze if the system possesses a unique solution and is stable. As stated earlier, Blanchard and Kahn (1980) demonstrated that for a model with rational expectations to have a unique solution, there must be the same quantity of unstable roots (eigenvalue greater

Table 7: Values of variables at the steady state.

Variable	Steady state
A	1
R	0.040
W	2.084
Y	2.338
I	0.508
C	1.829
L	0.729
K	20.338

than 1 in modulus $|\lambda| > 1$) plus forward-looking variables. Using the values in tables B.1 and B.2 and the script in box B.1, we arrive at the eigenvalues (λ) of matrix $\tilde{A}$:

$$\lambda = \begin{bmatrix} 0.9041 \\ 0.9500 \\ 1.0337 \\ 34.9758 \end{bmatrix}$$

In this case, the Blanchard and Kahn condition is satisfied and the model has a unique solution[13].

---

[13]The Dynare result for the analysis of the Blanchard and Kahn conditions is displayed in BOX B.2.

BOX B.1 - Analysis of the Blanchard and Kahn (1980) condition for the RBC model in chapter 2.

```
%Analysis of the Blanchard and Kahn (1980) Condition
%Chapter 2 - RBC Model

%Value of Parameters
sigma = 2;
phi = 1.5;
alpha = 0.35;
betta = 0.985;
delta = 0.025;
rhoa = 0.95;

%Steady State
Rss = (1/betta)-(1-delta);
Yss = ((Rss/(Rss-delta*alpha))^(sigma/(sigma+phi)))*...
(((1-alpha) *((alpha/Rss)^((alpha*(1+phi))/(1-alpha)))...
)^(1/(sigma+phi)));
Iss = delta*alpha*(Yss/Rss);
Lss = ((Rss/alpha)^(alpha/(1-alpha)))*Yss;
Wss = (1-alpha)*((alpha/Rss)^(alpha/(1-alpha)));
Css = (Wss/(Lss)^phi)^(1/sigma);

% The system is: E s(+1) = A0 S + D L + G e
E = [1 0 0 0;0 1 0 0;0 Rss (sigma/betta) 0;0 0 0 Rss];
A0 = [rhoa 0 0 0;0 (1-delta) -delta*(Css/Iss) ...
delta*(Yss/Iss);
0 0 sigma/betta 0;-1 alpha 0 1];
D = [0; 0; 0; (1-delta)];
L = [0 0 sigma/(1+phi) 1/(1+phi)];

%A_=E^-1 A
A = A0 + (D*L);
A_ = inv(E)*A;

lambda = sort(eig(A_))
```

BOX B.2 - Result of the analysis of the Blanchard and Kahn (1980) condition for the RBC model in chapter 2, on Dynare.

```
EIGENVALUES:
        Modulus           Real        Imaginary

          0.95            0.95            0
        0.9614          0.9614            0
         1.056           1.056            0
           Inf             Inf            0
```

There are 2 eigenvalue(s) larger than 1 in modulus
for 2 forward-looking variable(s)

The rank condition is verified.

Index

CPSIA information can be obtained
at www.ICGtesting.com
Printed in the USA
BVOW09s1114141117
500150BV00010B/69/P

9 781622 731336